OVER THE FENCE

with joe gardener®

Published by Cool Springs Press
101 Forrest Crossing Boulevard, Suite 100
Franklin, Tennessee 37064

Catalog in Publication Data is Available.
ISBN: 1591862620

First printing 2006
Printed in the United States of America
10 9 8 7 6 5 4 3 2 1

All photography by Joe Lamp'l and Courtenay Vanderbilt unless stated below.

Touchstone Accent Lighting (www.touchstonelight.com): 21 (top), 47, 206, 209 (top), 210-212
Kennesaw Landscapes: 197
Proven Winners: 69 (bottom)
David Gottlieb: 64
Becky Lamp'l: 104-1, 104-2
Nancy Malone: 37, 52, 53 (bottom)
Felder Rushing: 223 (top)
Photo ownership by Bell Laboratories, Inc.: 175 (bottom)
Korina Petrozzi, "The Plant Nerd": 46 (bottom), 49, 216
The Espoma Company: 106 (bottom)
Zeba: 149 (bottom)
Fiskars: 161-3
Joanna Amato: 61
Paige Jarvis: 179 (bottom)
Tom Vanderbilt: 4

Managing Editor: Ramona D. Wilkes
Cover and Interior Design: Jade Novak for Anderson Thomas Design
Production Artist: Bill Kersey, Kersey Graphics
Typesetting: S.E. Anderson

Visit the Cool Springs Press website at www.coolspringspress.net

OVER THE FENCE

with joe gardener®

by JOE LAMP'L

COOL SPRINGS PRESS

Franklin, Tennessee

Special Thanks and Acknowledgements

As with any book, there is usually an army of people behind the scenes that help to make it a reality. That was certainly the case here.

First, I am so thankful to my family. Becky, you and the girls put up with me a lot as I told you about the next deadline and how I needed to work on the book. I know with every utterance of the word "deadline" it became less and less meaningful, but you gave me the time to do what needed to be done. Thank you!

To Tom Vanderbilt, husband to my book partner Courtenay Vanderbilt: You gave up your spouse for many months and you barely uttered a grumble. Who knows what you were really thinking but thank you for your patience.

And especially to Courtenay Vanderbilt: I never really appreciated hearing or reading the words "I couldn't have done it without you" before this project. But now I KNOW what that really means! I am not aware of any writer talented enough to adequately put into words the expression of my gratitude. Thank you for your help at every step of the way as this book went from concept to completion. You gave of yourself from before sunrise until after midnight many days. You pushed me along and kept me on track. You'd work on the book when you could have been sleeping, and when you couldn't sleep, you'd work on the book. And with your camera you were unstoppable! You'd take pictures anywhere and everywhere they were needed, crawl on your stomach, approach strangers, and drive for miles, all to achieve that perfect shot. In the end, this book is, because of your help. Thank you!

Finally, some special friends contributed their skills and talents to make sure this book looked good and that the content was accurate. Thanks to all of you for the important part you played.

Joanna Amato: You alone got the sample chapters into a form that was actually readable and attractive enough to be accepted for publishing.

Cheryle Kerr: You went the extra mile! Thank you for generously giving of your time and hard work. You gladly accepted my request for help and exceeded my expectations.

Thanks also go to: Steve Pettis, Complete Horticultural Consulting; Gretchen Pettis, PhD, University of Georgia; Tony Johnson, Horticulturist, University of Georgia; Dan Cleveland, Atlanta, GA; Dr. Robert Gilbert, Kennesaw, GA; David Rolston, Landscape Architect, Dallas, TX; and Inta Krombolz, West Chester, PA.

The Dynamic Duo

Dedication

This book is dedicated to everyone who appreciates the beauty of nature and understands that we can have an influence starting with our own little corner of the world, and to those who care enough to do their part so future generations can experience the same pleasures.

Contents

Foreword

When I set out to write *Over the Fence with joe gardener®,* I knew I wanted to share some of the most important principles I've personally learned as a passionate lifetime gardener. But it's my unique perspective as a gardener in the public eye that has allowed me to stay on the cutting edge of the most current techniques and information for home gardeners, landscapers, and weekend warriors alike. That's what makes this book special.

Through television and various aspects of the media, as well through my own company, I have been blessed with fantastic opportunities to access many of the most respected gardeners, educators, and researchers and to go behind the scenes at the top public and private gardens in the country.

So, armed with a lifetime of experience, a love for horticulture, a heart for teaching, and an insatiable desire to stay in the know, I felt equipped and ready to write. The premise behind this book is that I wanted it to *teach,* more than I wanted it to *instruct.* Certainly there are plenty of how-to books out there.

As you spend time within these pages, I trust you will find the straightforward answers you're looking for, but also the *reason* behind the answer. I call it the "why-do behind the how-to." If you understand why a certain step is important, you'll then be able to apply the same information to new steps and projects as well.

I hope this book speaks to you just as I would if we were having a conversation over the fence, neighbor to neighbor. And if you don't find what you're looking for here, I'm just an email away through our website at www.joegardener.com. No matter what your experience or where you live, I'm your gardener-next-door, too. Let's get started.

Joe Lamp'l
learn, create, grow

"Having a place where I can work the soil and leave my mark is almost as important as the basic essentials of life."

Personalizing the Landscape to Suit Your Lifestyle

Assessing Your Landscape Needs

For many people, the opportunity to have a little corner of the world, a piece of earth where they can work the soil and leave their mark, is almost as important as the most basic essentials of life such as food, clothing, and shelter. I belong to this group.

For others, a yard is just something that comes with the house. Rather than looking at the landscape (or lack of one) as a place to exercise creativity and expression, to enjoy nature and the fresh air, the yard is considered more of an impediment to free time and greater weekend pleasures. Initially, it is likely that many more people belong in this group. My neighbor is a member here.

Often times the lack of enthusiasm in this group may be due to the perceived magnitude of just getting started. They simply might not know how to convert a random, untamed plot of land into a more subdued, manageable area, no matter what their lifestyle or interest.

And finally, there are those who have basic skills which simply need refining, a little direction on how to begin and what do to next. These people have a general idea of how they want their yards and gardens to look but just can't seem to tie it together in a flowing, rhythmic way.

Regardless of where you are, you'll need the same basic skills that apply to each individual task. There are reasons *why* we do each step in the process, and many times those reasons apply to other jobs as well. Having an understanding of why we do what we do is just as important as the actual steps themselves.

You decide how much work it will take to tame your garden space.

Getting Started

This book will take you through some of the most common home gardening and landscaping projects, providing you with more in-depth information and most importantly, equipping you with the mental "tools" needed to apply your newfound skills to approach *other* tasks with confidence, enthusiasm, and even excitement.

Many non-gardeners have been turned into gardeners by simply taking the first basic steps. If you consider yourself a non-gardener now, maybe you'll be a convert before you finish this book. You won't be the first! If you are already a gardener, you can look forward to having this book as a guide, reinforcing what you already know, but no doubt adding to your existing knowledge base as well.

As I am fond of saying, "No matter how much you know about gardening, there is always more to learn . . . if you want to." I am always looking to learn more, and I love to share with others what I know. So let's get started. Even a journey of a thousand miles begins with the first step.

QUICK FACT

The process of taming your garden or landscape simply breaks down to making the right choices on what you plant, where you plant it, and what to do afterwards to promote the best environment possible.

WHY: A healthy plant is a happy plant, and a happy plant is very undemanding.

Low Maintenance vs. More Maintenance: How Involved Do You Want to Be?

How often have we been held hostage by our own yards, feeling overwhelmed by work that seems to crop up overnight? Or it may be that we observe our neighbors' constant toil as they weed, mow, prune, water, fertilize, and fight off pests and diseases with a virtual arsenal of products, gear, and tools. Before you put this book down feeling discouraged, wait…there *is* hope!

You Control the Garden, the Garden Doesn't Control You!

The process of taming your garden or landscape simply breaks down to making the right choices on what you plant, where you plant it, and what to do afterwards to promote the best environment possible.

Making the Right Plant Choices

Do You Want Your Landscape to Be Just for Show or For Your Pleasure Too?

If your goal is to have a great looking landscape with the least amount of work, then you might consider hiring a landscape company if you can afford it. Otherwise, taking

Plant tags provide information regarding ideal growing requirements, including wet or dry soil conditions.

• *Full sun* is unobstructed, all day sun, or at least eight hours a day of direct sunlight.

• *Full shade* never gets direct sunlight. It is the type of light that you'll find on the north side of your house or under the canopy of evergreen trees.

• *Partial sun* is more sun than shade. If full sun is all day sun (eight hours or more of direct light), then any shade up to about four hours is partial sun.

• *Partial shade* works the same way. If full shade is all day shade (eight or more hours) then any sun up to about four hours is partial shade.

How Wet or Dry is Your Soil?

All plants have a preferred environment for growing and looking their best. Much of this has to do with the moisture level of the soil. In fact, plant survival can depend on having the right soil conditions. For example, a cactus would never make it in a bog and a water lily would quickly expire in dry, sandy soil.

Sandy soil allows water to drain too quickly. Roots do not have time to absorb sufficient water to remain adequately hydrated. Although some plants are adaptive and thrive in this type of soil condition, most prefer soil that retains some moisture.

Conversely, soil that is too compacted, such as hard clay, does not allow water to drain quickly enough. Excessive rains or over-watering can cause plant roots to rot. This is because water in the soil replaces air spaces which are

some time to learn about what grows in your specific environment will get you well on your way to a landscape that suits your lifestyle. Some specifics on what to consider as you learn about your unique environment are listed below. The happiest, healthiest, and best looking plants are the ones that are growing in the right place. They will reward you with less effort on your part.

⚠ Look around your neighborhood.

See what you like and how it is growing. Is it in full sun, partial sun, or shade? What exposure is it getting (east, south, etc.)? Is it growing in a wet, shady spot or on a sunny slope? It's okay to borrow ideas from other gardens. The professionals do it all the time!

How Much Sun vs. Shade?

When you look at a plant tag, one of the most important pieces of information pertains to the light requirements for the plant to grow best. Tags usually say "grows best in full sun, partial sun, partial shade, or full shade." Well what does that mean exactly? There are many variations on how these terms are defined, but here's my explanation.

essential components to healthy soil. Oxygen contributes to the right environment for root expansion and a thriving plant.

Fortunately, most plants are more tolerant of a broader range of soil moisture conditions. However, in most cases, well-drained soil is best. If you will take the time to get to know your soil before heading for the nursery, you can find plants that are appropriate for your environment and avoid some costly mistakes. Plant tags usually include this information.

 You may have microclimates.

Even within your own yard, soil conditions can vary greatly. While part of your yard may be sunny and dry, another part may be shady and moist. And yet another might be shady and dry, such as that area underneath a large tree. These various soil conditions along with fluctuations in temperatures, all within a smaller area like your yard, are referred to as microclimates: small unique climates or environments within a larger area.

What Are the Minimum and Maximum Temperatures for Your Area?

Just as there are preferred light conditions for best growth, plants thrive under the right temperatures and climates but cannot survive outside of a certain range. The United States National Arboretum in cooperation with the American Horticultural Society developed the "Plant Hardiness Zone Map." When the map was developed, it was believed that the most critical criterion to a plant's ability to adapt to its environment was winter hardiness.

The map indicates the average annual minimum temperature range for every area of the United States. Virtually all plants sold today include basic minimum information. One of the most important mentions is a listing of the "hardiness zone" rating. This information is intended to indicate excellent adaptability of plants to specific growing regions.

The map represents ten different zones, with each zone indicating an area of winter hardiness. Each zone is based on a 10 degree difference in average annual minimum temperatures. The map also indicates areas where the average minimum annual temperature is above 40 degrees F. These areas are considered frostfree and are represented by zone 11.

When shopping for plants in person at the nursery, and especially in a catalogue or through the Internet, be sure you know your hardiness zone and if the plant you are considering for purchase is suitable for your area.

microclimates allow the more adventurous to push the limits of a plant's ideal growing conditions

14

Sedum and hosta require different growing conditions and should not have been planted together.

different preferences for ideal growing conditions is just asking for trouble, and you are assured of at least some of your plants looking poorly.

Are the Plants Pest and Disease Resistant?

These problems affect many plants. Find out if plants you are considering have varieties that offer resistance to pests, diseases, or both.

Will Children or Pets Come in Contact with the Plants?

Some plants are poisonous to eat, some create a severe allergic reaction, and some are very dangerous because of their sharp thorns or spikes. Although many of these plants are beautiful, they may not be appropriate to have around pets and children. Later in this chapter is a list of plants that are poisonous. See also "Plants for Security" for a list of plants with thorns.

Will Plants Require Dividing, Deadheading, or Pruning to Look their Best?

Know the requirements to maintaining a healthy-looking plant. Make sure that you're willing to commit to doing these tasks.

Do You Know the Growing Conditions of the Plants You Want to Use?

Some plants require consistent moisture while others prefer to stay on the dry side. Grouping plants with similar preferences together will make a big difference in keeping your plants healthy and looking great. Trying to combine plants in the same geographic areas that have

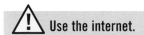

⚠ Use the internet.

Do an Internet search on "pest and disease resistant varieties of 'X' plant" to bring up a listing. You also may contact your local county extension office and speak with the agent or Master Gardener on duty. They are equipped to handle calls such as this and will be a great resource.

What is the Soil Quality?

If your soil is in good condition (rich, loamy, and full of organic material), you'll have a wider palette from which to choose. If you have sandy or compacted clay soil, plant choices become more limited.

How Tall and Wide Will the Plant Get?

Will you need to prune it to control the size for the space where you would like to plant it? The right plant in the right place rarely needs pruning to control its size. Don't be fooled by the size of the plant in the nursery. At the same time, don't assume your plant will look as good or always be as big as the one in the picture. It's important to know the expected dimensions of a plant when mature.

You wouldn't want to plant these *Cryptomeria japonica* 'Yoshino' under your family room windows!

Read the plant tag. Far too many plants are purchased solely on impulse, with no regard to the mature size.

If you encounter *"dwarf"* or *"miniature"* plants, these are slower growers than related plants that don't have these words in their title. It doesn't mean they will stay forever small. It really means that they will grow at a much slower rate and will not likely ever be quite as big as the non-dwarf alternative.

Are There Plants that Evoke a Special Memory for You?

Just as there are plants you may want to stay clear of, there are others you will certainly want to include. Maybe they bring back a favorite childhood memory or help you remember special people, places, or trips. It may be as simple as providing a certain fragrance that you love. Plants provide more than just something beautiful to look at. They can perfume the air and instantly take you back in time.

The Good News

It may seem like a lot of effort to find out what plants will work in your yard. There is, however, good news. As I've mentioned, today most plants purchased from a nursery or garden center have plant tags included that list the ideal requirements for that plant to thrive. Additionally, there should be knowledgeable staff on hand to guide you through the many choices.

The best step you can take to make the selection process easier is to become familiar with your home environment as it relates to the earlier questions. The more time you take to acquaint yourself with your personal landscape, the easier the process will be in selecting the appropriate plants. I'll guide you through some of the most important considerations in the following chapters.

Often there is a knowledgeable staff person to offer advice.

No fear about getting caught taking this picture!

More Work Can Mean More Fun

Now, if you don't mind a little work, the sky's the limit. Many folks discover that gardening really is fun! They enjoy getting their hands dirty after all. I can spend an entire day working in the yard, but my wife doesn't consider I've worked because I enjoy it so much. Who says work can't be fun! Plants grown in areas outside of their ideal environment, (whether it is a climate difference or growing a plant that prefers full sun in partial shade) usually require more maintenance to keep them looking good. This may be in the form of more watering or pruning or basic tender loving care but whatever the case, it's fun to experiment and push the limits if you have the time or desire.

Consider Your Particular Lifestyle

Do You Travel Often?

If you are away from home for more than a few days at a time you should think more carefully about your plant selections. First, watering becomes more of a concern. A simple solution to an otherwise challenging problem is simply to install soaker hoses or drip irrigation along with

electronic timers. That way, the watering needs of your plants and trees can be addressed in your absence. In my own case, even when I don't travel, I love the use of timers to ensure that the job gets done consistently. The risk of overwatering or underwatering is greatly reduced this way.

Another consideration for those who travel, as well as in general, is the use of certain plant material for purposes of security. Some plants are fantastic at providing a virtual shield around your home or property because they have vicious thorns. Conversely, you should consider eliminating tall shrubs and plants that block the view of windows and doors from the street. Dense shrubs do provide effective screening. If it's privacy you are seeking, plants provide many options. However, they are also the ideal hiding place for burglars or vandals as well.

In most cases, professionals and families who travel frequently will not want to devote their precious free time to maintaining a yard, garden or landscape. Fortunately there are many plants today that are considered "low maintenance". There are also tips and tricks to reduce the

QUICK FACT

It is fun to experiment and push a plant's limits in its growing environment.

WHY: If you're looking for a little adventure, pushing the limits can make you a better and more knowledgeable gardener. I love to see the cause-and-effect relationship of environmental conditions on plants. Observing these relationships and noting how the plant responds helps us learn to grow plants more successfully and deal with challenging conditions.

COMMON PLANTS TOXIC TO HUMANS		
Azalea/Rhododendron/Laurels	*Rhododendron/ Laurus nobilis*	All parts
Angel's Trumpet, Jimson Weed	*Datura*	Flowers, seeds, leaves
Baneberry, Dolls Eyes	*Actaea*	Roots, sap, berries
Bleeding Heart	*Dicentra*	All parts
Bracken Fern	*Pteridium*	All
Buckeye, Horse Chestnut	*Aesculus*	Fruit
Cardinal Flower	*Lobelia*	All
Castor Bean	*Ricinus communis*	Seeds
Christmas Rose	*Helleborus niger*	All
Daffodil, Hyacinth	*Narcissus, Hyacinthus orientalis*	Bulbs
Delphinium	*Delphinium*	All
Elderberry	*Sambucus*	Unripe fruits, leaves, twigs, roots
Foxglove	*Digitalis*	Flowers, leaves, seeds
Golden Chain Tree	*Laburnum anagyroids*	All
Irises	*Iris*	Rhizomes, root stocks
Larkspur	*Delphinium*	Young plant, seeds
Mayapple	*Podophyllum peltatum*	All
Pokeweed	*Phytolacca americana*	All
Skunk Cabbage	*Symplocarpus foetidus*	All
Wild Cherries, Black Cherries	*Prunus*	Seeds, leaves
Wisteria	*Wisteria*	All
Yew	*Taxus*	Seeds, twigs, berries, especially foliage

Do You Share a Gardening Passion?

Another consideration when setting up a landscape or garden is knowing who will most likely be interacting with it. Are you single, or do you share a gardening passion with a significant other? Allowing for differences in taste may or may not be a challenge.

The options for plants in the landscape can be much greater for those who are single or without children. A number of plants are mildly or highly toxic, especially to children. Many plants, although beautiful, have very sharp spines or thorns (see Plants for Security chart in this chapter) and may be inappropriate for children or unsuspecting visitors. Still other plants may be highly ornamental, yet severely caustic, such as poison ivy. (Yes, it *is* an ornamental plant.)

Are Pets a Part of Your Family?

Just after you complete that new landscape, Rover wears out the sod you carefully placed along the fence line. Or Daisy digs up your brand new perennial bed, making it her bed instead. Pets can create problems for backyard landscapes that you don't think about until it's too late. It

effort required to still get a great looking display. For example, reducing the amount of lawn you have can save you time and money. Lawns, although beautiful are considered by many to be the biggest maintenance component of an entire landscape. They require frequent fertilization, irrigation, weed control and disease fighting chemicals. Even with organic alternatives, the time or expense it takes to have a really great looking lawn can be unrealistic to many, especially for those who travel or simply work long hours.

Leaves of three, leave it be.

Looking like turf, this dwarf mondo grass makes an attractive, low-maintenance lawn alternative.

home—has inspired us to create an environment outside that is just as inviting and functional as the inside of our home. We simply want to enjoy our yards and gardens socially whenever, whether day or night. Fortunately there are now many ways to enhance the entertainment experience in our outdoor rooms, no matter what the time.

Does cooking outdoors appeal to you? It can be as simple or complicated as you like. Options abound, from a basic charcoal grill to a full-scale outdoor kitchen, complete with cook tops, refrigeration, icemakers, and dishwashers. Are you

may be that you go ahead and follow through on your original plan, then hold your breath. More often than not though, pets (especially large dogs) will undermine your best laid plans (or sod). Like many aspects of landscaping and life, there comes a time where you stop fighting and think of a better option. Once you know what damage has occurred, start making modifications.

Dogs and cats do chew on plant leaves. Usually their instincts tell them which plants are dangerous and which are not. Still, it pays to notice what they are chewing on and whether it may have the potential to be harmful. In Chapter 3, I've include more information about landscaping strategies with pets in mind and a list of some commonly grown plants that are toxic at some level to dogs, cats, or both. If in doubt, don't hesitate to contact the ASPCA in your area.

How Do You Like to Entertain?

Today, we are spending more time than ever in our yards, but less time actually gardening. With so many competing demands on our time, it's no surprise. Yet the allure of the garden setting—the desire to be outdoors and yet at

Pets can create problems for back yard landscapes you don't think about until it's too late.

COMMON PLANTS TO USE FOR SECURITY		ZONE*
Barberry 'Rose Glow'	Berberis thunbergii var. autropurpurea	3a-10b
Blackthorn	Prunus spinosa	5a-9b
Common Gorse	Ulex europaeus	7a-10b
Firethorn	Pyracantha	5a-8b
Fuchsia-flowering Gooseberry	Ribes speciosum	7-9
Hawthorne	Crataegus monogyna	4-9
Holly	Ilex sp.	3-9
Oregon Grape, Grape Holly	Mahonia aquifolium	5a-9b
Prickly Ash	Zanthoxylum americanum	3a-7b
Rose varieties	Rosa sp.	4-10
Sea Buckthorn	Hippophae rhamnoides	4-10

*hardiness zone varies with cultivar and variety

the type that enjoys dining alfresco, or do you prefer the protection of a screened room which can also serve as a focal point in the garden?

Do you envision dining casually or in a more formal atmosphere with a large table and many chairs? If so, an area that is level enough to accommodate such a crowd will be a necessary part of your planning.

Enhancing Your Outdoor Space

Outdoor Lighting:

One of the best and simplest enhancements to enjoying our outdoor living space after hours is attractive and functional lighting. Thanks to low-voltage power requirements and installer-friendly instructions and kits, most homeowners find outdoor lighting well within their budget and ability. Specifics on planning for outdoor lighting can be found in Chapter 16.

Hardscapes and Garden Art:

A good way to add visual interest to any garden is by using hardscapes, sometimes referred to as garden art. These are non-plant items that can be functional as well, such as a statue, birdbath, garden bench, or fountain. The possibilities are unlimited and bound only by your imagination.

Hardscaping provides four seasons of interest and can dramatically enhance the overall design, add flair and punctuation to an otherwise drab landscape, or divert attention from an unsightly area. Hardscaping should complement the surrounding landscape without completely detracting from it and should be appropriate in scale for its intended area.

Hardscapes should appear to fit or belong in their setting. The visual weight and size should feel balanced and right. Although hardscapes are often earth toned, use of color can complement other elements in your garden.

Outdoor rooms can be just as functional and inviting as the inside of our home.

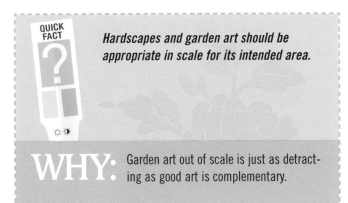

QUICK FACT

Hardscapes and garden art should be appropriate in scale for its intended area.

WHY: Garden art out of scale is just as detracting as good art is complementary.

Touchstone Accent Lighting

With proper lighting we are able to prolong the enjoyment of our gardens.

Furniture:

It's not your grandmother's wicker anymore! As we design our gardens to be outdoor rooms, furniture is an obvious accessory. Wood furniture has been the standard, with teak, cedar, cypress, redwood, and treated pine leading the way. Now, there are many other choices including plastic, wrought iron, composite plastics, bamboo, rattan, aluminum, and canvas.

Much of the outdoor furniture today including the material and cushions that go on them are weather resistant and can be left outdoors year round. However, your furniture will fade less and last longer if you store it indoors when not in use or out of season. Furniture designed for outside living is so popular, you can now find it at many garden centers, home improvement stores, and nurseries, right along with the all the plant material and potting soil.

Privacy and Mystery

Unless you plan on building physical walls around your landscape, trees and shrubs are the best way to provide natural *privacy*. The key is knowing the conditions of your area — including sun and shade levels, temperature zone, and soil type (wet or dry). Finding plants

Appropriately scaled garden art is another form of hardscape.

that grow best under your circumstances will provide the most satisfactory results for your privacy needs.

The first rule in choosing plant material for *screening* is to know what plants or trees grow best in your area for this purpose. A simple trip around the neighborhood may inspire you with ideas. If you don't know what that plant or tree is, don't be afraid to ask your neighbor. Another option is to take pictures of the plants and show them to a nursery professional for identification.

If this doesn't provide you with what you're looking for, another source of inspiration could be botanical gardens and arboretums in your growing region. Plenty of information is available in books, magazines, and on the Internet. Finally, an underutilized source available in many parts of the country is your local county extension service. They will have printed information relative to your particular growing conditions, and it's always nice to have an expert you can discuss your ideas with.

Once you decide on what to plant, know how to plant it correctly. All too often, we want instant results and get ahead of ourselves when we start to install the plants, not taking into consideration their mature sizes. As a result we place them too close together, and the outcome is almost always disappointing.

Tall trees and shrubs create natural "walls" around the pool area.

One landscaping technique to provide more immediate screening results and achieve long term success is to stagger the plantings in a triangular pattern. In this way, plants are allowed to spread out, but visual fullness is more quickly achieved.

Want to create mystery in the garden? Try creating *secret rooms* within your garden. Place plants so that an area is discovered as you round the corner, go through one part of a garden into another, or pass through a hedge or shrubs growing closely together. It's a "secret room" because it is hidden until you enter that area, often taking a detour off the main path to do so.

Any combination of plants or hardscapes can be used for this effect. The goal is simply to provide an enclosed space within your landscape or garden that is not immediately obvious. The pattern can be formal with all plants arranged like an actual wall, or more informal with plants working together to conceal what lies beyond. Secret rooms are fun and make outdoor spaces even more inviting.

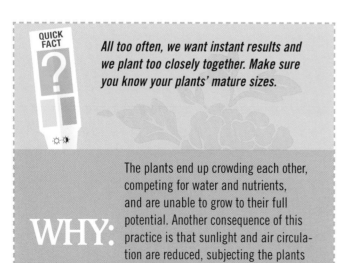

QUICK FACT

?

All too often, we want instant results and we plant too closely together. Make sure you know your plants' mature sizes.

WHY: The plants end up crowding each other, competing for water and nutrients, and are unable to grow to their full potential. Another consequence of this practice is that sunlight and air circulation are reduced, subjecting the plants to added stress and potential pest and disease problems.

Secret rooms are fun and offer an element of mystery.

"I love the way the texture and form of the plants along the pathway draw me in. It tells me this gardener has transcended the desire to have flower color dominate the design and relies instead on beautiful foliage to create visual interest."

Design Basics

Pathways to Striking Landscapes

There was a time when garden and landscape design focused primarily on flower color from annuals and perennials for most of the visual interest. Today professional designers and savvy home gardeners look to flower color more as a secondary issue for deciding what to plant where.

• *Foliage:* Thankfully plant breeders, nurseries, and designers have responded to our desire to have a more low-maintenance but interesting garden and landscape. Each year, more and more plants are being introduced that have highly ornamental qualities other than flowers. It is often seen in the unusual foliage color which can be every bit as brilliant as many flowers.

Even within one color family, such as green, there are so many tones and hues that entire gardens are designed around complementary and contrasting shades of it. Variations of tones can give even a monochromatic garden year-round interest.

• *Texture:* In plant foliage, texture has also taken on more importance in garden design as it is used to create diversity and variety among neighboring plants. Striking visual interest can even be achieved when working with two different plants with similar shades of green, simply by contrasting textures.

• *Form:* This relates to the overall shape of the plant, shrub or tree. Without regard to color or flower, form alone commands attention, creates diversity, or breaks up an otherwise boring design. Plant forms can

The striking foliage in this trough planting takes center stage.

provide the punctuation or blend shapes together into a unified vignette. Repeating the same plant shapes throughout the landscape can create rhythm and tie the entire design together. At the same time, throw in a unique form, and the eye stops—breaking the visual flow across the landscape.

There are many natural forms and shapes that can be used in landscape design. Plants and trees can be columnar, conical, oval, round, pyramidal, weeping, horizontally spreading, or arching.

• *Layers:* Nature creates the most beautiful combinations with no help on our part. As you observe a natural landscape you will note up to six layers of plants and trees.

Working from the ground up, the first layer is ground cover. In nature, ground cover consists of fields of various grasses and weeds. Think of goldenrod or dandelions in bloom. They are beautiful and yes, they look best when in *someone else's* landscape or in open fields. In our home landscapes this lowest layer is typically a lawn or one of many ground cover substitutes.

The second layer is low growing, up to about 12 inches in height. In nature, this layer could contain one or more of

QUICK FACT

Today professional designers and savvy home gardeners look to flower color more as a secondary issue for deciding what to plant where.

WHY: Actual flowers, although often times the first thing we notice, are only the center of attention for a relatively short time. Perennial blooms for instance usually last only a few weeks during the entire season, and annuals constantly have to be maintained to look their best.

TREES WITH INTERESTING FOLIAGE		ZONE*
Japanese Maple	*Acer palmatum*	5-8
Colorado Blue Spruce	*Picea pungens*	3a-8b
Eastern Redbud 'Forest Pansy'	*Cercis canadensis*	4a-9b
Eucalyptus	*Eucalyptus*	8b-11
Ginkgo	*Ginkgo biloba*	6a-9b
Hinoki False Cypress	*Chamaecyparis obtusa*	5a-11
Parsley Leaved Hawthorn	*Crataegus apiifolia*	7-10
Persian Parrotia	*Parrotia persica*	4a-8b
Robinia	*Robinia pseudoacacia* var. *aurea*	5a-9b
Smoke Tree	*Cotinus coggygria*	4a-8b
Variegated Dogwood	*Cornus alba*	3-8

* hardiness zone varies with cultivar and variety

SHRUBS WITH INTERESTING FOLIAGE		ZONE*
Acuba	*Acuba japonica*	6a-10b
Barberry	*Berberis thunbergii*	4a-8b
Blue Mist Shrub	*Caryopteris* 'Worchester Gold'	5a-9b
Gold Thread Cypress	*Chamaecyparis pisifera* 'Aurea'	5a-10b
Heavenly Bamboo	*Nandina domestica*	6a-9b
Ninebark	*Physocarpus opulifolius* 'Darts Gold'	2a-8b
Oakleaf Hydrangea	*Hydrangea quercifolia*	6a-9b
Purple leaved Elder	*Sambucus nigra*	3a-9b
Variegated Boxwood	*Buxus sempervirens* 'Aureovariegata'	5a-8b
Variegated Pieris	*Pieris japonica* 'Variegata'	5a-9b

hardiness zone varies with cultivar and variety

ANNUALS/PERENNIALS WITH INTERESTING FOLIAGE		ZONE*
Ajuga, Bugleweed	*Ajuga reptans*	3-9
Alum Root, Coral Bells	*Heuchera*	3-10
Canna, Canna Lily	*Canna*	7-11
Coleus	*Coleus blumei*	3-11
Cushion Spurge	*Euphorbia epithymoides*	5-8
Hosta	*Hosta*	3-8
Lambs Ear	*Stachys byzantina*	4-8
Lungwort	*Pulmonaria*	4-8
Persian Shield	*Strobilanthes dyerianus*	9-11
Caladium	*Caladium bicolor*	9-11

hardiness zone varies with cultivar and variety

many combinations of annuals and perennials which can be imitated in our own home landscape. You might imagine drifts of ferns or spreading perennials like daffodils and daylilies above the lowest layer.

In the third layer, we would see small shrubs up to 6 feet or so in height. A shrub can be defined as a woody plant, usually smaller than a tree, which produces several stems rather than a single trunk from the base. In our own designs these may include azaleas, rhododendrons,

hydrangeas, some hollies, etc.

Taller shrubs make up the forth layer. Again, the possibilities are many. Sometimes it is difficult to imagine that something 12 feet tall and shaped like a tree is still considered a shrub.

Making up the fifth or 'understory' layer, small trees take root and grow happily under the canopy of taller deciduous and evergreen trees. Dogwoods and redbuds are just two of many possibilities. They add an element of interest with spring blooms and fall color.

Finally, in the sixth layer, the tallest of trees dominate the upper canopy. These trees determine what is able to grow underneath them, based on the amount of light reaching through and the competition of the roots for moisture and nutrients.

In any case, what is seen in nature provides inspiration and illustrates ways we could think of creating a

Understory trees add an element of interest with spring blooms and fall colors.

This garden effectively reflects layers as seen in nature.

lines, symmetry, geometric patterns and relationships. However, in the home garden or landscape, this is more the exception than the rule. Rather, a casual, flowing design is more often the desired effect. Curved beds are generally more inviting, calming, and forgiving when creating the finished look. A bonus: curved bed lines are easier to mow.

natural looking design in our own gardens. Plenty of interest comes from the varying layers of plants and trees as well as their form, color, and texture.

Bed Lines

When it comes to designing your garden beds and landscape, you'll be faced with the decision of how to arrange the bed lines. Do you make straight beds, perfectly parallel with the sidewalk, or driveway, or house, or do you create curved, flowing beds that draw your eye down toward the next visual stopping point?

For most designs, curved beds may be the right choice. The main exception to this would be in the case of a formal garden design. This classic design technique uses straight

Even numbered plantings and mirror images work best with formal designs or when symmetry is the goal.

Flowing bed lines are easy on the eye.

The exception to this would be in a formal landscape design when you are deliberately trying to achieve symmetry, in which case even numbers and mirror images work best.

Using Focal Points

A focal point is anything that draws the eye to it. Examples in the garden include a statue or fountain at the end of a long narrow pathway or, a brilliant Japanese maple cloaked by a wall of dark evergreens. Focal points not only draw your eye to it, but they often draw the viewer towards it as well for a closer look.

Landscape designers agree the most effective step you can take to spruce up a landscape quickly is to sharpen the bed lines. The lines provide strong contrast between two distinct areas. The cleaner the definition, the greater impression you can make. When you're in a time pinch but you want to really spruce up your front yard or garden before guests arrive, the most noticeable thing you can do is sharpen up the bed lines where they might be walking.

Designing with Odd Numbers

When planting beds, especially when using shrubs or trees, think in terms of odd numbers. From a design standpoint, our eye tends to be more comfortable with odd numbers of plants such as one, three, five, nine, etc. It also contributes to soft curves and helps to get away from straight bed lines and tightly pruned geometric shapes.

PLANTS WITH STRIKING FORM		ZONE*
Agave, Century Plant	*Agave*	6b-10
African Mask	*Alocasia amazonica*	11
Australian Tree Fern	*Cyathea cooperi*	10b-11
Bamboo	*Phyllostachys, Borinda*	
	Fargesia, Pleioblastus, etc.	5-10
Banana 'Rowe Red'	*Banana Musa* 'Rowe Red'	8-11
Banana basjoo	*Musa basjoo*	3-11
Bear's Breech	*Acanthus mollis*	6-8a
Cactus	*Cactus*	3a-11
Canna	*Canna*	7-11
Castor Bean	*Ricinus communis*	2-11
Harry Lauder's Walking Stick	*Corylus avellana* 'Contorta'	4a-8b
Helleborus sternii	*Helleborus sternii* 'Blackthorn Strain'	5-9
Mugo Pine	*Pinus mugo*	3-7
New Zealand Flax	*Phormium tenax*	7b-10
Ornamental grass	*Panicum, Miscanthus*	
	Calamagrostis, Deschampsia, etc.	4-9
Sea Holly	*Eryngium* 'Miss Willmott's Ghost'	5-8

hardiness zone varies with cultivar and variety

Hardscapes can serve multiple purposes and should always be used to add visual interest to your design.

Usually this is for the intent of showcasing a unique or beautiful feature such as a piece of sculpture or a specimen tree with amazing branch structure or color. Another use of focal points can serve the dual purpose of cleverly distracting the eye away from an unsightly view. An example may be a utility pole, immovable structure, a car on blocks etc.

Any visually appealing object that can distract you away from that trailer or boat and call attention towards something else is the intent when focal points are used for this purpose. In your case, maybe it's your neighbor's rusty shed or garbage cans from which attention needs to be diverted.

Within any landscape, a great way to incorporate built-in variety, interest and visual punctuation is with focal points

in the form of hardscapes, garden art or strategically placed plants.

Hardscapes often serve as focal points. These are non-plant items placed in the garden to be enjoyed and viewed on their own merit, or to complement the choice of plant material around it. Usually hardscapes and plants work together, complementing each other in a visually pleasing way. Frequently they are objects of stone, wood or metal. They can be aesthetic, utilitarian or functional or any combination thereof.

Imagine an attractive retaining wall, stacked skillfully of native field stone. Imagine further that it is draped with attractive plants or covered with moss or lichen.

In this example the wall may serve multiple purposes as a hardscape. First, it is there to retain soil. It is utilitarian. It also happens to be at the perfect height to sit (by design) as one strolls through the garden and seeks a place to rest and take in a view of the landscape. It is functional. Now recall the beautiful native stack stone, draped with ground cover or spotted with moss or lichen. It is aesthetic. Hardscapes can serve not only one but multiple purposes

QUICK FACT

Landscape designers agree the most effective step you can take to spruce up a landscape quickly is to sharpen the bed lines.

WHY: As you look down or around the immediate vicinity, you are most likely to notice the area closest to your feet. That crisp sharp edge really makes a statement and will distract from other potentially less attractive views you'd rather your guests not see.

however they never have to be an eyesore and should always be used to add visual interest to your design.

Focal points can be just about anything. In fact, I can't think of an example that could not be a focal point if used in the proper application. However, common examples that can easily be used in the home garden and landscape include fountains and ponds, outdoor furniture such as one simple but unique chair, art or sculpture, a beautiful container, a specimen tree or even a bird bath or feeder.

Plant material used as a focal point is usually a striking specimen. I always think of a stately Japanese maple, reaching out with magnificent branch structure. Even when dormant, it commands attention because of its

Since focal points can be almost anything, add some whimsey to your garden with a humorous piece of art.

Shadows add punctuation to the bold form of this phormium.

beauty in the branching alone. But this is a tree with up to four seasons of interest. In the spring, emerging leaves may be lime green. In the summer they might turn to crimson red, and in the fall they can change again to shades of red, orange, and yellow. Set off by a background or dark ever-green foliage only helps to set the stage as this tree takes front and center.

Create Mystery

Focal points can also beckon you to come closer, and take a closer look. Many times you are first captivated as your eye is drawn towards the object. Quite often, because of its beauty or mystique, your body is drawn to it as well. To further entice the viewer, a focal point that is not completely in view or is framed tightly by hedges or visual barriers seems to call to us even more. There is something irresistable about geting a better look or seeing past the obstruction to get the great reveal.

Making Focal Points Stand Out

There are times when you have a special feature or specimen tree that you really want to show off. Depending on how you plant or design the landscape around it, you can accent that feature or detract from it.

Try painting chairs or a bench in the garden to give them punch.

WHY:

Painting objects can carry a color scheme through the garden or incorporate a color you'd like to use more.

Dense evergreens showcase the brilliant fall color of this Japanese maple drawing the eye and perhaps even the viewer towards it.

A good way to feature an object in the garden is to make sure the background is dense, monotone, and muted or in contrast to the object in the foreground. Said another way, don't put anything distracting behind what you want people to see. Keep the background subtle.

Conversely, an object that you are trying to feature can easily get "lost in the crowd" if too much is going on or if the colors of it blend in with the surroundings. Unless this is by design (and sometimes it is), objects will go unnoticed because they don't stand out enough.

Try *painting* chairs or a bench in the garden to give them punch, and carry a color scheme through the garden with color echoes. Use the paint color to introduce a color you would like to have more of but can't seem to get with plants or flowers. Painting objects such as furniture or accessories can do an excellent job of weaving the garden tapestry together.

The use of *contrasting colors* will pop a feature into view. For example, a specimen plant in a shady spot close to the ground may not be noticed if the ground underneath it is dark or has dark mulch. However, simply changing the mulch can instantly make that plant or garden bed come alive. Similarly, a special plant in a sunny spot may go unnoticed if the ground underneath is mulched with a light color. Simply using darker mulch can suddenly bring

In spring, these painted chairs and azaleas make a stunning combination.

Stimulating All the Senses

When we consider landscape design, we first think in terms of what we see. However, sight is only one of our five senses. In a complete landscape, we should strive to stimulate all the senses: sight, smell, hearing, taste, and touch. Beyond the seemingly infinite visual opportunities that exist, it is easy to incorporate elements that reach other senses as well.

that plant into view. Applying these techniques to any size project—from a single plant or object to an entire bed or beyond—is an easy way to get quick results.

The perfumed fragrances of jasmine, tea olive, gardenia, viburnum, roses, or native azaleas are just a few in a long list of aromatic plants. They can provide the scent that evokes the memory of a loved one or a special time or place. The sound of a bubbling fountain, a babbling creek, or the many tones of a wind chime can take you to a place far away. The opportunity to stimulate your taste can easily be provided by placing edible flowers, herbs, and fruit throughout your garden.

A monotone background allows this variegated dogwood to command attention.

QUICK FACT

A good way to feature an object in the garden is to make sure the background is dense, monotone, and muted or in contrast to the object in the foreground.

WHY: This technique will stop your eye at the object because there is nothing else of interest behind it that competes visually.

(1) The coarse texture of stone is softened by lichen and moss. (2) Beautiful bark can be found in the form of *Lagerstroemia* 'Natchez'. (3) Stone is used to compliment the fine texture of this Japanese maple.

Finally, there are so many textures to add to the overall sensory pleasures. From the soft foliage of lamb's ear and moss, the silky smooth bark of a sycamore tree, or the many surfaces of stone, closing your eyes and taking in all that you don't see can be an equally rewarding part of your garden experience.

Using Pathways

I think every great garden, no matter how simple or complex, should have pathways. Paths beckon and lead you along to discover that next great mystery that lies ahead. Paths are comfortable and reassuring under foot as they guide all who enter on a great adventure. Paths direct visitors and (usually) keep them from venturing to areas you don't want them to see.

Pathways give you a sense of security, and comfort. They let you know others have come before you. Paths can be nothing more than trodden earth, worn down from repeated use. They can be made of any number of materials, both natural and man-made. The material you choose to create your path can be as simple as collected leaves, wood mulch or bark, crushed stone, or bricks. There are many options.

Make a Splash with Large Drifts

Any time you want to make a visual splash within a garden bed, plant in mass—using many plants, not just a few. This is known as planting in drifts.

This concept is usually applied to bedding flowers or bulbs. However, the plant or flower color does not need to be bold, as in a large area of ferns planted beneath a canopy of trees. The mass planting will be all that is needed to create a statement.

The key to making a drift look natural is to make sure it has a bit of a random look to it. Although plants or beds may be laid out and planted in a symmetrical pattern, it is the large relaxed shape of the bed or plants in mass that gets noticed. In fact, to create the most natural looking drifts, try taking a large number of bulbs such as daffodils or tulips and tossing them onto the ground. Plant them where they lie to replicate what you might observe in nature.

Paths beckon and lead you along to discover that next great mystery that lies ahead.

EDIBLES THAT ARE SAFE IN THE GARDEN AS LANDSCAPE PLANTS			
COMMON NAME	BOTANICAL NAME	ZONE*	EDIBLE PART
American Persimmon	*Diospyros virginiana*	6a-9b	Fruit
Basil	*Ocimum basilicum*	10a-11	Leaves
Blueberry	*Vaccinium angustifolium laevifolium*	6-9	Fruit
Carnation	*Dianthus caryophyllus*	6a-9b	Petals
Cranberry	*Vaccinium macrocarpon*	2b-7a	Fruit
Daylilies	*Hemerocallis*	3-9	Flowers
Hardy Kiwi	*Actinidia arguta*	4-8	Fruit
Jersulam Artichoke	*Helianthus tuberosus*	4a-9b	Tubers
Lemon Verbena	*Aloysia triphylla*	8a-10b	Leaves
Marigold	*Tagetes tenuifolia*	Annual	Petals
Mint	*Mentha* sp.	4a-11	Leaves
Nasturtum	*Tropaeolum majus*	Annual	Buds, petals, leaves
Ostrich Fern	*Matteuccia pennsylvanica*	2-8	Fiddleheads
Pansy	*Viola* x *wittrockiana*	5a-9b	Petals, leaves
Sunflower	*Helianthus annuus*	Annual	Unopened buds, petals seeds
Violets	*Viola odorata*	4a-9b	Leaves, flowers
Yellowgrove Bamboo	*Phyllostachys aureosulcata*	5a-10b	Young shoots

These tulips make a visual splash with one color.

You will need:

- ❏ string or garden hose
- ❏ wooden stakes
- ❏ marking paint
- ❏ small sledge-hammer
- ❏ fieldstone
- ❏ gravel dust
- ❏ all-purpose sand
- ❏ grading rake
- ❏ tamping devise
- ❏ a level

project Installing a Walkway

Give consideration to the shape that you would like your path to have. If it is a curved path, mark it out with a garden hose. A straight path can be lined with stakes and string. If using stakes, drive them into the ground every 3 to 6 feet. Attach string close to the ground so the entire path is outlined.

Measure the length and width and multiply these to get the number of square feet. You'll need this information for ordering the proper quantity of stone and gravel base and sand. If your path is curved, use a rectanglular pattern for measuring to get an approximate total.

Spray the outline with marking paint. This step is optional but allows you to remove the hose or string making it easier to excavate your walkway.

Dig out the pathway to the depth of the stone plus 4 inches. This will allow for the base material that you add first. If you encounter any roots or large stone, it is advisable to remove them at this time. Otherwise the path could become unsettled or disturbed later.

Smooth out the excavated area so that it is basically level.

Apply a 3 inch layer of stone dust evenly across the base. Smooth this out as much as possible with a grading rake or steel tined rake. Pack this layer with a handheld tamper or other tool to provide a firm and even base.

Just above the stone dust, **apply an inch of coarse builder's sand or all purpose sand.** Note this is NOT play

sand (the kind you add to a child's sandbox which is too fine for use here). Again level and smooth this layer as you prepare it for the stone.

Place the stone pieces into the sand. Work them in enough so they are stable and level. Use a rubber mallet and the handle base to firm the stone. Use a level to make sure that the stone is even from one to the next.

Once you are satisfied with the layout and the stones are level and secure, **add more of the sand** to fill in the gaps between stones. **Moisten the sand** with a light spray of water to settle it.

Continue to **add sand until it is level** with the stone surface.

project Creating Sharp Bed Lines

You will need:

- ❏ garden hose
- ❏ marking paint or powder
- ❏ garden spade or equivalent

Decide how you want the bed to look.

Use a flexible garden hose or rope to **define the bed lines.** (TIP: broad, gradual curves generally look better than tight wavy curves.)

Adjust this line until you are satisfied with the look. (TIP: look at the line from several directions to get a feel for it from different perspectives.)

Use marking paint or powder such as lime or chalk **to track or copy the hose** outline.

Remove the hose. You should now have the entire bed line clearly marked.

Use a sharp, squared, flat blade or spade to **cut at least 6 inches into the** turf.

Pull the handle back towards your body with blade still inserted in turf. This will force the soil into the bed.

Proceed along the line until the project is complete.

Maintain sharp edges with a mechanical edger or spade.

“Once you achieve privacy, the sky's the limit to what you can do in your own backyard.”

Landscaping and **Gardening** with a **Purpose**

Outdoor Space to Suit Your Lifestyle

Gardens and gardening mean different things to different people. Some live to spend as much time in their gardens as possible. They are just as happy working in it as they are entertaining there. The garden is pure pleasure at all times. Unless they have physical limitations, these individuals would never consider hiring someone else to do their gardening. I am one of these!

Then there are those who are most happy looking at their yard or garden from the comfort of a climate controlled environment, safe and secure from weeds, bugs, dirt, and sweat. They are far happier writing a check to have the work done by someone else than doing it themselves. My neighbor is one of these!

Then there's everyone else. They fall in between the first two groups. You may see that you are somewhere in this middle group. A little work is okay now and then, or you may enjoy parts of gardening but don't want anything to do with other parts. Most homeowners fit into this group.

No matter which group you find yourself in, almost everyone enjoys the opportunity to entertain outdoors. Now more than ever, it is popular to create outdoor living spaces that rival the comfort and conveniences of the indoors.

So, to create a perfect outdoor room for one or one hundred, there are several options you will want to consider as you prepare the appropriate space.

Outdoor living spaces today rival the comfort and conveniences of the indoors.

Privacy: Seclusion, Screening, Mystery

In a room for one, that place where you go for some outdoor peace and quiet, it may be as simple as stringing up a hammock between two well-spaced trees. We just want a quiet spot to get away, and we don't necessarily want to be seen either.

"Outdoor walls" are easily created by using appropriate shrubs and trees to create a lush enclosed area. The key to pulling this off is to select plants or trees that have the growth habit to provide density and that will do well based on your cultural conditions such as sunlight, temperature, and soil. I'll say it often

Dense shrubs create a lush, enclosed area.

EVERGREEN SCREENING PLANTS		ZONE*
Acuba	Acuba japonica	6a-10b
American Holly	Ilex opaca	5-10
Bamboo	Bambuseae (1,000 species)	5-10
Boxwood	Buxus sp.	4-9
Camellia	Camellia japonica	6b-9b
	Camellia sasanqua	7a-9b
Canadian Hemlock	Tsuga canadensis	3a-7b
Carolina Hemlock	Tsuga carolininana	4-7
Cherry Laurel	Prunus caroliniana	7a-9b
Chinese Juniper	Juniperus chinensis	4a-9b
Cryptomeria	Cryptomeria japonica	5a-9b
Eastern Arborvitae,	Thuja occidentalis	2a-8b
Eastern Red Cedar	Juniperus virginiana	3a-9b
Eastern White Pine	Pinus strobus	6a-9b
Holly 'Nellie R. Stevens'	Ilex aquifolium x I. cornuta	6a-9b
Holly varieties	Ilex sp.	2-10
English Laurel	Prunus 'Otto Luyken'	5b-8b
Lusterleaf Holly	Ilex latifolia	7-9
Leyland cypress	Cupressocyparis leylandii	6a-10b
Magnolia 'Little Gem'	Magnolia grandiflora	6a-10b
European Privet	Ligustrum vulgare	4-11
Viburnum	Viburnum sp.	3-9
White Fir	Abies concolor	3-7
Yew	Taxus sp.	3a-8b

hardiness zone varies with cultivar and variety

throughout this book, but putting the right plant in the right place gives you a tremendous head start on achieving success.

Another aspect of creating privacy around your garden is to create mystery *in* your garden. Utilizing the same plants and trees to screen the public view can be incorporated to tease visitors within your garden. Curved pathways lined with tall shrubs create a sense of enclosure and mystery. They draw the curious around the bend. Mark the point of entry by creating a keyhole or narrow opening and you will make it irresistible for guests to want to see what is through the opening to that mysterious enclosed space.

Public vs. Private Space

With *private* outdoor space, you have permission to make it as cozy, messy, or intimate as you want. This area is designated as that part of your landscape which is generally not part of one's visit to your backyard. It's like your bedroom in your house. Since visitors rarely happen upon it, maybe you choose not to make up your bed or pick up your clothes every day.

Create mystery with curved paths and tall shrubs.

Imagine a quiet, tucked away spot with a big hammock or a favorite chair or two. You could encourage chirping birds by including well-stocked feeders. The sky is truly the limit on what you can do in your own backyard hideaway.

That part of your landscape which is viewed from the street or any place where visitors will have access is the *public space*. You always want to keep this place neat and attractive. This part of your landscape is where you can really show off your gardening and design skills. Not only do you want to have this area looking good most if not all of the time, but it needs to be functional for all who visit as well. Think of your

The public area is a place where you can showoff your handiwork, gardening and design skills.

living room in your house. If there are children either living there or visiting, then make sure the public area (and private) is safe and secure.

If there are senior adults or people with physical limitations, make sure that access to all areas of the public space is as safe as possible. One of the biggest obstacles when physical limitations are an issue is with slopes, steps, and pathways. Make sure paths are basically smooth, level, and even for ease of navigation. Steps should have an appropriate rise over run relationship, and slopes should never be slippery or so steep that anyone is challenged with negotiating an up or down climb. In these cases, cutting into the slope to create some level walking areas would be a simple but far safer solution than the "cross your fingers and hope they make it" option.

Fragrant Plants: An Added Dimension

To me, a classic example of a "welcome sign" for the public area of a home landscape is the heavenly scent of a gardenia plant or oriental lilies in bloom. Now imagine that fragrance beckoning you from a location near the front entryway. Imagine what sort of impression the sweet perfumed fragrance will have on all who come to visit. Fragrance, the sound of moving water or wind chimes, and the display of beautiful plants and flowers all come together to make the public area a memorable and relaxing place for you and your guests.

Fragrant plants should be placed all around your yard for an extra dimension to a pleasing garden. Look for plants that are fragrant at different times of the year to prolong the enjoyment.

 How well do you know your neighbors?

If you don't like frequent or surprise visitors, you may not want to plan for fragrance in your front yard. Its magnetic affect will draw even strangers to your door!

Service Area

Do you have or need a service area? The service area is probably not a place that will be visited by company. This area is set up for storage of tools and equipment, a potting area, as well as a likely place for trash cans or air conditioning units. It is usually easy to screen these places from public view with shrubs, lattice, fencing, etc. We all usually have at least one service area. Keeping these areas out of the way and out of view will be to your advantage as you plan for the overall design.

Children's Play Area

A children's play area also may be a place that is specially designated as such, with swings, toys, and anything else

FRAGRANT PLANTS			ZONE*
Angel's Trumpet	*Brugmansia*	Perennial	7b-10
Banana Shrub	*Michelia figo*	Shrub	7b-10
Butterfly Ginger	*Hedychium coronarium*	Perennial	7-11
California Lilac	*Ceanothus concha*	Shrub	8-10
Clove Currant	*Ribes odoratum*	Shrub	5a-8b
Confederate Jasmine	*Trachelospermum jasminoides*	Vine	7b-10
Daphne	*Daphne odora*	Shrub	7-9
Fragrant Tea Olive	*Osmanthus fragrans*	Shrub	7-10
Gardenia	*Gardenia jasminoides*	Shrub	7-10
Hosta 'Royal Standard'	*Hosta* 'Royal Standard'	Perennial	3-8
Hyacinth	*Hyacinthus orientalis*	Bulb	4-8
Korean Spice Viburnum	*Viburnum carlesii*	Shrub	4-7
Lavender	*Lavandula* sp.	Perennial	5-10
Lemon Verbena	*Aloysia triphylla*	Herb	7-10
Lilac	*Syringa*	Shrub/tree	3-9
Lily of the Valley	*Convallaria majalis*	Bulb	4a-8b
Mock Orange	*Philadelphus*	Shrub	4a-8b
Oriental Lily	*Lilium* sp.	Bulb	4b-9b
Passion Flower	*Passiflora*	Vine	6b-10b
Roses	*Rosa* sp.	Shrub	4-10
Sweet Box	*Sarcococca hookeriana* var. *humilis*	Tall ground cover	6a-9b
Tall Stock	*Matthiola incana*	Annual flower	6-10
Thyme	*Thymus vulgaris*	Ground cover	4-7
Vernal Witchhazel	*Hamamelis vernalis*	Shrub/small tree	4b-8b
Virginia Sweetspire	*Itea virginica*	Shrub	5-9

hardiness zone varies with cultivar and variety

Simple and well designed barriers can effectively conceal equipment and trash cans.

that can draw and keep them and their toys in a particular part of the yard.

Points to Consider When Planning a Children's Play Area:

If play structures and fencing are made of wood, use ***non-treated, rot resistant material.*** Other choices include recycled wood composites that will last until your children's children are ready to play at your house.

Consider recycled ***rubber mulch to soften the play area*** under foot. Note: This is the only time you'll see me suggest rubber mulch, but for this application, it makes for a soft landing pad and doesn't attract bugs. One word of caution: If your play area will be in direct sun, rubber may have the potential of being a little too good at absorbing heat. Keep this in mind, and plan accordingly.

If using ***herbicides*** and ***pesticides*** in your home landscape, avoid the use of these products around the children's play area. Although there are products on the market labeled as safe for children, it's best not to use anything.

⚠ **Kids and cats love sandboxes.**

If you incorporate a sandbox, be sure to cover it when it's not in use. Sandboxes are famous as outdoor litter boxes for the entire neighborhood!

Locate a play area within adequate view from inside the house. If adults are not immediately present, they at least should be able to see the children at all times.

Entertaining

In former days, entertaining outside consisted of throwing a few burgers and dogs on the charcoal grill, bringing out some folding chairs, or brushing off the picnic table. If you were really feeling wild, maybe you strung some colored lights across the patio.

These days, entertaining in our own back yards has never been more popular or sophisticated. With built-in fireplaces, kitchens (complete with sinks, cook tops, and refrigeration), all-weather furniture, stereo speakers

Perhaps a children's play area is part of your landscape plan.

Attract birds to your private retreat as an added benefit

HOW: Keeping feeders well stocked with their favorite foods will have the birds chirping and you relaxed. Although birds will naturally be present, the sound of their chirping and the sight of them foraging about is one of the most relaxing pastimes I know. I equate it to the sound of flowing water or the sight of a well-stoked fire.

Kitchen or Vegetable Garden

As I've taped shows for *Fresh from the Garden*, I have had many opportunities to visit and create gardens within the landscape that were both functional and beautiful. Most often, these were kitchen or vegetable gardens. When incorporating them into your landscape, it is important to understand the cultural requirements of vegetables and herbs so they will grow, look their best, and produce well. Having those plants convenient to your kitchen is almost as important.

A kitchen garden is the ideal way to provide fresh herbs and vegetables at your fingertips for your cooking pleasure. Gardens of this type don't need to be large, especially if you are really just in it for the culinary herbs. A little goes a long way as they say. Just a few small raised beds will do the job. If you would like to have access to fresh vegetables as well, you will need more space.

More About Herbs

Herbs, depending on the part of the country you live in, can be annual or perennial. There are also many different

concealed inside faux rocks, and low voltage/high intensity outdoor lighting, we've entered a whole different world.

Preparing a landscape to incorporate such a room in detail is beyond the scope of this book. However, we will address different aspects of enhancing our outdoor living space after hours, in a later chapter.

If you have plans for future projects such as an outdoor kitchen or pond, having the vision for that today and planning ahead as you get started makes implementing the plan much easier later on. Even consider where you'd like to place a specimen tree or piece of garden art. This gives you a head start on a mature looking design when you finally do move on to additional phases of the plan.

Outdoor kitchens extend the living space.

cultivars and varieties. I have not included zones in this list, only the species name so you can decide which variety you would like to grow, then research whether it might be annual or perennial in your area.

To make a functional kitchen garden, you need a location that gets at least six hours of direct sun each day. You also need well-drained soil. I find the easiest way to achieve this is to make raised beds and create the ideal soil that goes into them. Then, not only can you avoid the challenges of trying to grow in poor soil, the options of growing in raised beds can add an element of beauty as well.

Whatever space you end up using, herbs and vegetables both benefit from well-drained soil. Since many herbs prefer conditions that are dryer than most vegetables, it would be ideal to have at least two raised beds to provide optimal conditions for each.

CLASS HERBS FOR THE KITCHEN GARDEN	
Basil	*Ocimum basilicum*
Chives, Garlic	*Allium*
Dill	*Anethum graveolens*
Fennel	*Foeniculum vulgare*
Lavender	*Lavandula*
Lemon Balm	*Melissa officinalis*
Lemon Grass	*Cymbopogon citratus*
Lemon Verbena	*Aloysia triphylla*
Majoram	*Origanum majorana*
Mint	*Mentha*
Oregano	*Origanum*
Parsley	*Petroselinum crispum*
Rosemary	*Rosmarinus*
Sage	*Salvia*
Savory, Summer	*Satureja hortensis*
Savory, Winter	*Satureja montana*
Tarragon (French)	*Artemisia dracunculus*
Thyme	*Thymus*

The Approach: Great First Impressions

For some reason, we tend to spend most of the time working on our back yards when it comes to gardening and landscapes. But, creating that welcoming, inviting approach from the street or driveway to our front door is what really sets the stage. This is what the real estate industry terms "curb appeal."

When Designing a Pleasing Approach:

- *Keep shrubs pruned* back below window level.

- *Soften stark wall areas* between windows with appropriate taller plants or vines.

- *Accent the pathway* to the front door by planting low growing shrubs, flowers, or ground covers.

- *Place containers* of healthy looking plants at the location you are leading your guests towards. One container or a grouping of

A neat, tidy approach makes a great first impression.

Notice how the burgundy tones of the cannas echo the window trim color.

containers on each side of the doorway or stoop works well. Just be sure that the containers are in scale, neither too large nor too small in relation to the entry and landing.

- ***Don't overdo the planting.*** You don't want a busy look that is distracting and overpowering. Complement the house design and color scheme. Plants and flowers are an excellent way to unify the house with the garden, using complementary and contrasting colors. With so many choices in flower and foliage color, there is no reason to clash.

- ***Choose colors that set the mood.*** Do you want guests to feel calm and relaxed when they arrive at your front door? Then choose the cooler colors of greens, blues, purples, pastel pinks, and silvers. If you want to evoke excitement and energy, then use hot colors such as yellow, orange, and red. Again, be sure to work with existing color schemes of the house itself. It is usually much easier to work with the plants to match the house than changing the house to match the plants (although I know some people who do!).

- ***Pick a walkway style.*** If you are designing a walkway or path to the front door, a *curved path* has a similar effect as using cool colors. It slows you down a bit, relaxes, and calms. A *straight path* from the street or driveway is more formal. It speeds you up and directs visitors toward the front door.

In a formal landscape or for simplicity or other reasons, a straight path or walkway is appropriate and looks great. It's classic, traditional, and easy to navigate.

- ***Keep it neat.*** In an approach garden (that area first seen as guests approach an entrance to your home), it is especially important to keep your lawn, plants, flowers, and trees looking ***neat and tidy*** for great first impressions.

Well chosen containers add visual appeal.

Don't overlook the need to look up toward the trees. If you are fortunate enough to have large trees in your front yard, one of the most important steps you can take to improving the look and opening up the front view is to limb up the trees. To *limb up* means to raise the canopy of the tree branches.

• *Use outdoor lighting.* Many of your visitors will arrive or depart after dark. Incorporating outdoor lighting along the walkway and spotlighting dark areas will speak volumes to your guests. It will tell them that their comfort and safety are important to you. Beyond safety, placing mood lighting to soften a wall or to feature a special tree or object can be simple extras that make your landscape stand out. More details on outdoor lighting are covered in chapter 15.

A lighted pathway tells your visitors their comfort and safety are important to you.

Assessing and Preparing a New Site

Every yard presents a mix of conditions regarding sun exposure (including lack of sun), flat or sloping terrain, wet or dry ground, sandy or compacted soil, etc. We're all faced with conditions that require some advance thought in order to plant appropriate material. If plants are to thrive in our landscapes, it is important that they be ideally suited for the environment. My mantra again: Put the right plant in the right place for best results.

Most physical conditions can be altered to what you need, but the amount of work required to bring those conditions in line may be unrealistic. However, there are a few basics that you should look for when selecting the ideal environment: *sun, shade, slope, screening, and drainage.*

How Much Sunlight is Available?
Whatever the case, there are plants that will work. But planting anything that loves full sun into full shade or vice versa is asking for problems.

What Type of Soil Do You Have?
The goal for any garden soil is for it to drain well yet hold enough moisture to be available for plant roots until the

next watering. This is an unusual condition naturally. Usually soil is either too dense or compacted and water does not drain well enough. Other times, the soil is too sandy and moisture is not retained long enough. Either condition is correctable by adding organic material.

How Much Work Will You Need To Do?
On occasion, you may find that the natural planting conditions in your yard are perfect: not too loose and not too compact. Unfortunately, most of the time, our yards are one extreme or the other. In those cases, improving the soil will be to your advantage.

For many years, the widely accepted rule for planting and transplanting shrubs and trees was to amend the new planting hole with lots of organic matter to provide more drainage, improve water holding capacity, or both. As it turns out, studies show that amending this soil is not necessarily the best thing for woody ornamental plants and trees after all. Chapter 8 gives more specific advice for planting trees and shrubs.

Appropriately scaled shrubs would give this house some much needed curb appeal.

In a nutshell, trees and shrubs will ultimately respond better when they begin growth in their native soil. This way they can more quickly adapt to the long term conditions of their surroundings while continuing to grow roots out into a larger area.

One exception to using non-amended soil: You may want to amend soil if you have the opportunity to improve the *entire* planting area where the roots will be, even at full maturity. Amending such a large area is often not practical, but it helps in creating optimal growing conditions and nutrition. This is especially true when planting annual and perennial beds. These beds should always be full of deep, loamy, nutrient-rich soil. Unless you begin with outstanding soil, it is recommended that you improve as much of the area as you can.

Prepare for Planting

Have you ever stood in front of your house, either on the street or sidewalk and tried to imagine how to add that much needed curb appeal? Many of us start with a boring front yard, lacking personality and charm. New homes are often under-planted and somewhat stark. Other times we either inherit an overgrown, rundown yard, or it simply happens over time under our watch (or lack of it).

So how do we go about reclaiming and taming that overgrown yard, or adding some punch to our less than curb-appealing landscapes? The following are some important questions and suggestions on where and how to begin.

What's Not Working in the Old Landscape?

Undoubtedly there will be a few things you like and quite a few things you can live without. This is a good time to be ruthless. In many cases plants that were original to the house should never have been planted there in the first place. If your gut is telling you something doesn't look quite right, listen to it. Imagine the view without those plants, large overgrown shrubs and trees. There will always be something to replace it with. This may be one of the hardest obstacles to overcome as you do your front yard makeover.

Right Plant, Right Place (Have I Mentioned That?)

I don't know about where you live but I suspect it's pretty much the same overall. If you live in an "older home" chances are you still have a lot of the original landscaping

QUICK FACT

Amending soil is not necessarily the best thing for woody ornamental plants and trees.

WHY:

When the feeder roots or root tips encounter less favorable conditions beyond the amended area, they will most likely stop pushing out. Instead, they will stay in the improved soil. Root and plant growth will subsequently slow down significantly.

This photo shows an obscured entrance and hidden windows.

that was placed there by the builder. At the time, it probably looked okay, maybe a little on the sparse side. Then, a few years later, it really looked nice. The plants had established themselves, grown up a bit, and looked in scale with the rest of the house and yard. The problem was, the plants and trees kept growing! Now they're taking over the house, concealing the windows and entryway, uprooting the walkway, front stoop, and driveway. In some cases, even the house foundation is being compromised.

In these cases, with plants growing so well, they were getting the amount of sunlight and water to help them thrive. However, there's another consideration: mature height and width. The right plant in the right place should never require any severe pruning because its mature habit was taken into consideration when purchased and planted.

⚠ **Don't be afraid to start over.**

Planting fast-growing shrubs and trees too close to each other or too close to the house is simply asking for

trouble. It will guarantee more work for you later. If you find that you have a landscaping challenge such as this, don't be shy about starting over. It can be traumatic to think about severely cutting back or removing a healthy, full-grown shrub. But, if it's taking over the house or foundation, it's time for it to go! Pull out the loppers, pruning saw, ax, or chain saw and erase the errors.

It seems harsh and drastic and I'm not saying it must always be done (I am a tree hugger at heart!). But if it's the wrong plant for that location, unless you do cut it down, you'll likely be faced with an annual chore of pruning, lopping, and cutting to resize it to stay in bounds. Eventually that gets old!

Limbing Up

One of the most important outdoor activities I save for the dormant months is to limb up trees. I have a lot of them, and left unchecked, they could easily shade out the entire yard and conceal the front part of the house from view. However, with some selective cutting, I am able to enjoy

The window is cleared and the entrance is open and welcoming.

the beauty of the trees, open up the view from the street to the house, and allow more light to filter down to the lawn and other plants. The light filtering through is sufficient to keep my turf lush, and the sun-loving plants happy.

This annual or semi-annual exercise is well worth it. I am constantly getting comments from my neighbors and other gardeners surprised at how well my lawn and other plants do, in spite of having so many trees. Limbing up your trees can be a do-it-yourself project, but I don't advise it. The older I get, the more inclined I am to hire a professional. There are several things to keep in mind if you decide to have your trees limbed up.

Which Trees Should You Prune?

As you survey your landscape, examine all the trees that overhang your roof, block windows, or excessively obstruct the view of your house from the street. Also examine trees that affect sunlight reaching the ground. In woodland areas, you may not need to do any pruning. However, if there are areas where your plants are looking "leggy", or places where you are struggling to grow grass, or if certain shrubs just are not flowering like they should, you'll need to see what you can do to bring more light to the ground. Short of cutting the trees down, limbing up is the next best thing and gives a neater look to your entire yard.

Limbing up is one of the stealth landscaping techniques that makes a big difference without being noticed. Unless

Limbing up is best completed in late winter when you can see the branch structure more easily.

one is really observant, a landscape that has had the tree canopy raised (limbed up) seems more open without feeling thin. I've had many visitors comment about my yard as it relates to this. They notice something different about it vs. other yards, but they can never put their finger on just what that difference is.

To really open up the area underneath the canopy, have as many of the lower limbs removed as possible. The higher you can make the canopy, the better. Be sure to keep in mind the aesthetic consequences of these cuts. You'll be surprised to find you won't even miss those limbs.

Your trees might look even better if proper attention is given to uniformity during the pruning process.

⚠️ Do not paint wounds or pruning cuts.

The old standard recommendation was to paint or dress pruning wounds to protect the cut surface from drying out and cracking and to seal the wound from pest and disease entry. This practice is no longer recommended. In

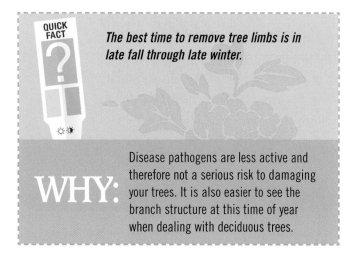

QUICK FACT

The best time to remove tree limbs is in late fall through late winter.

WHY: Disease pathogens are less active and therefore not a serious risk to damaging your trees. It is also easier to see the branch structure at this time of year when dealing with deciduous trees.

fact, research has shown that it can exacerbate the problem. Tree wound paint does not prevent rot and in some cases promotes it by sealing in moisture. The tree is best equipped on its own to deal with the situation. The best we can do is make the right cut.

Some people think that if they prune trees early in the year they will bleed to death. This is a myth. Although some trees such as maples and birches do bleed when cut early in the season, this will not harm the tree. This bleeding is merely sap. Some trees that are especially prone to bleeding include beech, birch, elm, maple, and yellow-wood. Although it is unsightly, the tree is fine.

One other thing to consider when deciding which limbs to remove is where you would like limbs to shade certain plants. For example, I have a bed of azaleas that happily grow under several tall trees. But, there are lower branches on these trees that could be limbed up. However, I don't want to remove the branches on the west side of the tree because they provide shade and protection to my azaleas

Limb up trees that overhang your roof, block windows, or obstruct the view of your house from the street.

below from the harsh, late afternoon sun. In this case, judicious pruning is best.

The 3-Step Approach to Pruning

A three-step approach is the proper way to prune tree limbs. Make the first cut about 1 or 2 feet out from the tree trunk. Start this cut *on the underside* of the limb and go into it, but only *about half way*. This is a very important step in the process.

The second cut is out beyond the first cut another foot or two. This cut goes down and all the way through the branch. The branch is likely to break away as you make your way through the limb. Because you've already made the first cut properly, the bark will not continue to tear down into the tree trunk.

The final cut is right at the branch collar (where the branch meets the trunk). You'll notice a flared area here. Make the final cut so that the flare is just evident. If cut properly, this flare will heal over and eventually fill in with new bark or scar tissue. You'll know the tree is healing properly when you notice what looks like a doughnut forming where you made the cut.

Hire a Certified Arborist

There was a time when I would tackle this limbing-up project myself. Now that I am older and wiser, I realize this job is best left for a professional "Certified Arborist." Mature trees are not easily replaced and improper pruning could lead to their demise. Certified Arborists have the training and equipment to get the job done right, while protecting your trees. You can find them listed in the phone book under "Tree Care." Look for the "Certified Arborist" logo or designation by their name.

 **Buyer beware!**

Stay clear of economy tree services. Just because someone has a chainsaw and a pick up truck, doesn't mean they know what they are doing. Rather, their interest is likely

(1) Make the first cut underneath the branch but only halfway through. (2) Make the second cut beyond the first and through the branch. (3) Make the final cut at the branch collar.

in getting the job done as quickly as possible, with little to no regard to the long-term health of your trees. If your hired help pulls out tree climbing spikes to prune your trees, send them on their way. These are very harmful to trees and should only be used for complete tree removal.

A true Certified Arborist will have credentials. Ask to see them. In all cases, you'll want to inspect that they have the proper insurance. The professionals pay dearly for this, and they expect you to ask.

And, if these are not enough reasons to hire the work out to a professional, consider the consequences of even one fall from a ladder. No matter how much you think you're saving, it is not worth it!

QUICK FACT

Limbing up is one of the stealth landscaping techniques that makes a big difference without really being noticed.

WHY: One of the primary reasons to prune tree limbs is to open the canopy of your landscape, allowing more sunlight to reach the grass and low growing shrubs. It also makes for a more balanced, aesthetically pleasing look.

Pet Friendly Gardens and Landscapes

If you have a pet that spends any time outdoors, especially dogs, chances are it might be a challenge to keep the yard looking great and be reasonable on Fido as well. Since the bulk of destruction comes at the paws and mouth of dogs, we'll focus our discussion here first.

To start, be patient, keep your sense of humor and know that most dogs will eventually learn what it is you are trying to teach them if you are consistent and just show them. They're only doing what comes naturally and it's their turf too.

Your Pet's Path to Happiness

Keeping dogs from wearing out the backyard grass is an ongoing battle. A designated path is usually the best alternative. Either create the path directly on top of the worn area, or create a new path and encourage your pet to use it instead. A clever way to train your dog to use this new path is to walk him on it regularly and sweeten the pot (or trail) as well. You'll keep Fido coming back for more if you drag some raw meat wrapped in cheesecloth along the path. You may need to repeat this a few times or after it rains, but in time, you should get the results you are after.

For example, let's assume Fido has worn a clearly marked path along your back fence line where sod once grew. As long as Fido is part of the family, sod will likely never grow there. Mulching that pathway will at least keep dust or mud off of Fido and out of your house.

One of the biggest challenges is trying to get dogs to use the bathroom outside of the public space. Assuming your dog has no designated space to relieve himself, all parts of the yard are equally suspect. As an alternative, train your dog to go in a certain area each time. Lead your dog from the house to a designated area where you want him to consistently go. On leash, guide him to this area and patiently wait until the job is done. Reward Fido lavishly and then remove the leash.

Incorporate your pet's natural path into your landscape design.

New motion-activated sensors can be used to deter pets and other animals from entering an area you have designated as off limits. They are quite effective as a deterrent and also work for many types of pests. They are reasonably priced and readily available. The biggest downside to these devices is they can't tell the difference between pets, pests, and people. So be sure to shut off the water before approaching the area, and remember to deactivate the devices before you plan to work in that area.

⚠ **Keep your yard pet-friendly.**

Poisonous plants can be a problem for pets as well as people. If you have pets that spend time unsupervised in your yard, review the list of poisonous plants on the next page. Most plants will not cause severe problems but rather temporary discomfort. However, some can be deadly to pets when ingested, so it is important to be cautious.

Certain plants aren't the only risk to pets. According to the AICPA, the use of cocoa bean shell mulch in landscaping should not be used around unsupervised dogs. Cocoa bean

shell mulch has an attractive odor and smell. Some dogs will eagerly eat large amounts. It can be toxic with symptoms such as gastrointestinal upset, muscle tremors, and seizures. Death may result.

Products formulated with Metaldehyde as the active ingredient should not be used anywhere near the presence of children or animals. Unfortunately, this is still a commonly sold product for snail and slug control. There are safer options. See Chapter 12.

Dogs Will Be Dogs

- *Burned Spots in the Lawn*

On a separate but related note, you may be dealing with burned out spots in your lawn. Although there are several reasons for this, the one I am referring to is caused by dog urine. The burning is the result of a high nitrogen content in the urine. There are products on the market that are designed to neutralize the effect of this somewhat, but these products are not without controversy. Changing

The best way to deal with urine spots in the lawn is to flush the area immediately with water.

Fido's diet to the point that it significantly changes the chemistry of his urine can be unsafe. The rewards are not worth the risk to your pet.

The simplest way to neutralize the burning effect of urine is simply to flush the area with water immediately after your dog has relieved himself.

• *Digging*

Certain dogs were born to dig, and that's what they do in your yard. In these cases it may be a combination strategy that works best. If the dog is a digger, you're not likely going to change him into a non-digger. So, as Fido claws his way to China, interrupt this action in a firm voice and redirect him to the DDA (Designated Digging Area). You can make this most inviting to him by burying favorite

COMMON PLANTS TOXIC TO DOGS	
Amaryllis	*Hippeastrum*
American Bittersweet	*Celastrus scandens*
Autumn crocus	*Colchicum autumnale*
Azalea	*Rhododendron*
Buckeye	*Aesculus*
Caladium	*Caladium hortulanum*
Calla Lily	*Zantedeschia*
Castor Bean	*Ricinus communis*
Clematis	*Clematis*
Daffodil	*Narcissus*
Daylily	*Hemerocallis*
Foxglove	*Digitalis*
Holly	*Ilex*
Hyacinth	*Hyacinthus orientalis*
Hydrangea	*Hydrangea*
Iris	*Iris*
Lilies (Asian, Easter, Tiger, Oriental)	*Lilium*
Lily of the Valley	*Convallaria majalis*
Morning Glory	*Ipomoea*
Nandina, Heavenly Bamboo	*Nandina*
Rhododendron	*Rhododendron*
Tomato	*Solanum lycopersicum*
Tulip	*Tulipa*
Yew	*Taxus*

COMMON PLANTS TOXIC TO CATS	
Castor Bean	*Ricinus communis*
Almonds	*Prunus dulcis*
Amaryllis	*Hippeastrum*
Caladium	*Caladium hortulanum*
China Berry Tree	*Melia azedarach*
Chrysanthemum	*Chrysanthemum*
Daffodil	*Narcissus*
Delphinium	*Delphinium*
Foxglove	*Digitalis*
Larkspur	*Delphinium*
Mock Orange	*Philadelphus coronarius*
Morning Glory	*Ipomoea*
Nutmeg	*Myristica fragrans*
Periwinkle	*Vinca minor*
Poinsettia	*Euphorbia pulcherrima*
Pokeweed	*Phytolacca americana*
Privet	*Ligustrum*
Skunk Cabbage	*Symplocarpus foetidus*
Wisteria	*Wisteria*
Yews	*Taxus*

toys, snacks, or anything that might interest him.

The digging area can be filled with softer, safer sand and organic material, tilled deeply enough for even the most aggressive dogs. To further delineate this DDA, line it with plants, pots, or stones so there is actually a physical area that is clearly marked for this purpose.

As a final touch for keeping him in bounds, line the dog run with low growing shrubs to encourage him to stay on the beaten path. Know that dogs will likely hover along the fence line if one exists. They are territorial and will want to greet or warn all creatures that pass by.

project Measuring Your **Drainage**

You will need:
- ❏ tape measure
- ❏ timer
- ❏ water
- ❏ shovel

Soil that is sandy or loose may drain too quickly. Water can pass by the roots before they have a chance to absorb the moisture and nutrients. On the other hand, soil that is too dense or compact may not drain quickly enough, causing plants to drown or rot.

Ideally, soil should drain neither too quickly nor too slowly. A good way for you to assess the percolation qualities in your home garden is to conduct a simple "perc test." It's a quick and easy project and will provide key information on how to amend your soil if necessary. Here are the steps to conduct your own soil perc test at home:

1. **Dig a hole** a foot deep and about a foot wide.

2. **Fill the hole with water** and let it drain completely.

3. **Fill the hole again** and time how long it takes to drain completely again.

If the hole is drained of water in less than three hours, your soil is draining too quickly. This may be due to being excessively sandy. Consider amending with peat moss or other moisture-holding organic material.

If the hole takes longer than eight hours to drain, that too is a problem. In this case the ground is too compact or too heavy with clay. You may need to incorporate ground bark or compost to improve drainage.

If your hole drains completely in about four to six hours, conditions should be about right and drainage should not be a problem.

When proper landscaping principles are applied the results can be breathtaking. This was the scene that greeted me when I got off a tour bus at Minter Gardens near Vancouver BC one September.

4

Essential Landscape and Gardening Principles

Fundamentals to Success

The long-term success of any landscape or garden revolves around some fundamental principles such as site selection, planting, fertilization, pruning and mulching. A basic understanding of these important factors has everything to do with the results experienced in your own yard and garden.

Site Preparation

If you only have a fixed amount of time to work on a particular planting or outdoor project, devote the majority of your time to preparing the site. I cannot say enough about the long-term value of this extra time and effort on the front end.

- *For planting:* If you are planting a garden, do all you can while the plot is empty and there is nothing to disturb. The most important ingredient in a successful garden is rich, loose soil. The best time to prepare your garden area quickly is before planting. Furthermore, almost all trees, plants, flowers, and vegetables do best when the growing environment drains well and includes plenty of organic material.

In the home garden and landscape, these conditions rarely exist naturally. It requires thorough planning and a little extra care to create this highly productive growing environment. However, when plants are provided with these conditions, they are more vigorous, more pest and disease resistant, and more tolerant of stressful conditions such as heat and drought and are more likely to please you in the long run.

Be sure not to cut corners here; soil prep is essential.

• *Non-planting projects:* Site preparation is essential in non-planting applications as well. For example, ensuring that the first tier of a retaining wall is set on a firm, level foundation is so important. The look and integrity of the entire wall, no matter how many levels, will depend on how well the foundation base was prepared and how evenly it was positioned.

The same principles apply to any other planting or landscape project such as making a stone pathway. The base into which the stones or pavers are set determines the longevity, ease, and functionality of navigating the walkway.

Yes, the extra effort required during the early phases of a project can be labor intensive, but the amount of time saved later in maintenance or repair is more than covered.

Planting Basics

"Dig a ten-dollar hole for a one-dollar plant." You've heard it before, and it is so very true. So just what is a ten-dollar hole? It is a growing environment that allows roots to spread and thrive. It doesn't hold water like a bucket, yet allows enough moisture to be retained and available to plant roots over an extended period. So, it is no accident that site preparation and planting sound similar. They are related. With planting, some extra steps will help plants and trees not only establish quickly, but excel as well.

Prepare the soil. The ideal soil will be the single most important contribution you can make to the success of your flower or vegetable bed. If you've ever grown annuals or perennial flowers before and were disappointed with the

results (assuming all other conditions were right), the most likely reason for poor results is soil quality. Don't cut corners here—invest in well-amended, well-drained beds! I'll tell you more about the importance of good soil in chapter 5.

Adding organic matter to your soil will keep it healthy and productive. Newly planted perennials and especially annuals benefit from nutrient enriched soil. I'm a big advocate of

QUICK FACT

If you only have a fixed amount of time to prepare a new site, devote the majority of it to improving the soil.

WHY: To begin with, there is no better opportunity for unlimited access to the site or area in which you are working. It's not likely you will have an as unencumbered a chance to mix in soil amendments, level the site, or adjust the nutrient balance or soil pH than you will at this time.

Periodically adding organic matter to your soil will keep it healthy and productive.

QUICK FACT

You can have flower beds that look professionally maintained.

HOW: You have likely noticed the entrances to office buildings, subdivisions, and apartment complexes that are professionally maintained. The flowers are bold, beautiful and vigorous. If you look closer, you'll see that the soil was mounded up high and full of coarse organic material such as fine bark and compost. This method provides terrific drainage yet retains adequate moisture, and it looks great.

periodically improving soil with organic material such as compost. There's never a bad time, but fall is a great time to for this task. Typically you are cleaning up, clearing out, and putting the garden to bed at that time.

In addition, mixing a small amount of slow release, all purpose plant food into the soil at the start of the growing season will provide supplemental nutrients that flowers can utilize to put on an all-season display. While I'm not necessarily advocating this, there are many "bloom boosting" fertilizer type products made for this purpose. You'll find them in the garden center and they are well labeled. Just be sure to read the directions on the package so you apply it at the right rates.

More is not better when adding fertilizer. It can potentially harm your plants and the soil when applied in excess. Be sure to use only the recommended amount or

Soil that is mounded high and full of coarse organic material yields beautiful results such as this.

even less. If you are truly creating healthy, nutrient rich soil, using compost and organic material should be all that is necessary.

You may choose to add supplemental fertilizer to give your plants a boost, but understand that excess fertilizer can be over-kill and potentially disruptive to the natural soil balance. Over-fertilizing can cause excess salts to build up in the soil leading to desiccation of beneficial microbes.

The Big Three

Just like people, plants need proper nutrition to grow. There are eighteen nutrients considered essential for plants. The soil supplies fifteen of them, which are taken up through the roots. Air and water provide the remaining three: oxygen, carbon, and hydrogen.

With that in mind, it's no surprise that any time I go into a garden center, I see people staring at the wall of fertilizers with a rather perplexed look on their faces. There are so many fertilizer products on the market, it is easy to become confused. Fortunately, it is not necessary to know all the details. Simply recalling some basic points will give you new confidence the next time you make a trip to the fertilizer department.

First, any fertilizer product will list three numbers prominently on the package. They represent the *Primary (or Major) Nutrients* and always represent *nitrogen, phospho-*

rous, and *potassium*, in that order. In simplest terms, each number indicates an ingredient's percentage of the package's total weight.

For example, a general all-purpose fertilizer commonly used is 10-10-10. For instance, in a 40-pound bag of 10-10-10, there are four pounds each (10 percent) of nitrogen, phosphorous, and potassium, for a total of 12 pounds of actual nutrients (4 lbs + 4 lbs + 4 lbs). The balance of the bag weight (28 lbs in this case) is what is referred to as inert or inactive ingredients.

What Do Those Numbers Mean?

N = Nitrogen

The first number represents nitrogen. It is responsible for foliage growth and is the primary nutrient for making plants lush and deep green. Fertilizer with a high nitrogen content is great for your lawn, but not necessarily good for your plants unless you want lots of leafy green at the potential expense of flowers or fruit.

P = Phosphorous

The second primary ingredient is phosphorous. Its primary contribution is to develop a good healthy root system and is vital in fruit and flower production. If you want lots of fruit, vegetables, or flowers, a fertilizer with a high middle number is important.

K = Potassium

The third number represents potassium. It is involved in overall plant health, hardiness and disease resistance.

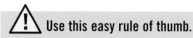 **Use this easy rule of thumb.**

An easy way to remember what each of these nutrients does is to remember "up, down, and all-around." The "up" stands for growth above the ground. The "down" refers to strong roots and shoots. And "all-around" addresses all around plant health.

Although the major nutrients are needed in the greatest quantities, secondary and trace nutrients are just as impor-

Fertilizer packages will prominently list values for nitrogen, phosphorous, potassium.

tant. A deficiency in any one can make the plants less vigorous or more susceptible to disease.

The Other Important Nutrients

• *Secondary nutrients (or minor nutrients):* These are nutrients that are also needed by the plants but in smaller quantities. They are calcium, magnesium and sulfur. They are no less important to the plant. These nutrients are listed on fertilizer packaging as a percentage of weight.

• *Trace nutrients (or micronutrients):* Also just as important to healthy roots and shoots, these nutrients are necessary, only in much smaller quantities. These include boron, cobalt, chlorine, copper, iron, manganese, molybdenum, sodium and zinc. If purchasing a balanced, all-purpose fertilizer, look for ones that say "includes micronutrients."

Liquid vs. granular fertilizer

Nutritionally, there is no difference between liquid and granular products. However, *liquid* applications can deliver a more immediate response. Roots *and* foliage are

able to absorb liquid fertilizers faster. Also be aware that liquid products will leach through the soil more quickly. If you choose to fertilize your plants using liquid, understand that you may need to keep up the regimen every week or two during the growing season.

Dry, *granular* products offer other options. The nutrients will be *released* over several months with one application— activated by chemical reaction, soil-temperature, or dissolved over time by breaking down the outer coating. However, unless the package says "slow or controlled release" or something to that affect, don't assume you will get a season-long feeding period from these products.

Another practical benefit of using dry products is the ease of fertilizing a larger tree, or shrub, or an entire bed. A common method of applying granular fertilizer to a large area is to "broadcast" it, simply by tossing it across a wide area. Applying liquid fertilizer would be less practical in this instance unless using a sprayer attached to a hose. *Caution: Fertilizers can burn; be sure to wear gloves.*

Non-organic vs. Organic

Fertilizers are also available as man-made non-organics and as organic plant and mineral products. Generally, the non-organic (also commonly referred to as "synthetic" or "traditional") products can be fast-acting, available in many formulations, and inexpensive. On the downside, excessive use of non-organic products could harm plant foliage and adversely affect the soil pH and beneficial microbes that live in the soil. These outcomes are due to

Applying liquid fertilizer delivers a more immediate response.

high concentrations moving through plant tissue, or the cumulative effect of excess salt buildup in the soil.

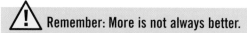 **Remember: More is not always better.**

Non-organic (synthetic) fertilizers are very effective and fast acting. But be careful to apply no more than the recommended amount. Just because some is good, more is not always better! Excess amounts could burn plants, alter the soil chemistry, and destroy beneficial microorganisms that make soil healthy and alive.

Although *dry organic choices will take longer to work,* they'll be available longer and at the time most needed by the plants. Organic fertilizers must first be broken down and digested by beneficial soil-dwelling creatures which then release the nutrients in a form that can be taken up by plant roots. This process can take several months.

As soil temperatures rise and plant growth becomes more active, the need for nutrients becomes greater. Because microbial activity increases with rising temperatures, these organically derived nutrients are available at the optimal times.

Fortunately, there are liquid organic fertilizers on the market that are fast and effective. One of the most popular and effective choices is liquefied worm castings. This is simply worm waste that has been converted into a solution that can be added to soil or directly onto plants. It is safe in that it can't be over-applied. There are many scientific and personal testimonials as to its effectiveness for growth as well as in helping fight off pests and diseases.

Organic fertilizers are non-burning because they are extremely low in salt content. This greatly reduces the risk of burning during a drought or if fertilizer is accidentally spilled or over-applied. You'll often recognize fertilizer burn because it appears rather quickly after you or your lawn company applied it. The symptoms are wilting and brown spots or patches—which eventually can kill the tissue.

More Benefits of Organic Fertilizers

Although organic fertilizers have been around for years they are gaining in popularity. They are an excellent choice because they are long lasting and do not create adverse effects. They are not considered hazardous or toxic to children, pets or the environment. They are an easy and safe way to improve the health and structure of your soil.

Organic fertilizers are comprised of naturally occurring minerals and plant and animal material. These products originated from the earth and are returned to it as fertilizers and soil amendments. Some of these products will break down more slowly than others. Because many of them are somewhat coarse, they serve to add diversity to the soil structure as well. This helps with drainage and aeration.

The soil structure is also improved because as microbes digest the nutrients, they create a by-product referred to as humus. Humus is important in improving the soil's ability to retain water, air and nutrients in the proper balance.

Build soil quality over time by adding natural, organic amendments.

The soil structure created by humus contributes to an ideal environment for vigorous root growth which leads to greater drought tolerance.

A good way to monitor and know the overall nutritional state of your soil is to have it tested periodically. I prefer the tests available through most county extension services. The report provides detailed information to bring your soil into peak condition. Refer to chapter 5 for step by step instructions and more on soil testing.

Fertilizing Annuals and Perennials

For newly planted annuals and perennials, you may choose to incorporate a slow release granular fertilizer into the soil before planting which will provide a steady supply of nutrients during the growing season. Some people even use a supplemental biweekly application of liquid fertilizer for an additional boost. There are many fertilizer formulations on the market that are engineered for maximum health and vigor no matter what you are growing.

There seems to be a fertilizer for anything you want to grow from the basic (for vegetable, lawn, or flower) to specialty products (for orchids, African violets, and even cactus).

If you're looking for flower power in your fertilizer, make sure the middle number is higher than the first, on the fertilizer formulation. This second number, representing phosphorus, helps build strong roots, flowers and fruits. However, in this case, don't use a fertilizer that has a higher first number. The first number represents nitrogen. Too much of that and you'll have lots of green leaves, BUT at the expense of flowers and fruit.

Liquefied worm castings is a valuable fertilizer and safe for the environment.

From Joe

One time I was preparing to fertilize my lawn with a standard non-organic lawn product. I filled my spreader to a safe level and headed for the next area of my grass. As I rounded a corner, I hit a rock. Most of the contents of the bucket spilled out onto the lawn in a rather large pile. I KNEW I had a problem here and would be facing some serious burnout issues if I didn't come up with a way to pick up all the spilled granules quickly. After several moments, I had the bright idea of hauling the shop vacuum out to the back yard. I sucked up every granule of fertilizer I could find, thinking I had averted disaster.

As a final step, I watered the area thoroughly, making sure there was no concentrated build-up of granules that had escaped detection. I patted myself on the back for a job well done and finished my work. Two days later, that area of my grass was completely burned to a crisp! I had a large chemically burned circular area, precisely where I had spilled the fertilizer.

Burn out in lawns and flower beds is a common mistake among gardeners and lawn warriors. I have fielded many questions along these lines and know you and I are not the only ones who have made this mistake. The moral of the story is to always apply at the recommended rate. More is not better!

COMMON ORGANIC FERTILIZERS AND WHAT THEY DO	
To improve Nitrogen:	Blood meal, fish emulsion or liquid fish meal, cottonseed meal, poultry manure, soybean meal, bat guano
To improve Phosphorus:	Bone meal, cottonseed meal, rock phosphate
To improve Potassium:	Crushed oyster shells, greensand, gypsum, granite dust, and wood ashes, potash

Just because a plant or tree is looking sickly, don't assume it needs fertilizer. That may be the worst thing you can do. Usually a plant or tree looks bad, not because of nutritional deficiencies, but because of improper pH or other environmental conditions such as too little or too much water. If you add fertilizer to a plant in stress, it's like adding fuel to the fire. The plant is then stimulated to grow in an already stressed state, which makes it more susceptible to pests and diseases.

To illustrate the point, imagine you are working on a hot summer day. The last thing you want to do is have to kick into high gear to take on a new, physically demanding project. All you want to do is take it easy and use whatever energy you have left to make it through the day without passing out. Well, fertilizing an already stressed plant can have a similar effect.

Fertilizing Trees and Shrubs

Wait several months after planting to apply fertilizer. With the exception of annuals, there is no great rush to force plants into production right away. The primary objective at the time of planting is for trees, shrubs and perennials to become established in the ground, first by developing a strong root system.

One of my favorite things about gardening is that I'm always learning. Fortunately, I learned something recently that changed my approach to fertilizing established trees and shrubs.

For most of my gardening life, trees and shrubs that needed a nutrient boost got their annual fertilizer application in early spring, right before active growth began for

Using organic options is a great way to promote environmental stewardship.

For beautiful spring color fertilize trees and shrubs in late fall so roots can store nutrients and release them at the appropriate time.

Deciduous trees and shrubs have lost their foliage for the year, and active growth of plants and trees has slowed. Rather than put on new foliage growth, established trees or shrubs take the nutrients from the soil and apply them to important health-promoting functions, such as disease resistance and root development. The excess nutrients are stored in the roots and become immediately available when needed for new growth in spring.

the year. This timing has been the generally accepted practice by gardeners and experts everywhere for years. And although early spring is a *good* time, research indicates there is an even *better* time.

Fertilize trees and shrubs in late Fall

Contrary to traditional wisdom, many experts now consider late fall, or about a month after the first killing frost, to be the ideal time for applying fertilizers to trees and large shrubs. We now know that plants utilize nutrients throughout the year in different ways.

In the past, the most common reason against fertilizing in the fall was the fear that plants and trees would put on new growth if unseasonably warm weather returned, only to be burned or damaged by the coming colder temperatures. They key is to understand the difference between *early* fall and *late* fall timing. If you fertilize in late summer or early fall, when temperatures are still warm and plants actively growing, it is likely new growth could occur and damage to tender new foliage will be the unhappy result.

The rationale for late fall fertilization goes like this:

⚠ Don't over-fertilize.

Keep in mind that not all established plants and trees are candidates for a regular fertilization program. This is another reason why it helps to have your soil tested.

I'm not saying that supplemental fertilizer is bad, just that the collective effect of over-application can be detrimental. Excess non-organic nutrients are usually wasted and can end up contaminating the soil and watershed areas. As we all work to beautify our own little corner of the world, we should be mindful of the cumulative impact we have on the environment beyond our own backyard.

Mulch

Spreading mulch is almost always an excellent step to take after every planting. Mulch, for the purpose of this discussion, is any type of natural product—such as wood chips, leaves or grass—broken down into small pieces. It is spread over soil and at the base of plants and trees. Mulch retains moisture, suppresses weeds, and helps keep soil temperatures more constant.

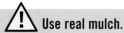
I prefer mulches that decompose and enrich the soil. It's one of the best benefits of using mulch. Rubber mulch is great on a walkway or in a children's play area, but it doesn't break down.

Mulch is also excellent at cutting down on certain soil-born plant diseases; it helps keep disease spores from splashing back to the plant due to rain or irrigation. Don't overdo it though. A 3-inch layer of mulch is sufficient. And, keep in mind that it shouldn't come in contact with the base or stem of the plant or shrub or the trunks of trees. Mulch that is right up against the stem or trunk could contribute to rot, create an access point for various pests and diseases, or both. Pull the mulch a couple of inches away from any contact with the plant.

Sometimes too much mulch around plants interferes with reseeding or shades out the seedlings from getting established if they do germinate. If you want your plants from this season to produce seed that will sprout and add to your garden next year, pulling the mulch away from those plants will keep it from interfering with good seed to soil contact.

A bonus: Adding mulch to any bed gives it a finished

Too much mulch only contributes to plant health problems.

look. It can really showcase your plants and flowers when you use a nice contrasting shade.

Don't Be Afraid of Pruning

Many people fear pruning, simply because they don't understand the concept of cutting something back to help it grow more! It seems counter-intuitive, and it was that way for me, too. Why would you cut something back that looks perfectly healthy? The concept is a funny one, and consequently, I have several friends who are *prunaphobic*. A basic understanding of the following principles will equip you to prune with confidence.

Contrary to what many think, cutting or pruning a tree, shrub or plant can be good for it by stimulating new growth, because a growth suppression hormone called auxin is removed.

This lack of auxin allows new buds or branches to begin to grow, quickly replacing the one removed. If leaf buds are present on both sides of the branch, you will likely get two new branches for each one that is cut.

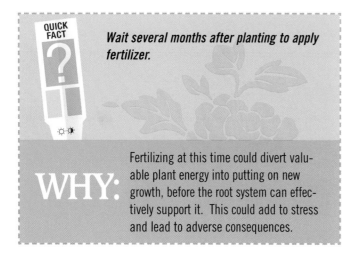

QUICK FACT
?

Wait several months after planting to apply fertilizer.

WHY: Fertilizing at this time could divert valuable plant energy into putting on new growth, before the root system can effectively support it. This could add to stress and lead to adverse consequences.

Why is Pruning Necessary?

Pruning is done for several reasons: to control size or shape, to remove dead, diseased or crossing branches or limbs, to improve structure or to stimulate new growth or flowering. Pruning can improve the health and look of a plant by allowing more light and air into the center.

What Time Should You Prune?

As you consider whether to prune a particular plant, you should know that there are better times of the year to prune. *Generally, the best time to prune is just prior to new growth starting to develop in early spring.* Most plants and trees utilize stored energy from fall and winter. New growth is produced just below the pruning cut.

The next best time to prune would be in late winter, before new growth occurs. Although pruning does stimulate new growth, in winter plants will typically not break dormancy until temperatures signal the appropriate time, even if pruning has recently taken place.

Early to mid-summer, after full leaf expansion, is an acceptable time. However, much of a plant's stored energy has gone into producing the new growth of spring. If you

QUICK FACT

?

Contrary to what many think, cutting or pruning a tree, shrub or plant can be good for it by stimulating new growth.

WHY: When a terminal bud or growing tip is removed from the parent plant, a growth suppression hormone called auxin is removed as well. Auxin, which is located in the terminal buds, suppresses the growth of other buds, signaling them to remain dormant. By removing the tip, nearby buds are no longer suppressed and may grow rapidly in response.

cut this new growth off, you've wasted the plant's energy. It will then be stimulated to put on new growth, yet the normal reserves for this process may have become depleted. This extra demand can be stressful to the plant in summer when conditions are likely to be dry and hot.

The least favorable time to prune is in early- to mid-fall. Pruning at this time can signal the plant to produce new growth, just as it is sending nutrients and energy into reserves for the cold months ahead. Not only can valuable reserves be diverted back into new growth, new growth can be damaged or killed by colder temperatures. This is especially true for evergreens. Any damage at this point could also create access points for over-wintering pests and diseases.

Pruning just above the bud releases a growth signal allowing dormant buds to develop.

Proper timing of pruning also needs to be considered for flowering shrubs. Certain shrubs bloom on new wood, such as (1) *glossy abelia* (2) *beauty bush,* and (3) *summersweet clethera.* These shrubs produce flowers on the current season's growth. They can be pruned in late winter and still produce flowers the same year.

Irrigation — Watering Wisely and Efficiently

In my observations, lawn and garden irrigation is an often-misunderstood topic. Most mistakes I see with watering center around when and how much water is applied. *Most plants and lawns thrive on about one inch of water per week.* This should be considered in total, which includes any rainfall.

Many people think watering should be a daily or every other day event. This is a common misconception. First, plants and lawns that receive frequent, but short watering cycles fail to develop a root system that grows deep beneath the soil surface. Consequently, the risk lies when frequent, shallow watering is interrupted for an extended time. These roots can rapidly dry up, and the entire plant or lawn can quickly die.

It's better to water infrequently and deeply, only once or

SPRING-FLOWERING SHRUBS COMMON NAME	PRUNED AFTER FLOWERING UNTIL END OF JUNE SCIENTIFIC NAME
Azaleas and Rhododendrons	*Rhodendron* sp.
Black jetbead	*Rhodotypos scandens*
Barberries	*Berberis* sp.
Beautybush	*Kolkwitzia amabilis*
Common, Chinese, and French lilacs	*Syringa* sp.
Cornelian cherry	*Cornus mas*
Deutzias	*Deutzia* sp.
Firethorns	*Pyracantha* sp.
Flowering quince	*Chaenomeles* sp.
Forsythias	*Forsythia* sp.
Hollies	*Ilex* sp.
Honeysuckles	*Lonicera* sp.
Japanese snowbell	*Styrax japonica*
Magnolias	*Magnolia* sp.
Mock oranges	*Philadelphus* sp.
Mountain laurel	*Kalmia latifolia*
Pea shrub	*Caragana* sp.
Pieris, Andromedas	*Pieris* sp.
Privets or Ligustrums	*Ligustrum* sp.
Smoke tree	*Cotinus coggygria*
Sweet shrub	*Calycanthus floridus*
Thunberg spirea, Bridalwreath spirea	*Spiraea* sp.
Viburnums	*Viburnum* sp.

Reprinted with permission from The University of Kentucky Cooperative Extension Service.

SUMMER-FLOWERING SHRUBS COMMON NAME	PRUNED BEFORE SPRING GROWTH BEGINS SCIENTIFIC NAME
Beautyberry	*Callicarpa* sp
Butterfly Bush	*Buddleia davidii**
Clematis	*Clematis* sp.(some)
Crape myrtle	*Lagerstroemia indica*
Fiveleaf aralia	*Acanthopanax sieboldianus*
Glossy abelia	*Abelia grandiflora**
Hills of snow hydrangea	*Hydrangea arborescens* 'Grandiflora'
Hybrid tea rose	*Rosa* hybrid
Oakleaf hydrangea	*Hydrangea quercifolia*
Peegee hydrangea	*Hydrangea paniculata* 'Grandiflora'
Rose of Sharon	*Hibiscus syriacus*
Summersweet, clethra	*Clethra alnifolia*

Reprinted with permission from The University of Kentucky Cooperative Extension Service.

Some shrubs produce flowers on old season's growth or wood produced from the previous year, such as (1) *sweetshrub*, (2) *holly*, and (3) *azalea* (below). Pruning these shrubs in late winter would remove all the flower buds already formed. They were set in the previous year. Shrubs blooming on old wood are best pruned immediately after flowering.

SHRUBS PRUNED BOTH BEFORE AND AFTER BLOOM	
COMMON NAME	SCIENTIFIC NAME
Anthony Waterer and Frobel spirea	*Spiraea bumalda*
Butterflybush	*Buddleia davidii*
Chenault coralberry	*Symphoricarpos chenaultii*
Cranberry cotoneaster	*Cotoneaster apiculatus*
Glossy abelia	*Abelia grandiflora*
Multiflora cotoneaster	*Cotoneaster multiflorus*
Oregon grapeholly	*Mahonia aquifolium*
Red twig dogwood	*Cornus sericea*
Snowberry	*Symphoricarpos albus*
Spreading cotoneaster	*Cotoneaster divaricatus*
Weigela	*Wiegela florida*

Reprinted with permission from The University of Kentucky Cooperative Extension Service.

twice a week, while working to provide a total amount of one inch.

Water early in the day. Watering early decreases the time foliage stays wet. This is a benefit because the longer the foliage stays wet, the greater the likelihood disease spores will become established.

- **Overhead watering:** Overhead watering is an easy and efficient way to cover a large area. But note that a good rule of thumb for overhead irrigation, especially turf irrigation, is to water during the dew cycle, which is generally between 10 P.M. and 10 A.M. Utilizing this period when foliage may already be wet provides ample opportunity during the day to dry and minimizes the risk of disease.

- **Soaker and drip hoses:** Other methods of irrigation include soaker and drip irrigation hoses. These are great options for keeping foliage dry and delivering water right to the roots, where it is needed most. A simple battery operated timer makes this job a snap to ensure that watering occurs when you want it and for how long. Then you don't run the risk of too little or too much water.

- **Drip irrigation:** For beds and containers, the best way

I've ever seen to keep plants hydrated right at the root zone is with drip irrigation. The water is delivered through a supply line made of flexible, plastic tubing. Along the supply line, small holes are punctured into it where needed, allowing water to drip out at those points. Additional tubing can also be tapped into the line, extending and directing water precisely to the base of any plants or containers.

Some shrubs such as 1) *butterfly bush*, 2) *Oregon grapeholly*, and 3) *wiegela* (below) may be pruned before or after bloom.

(1) A soaker hose allows water to seep evenly along its entire length. (2) Drip irrigation tubing and emitters allow for precision watering right where you want it. (3) Add an automatic timer to either and you'll have a worry-free way to water effectively.

The rate at which water drips from the end of the tubing is controlled by a plastic tip called an emitter. They come in different sizes depending on your desired flow rate. Drip irrigation kits and supplies can be purchased at garden centers and home improvement stores. They're easy to install.

Portable Drip Irrigation in a Bag

There comes a point where it becomes impractical to extend a drip irrigation line too far into your yard or landscape. There are products that address that very issue. One is essentially a portable drip irrigation system in a bag. The "bag" is a bladder that has tiny pinholes in the bottom. Wrap it around the trunk, fill it with water and over the next 6 to 12 hours water is released slowly into the soil. It's the ideal solution for watering trees and shrubs in a way that allows the water to slowly soak the area around the roots Getting sufficient water to the roots while they are becoming established is critical. Having a way to deliver that water slowly enough to soak deeply into the soil is essential.

QUICK FACT

If you don't know how long it takes to apply one inch with your watering system, you can find out with a simple technique.

HOW: Place empty tuna cans around the area you are watering. Periodically, check the cans. When they are full, you've delivered an inch of water. The time this takes will tell you how long to run your sprinklers each cycle.

Making a New Garden Area

Adding a new garden area can be exciting. Thinking ahead before you plant can save a lot of time and aggravation in the long run.

As you work with your existing site, you will either be dealing with full sun, full shade, or something in between. Unless you are willing to alter the existing conditions, such as cutting down trees to allow more light, then simply work with what you have. There are plenty of plant choices that are suitable for whatever growing conditions currently exist.

Some of the most important considerations are listed below as you decide where you will place your garden:

• *Proper Sun Exposure:* Choose your plants based on the spot you have picked out for your garden, or find a site that is suitable for the plants you want to grow. For example, if you want to start a vegetable garden, find a site that gets at least six hours of direct sunlight. That's not to say that you won't have some success with less. I've grown tomato plants and enjoyed a decent harvest on four hours of direct light. But, I was challenged the entire time. Giving plants their ideal environment from the beginning will get them off to a good start and help them thrive as they mature. Again, right plant—right place.

Many plants, especially tall growing ones, benefit from wind protection such as that provided by these tall pines.

natural wind break such as a dense planting of tall trees nearby, fencing, or a wall will help to block the wind and give your plants a better chance of staying upright.

Harsh, western exposure sunlight that comes in the late afternoon is the most intense light of the day. Some plants have a difficult time adapting to this hot, strong light—especially some of the larger leaved or more tender plants. Keep an eye out for excessive wilt that does not recover by the next morning. A bleaching effect on the foliage also could be an indicator of the plant's inability to take on that much light intensity.

Providing mid- to late-afternoon shade will be advantageous to many plants. The same screening that helps plants stand up to strong winds can serve to screen them from the burning sun as well.

- *Protection from wind and harsh sun:* Many plants and especially tall growing vegetables benefit from wind protection. Even shorter plants, laden with heavy fruit or large flowers can fall over in strong winds. Having a

- *Access to water:* Although it sounds like I'm stating the obvious, the closer the water source is to your garden, the more likely it is you will actually keep it watered.

- *Soil (sand, silt & clay):* Soil is rarely perfect right out of the ground. If your's is, consider yourself ahead of the game! For the rest of us, we'll need to make sure that the ground is soft enough to work in, but not so soft the moisture runs right through. Incorporating organic material such as compost, aged manure and mulch will help in either case.

- *Convenience:* Let's face it. We're a society that likes convenience. The easier it is for us to do something, the more likely it is that we'll follow through on the task.

Treegator® at work.

From Joe

Believe it or not, on the television set of *Fresh from the Garden,* we irrigated our garden almost every day by hand, using a hose attached to the house about 200 feet away! It was a hassle dragging the hose out and back everyday. It would have been easy to skip the watering duties because it was often so inconvenient, and I likely would have done so if it were not a TV garden where failure was NOT an option. Finally, toward the end of the second year of taping, we installed a permanent irrigation system. It made all the difference in the world. It really improved the health of the plants and made it much easier on me, since I was the official "waterer."

Gardens are the same way. The more convenient it is to our house or kitchen or water spigot, the more likely we will do the necessary chores to keep things looking good. Out of sight, out of mind applies to gardens too. If you have the option to keep it close in or easily accessible, then by all means, do so.

This site provides plenty of exposure for sun loving plants or vegetables.

I wish I had thought to mention irrigation installation as a topic for *Fresh from the Garden* in the first year of the show, rather than right before we moved the gardening set at the end of year-two.

You will need:
❏ hand pruners
❏ loppers
❏ gloves

project Pruning Tips

Pruning is done for several reasons: to control size and shape, to remove dead, diseased or crossing branches and to stimulate new growth or flowering. As you approach a shrub that needs general pruning, take the following steps:

Examine the shrub for any dead or diseased branches and remove them at ground level or back to a healthy stem.

Look for any crossing branches and cut them out so they don't rub against each other, exposing tissue to pests or diseases.

Cut out inward growing branches.

Thin out the shrub by cutting out crowded branches. When deciding between two branches, consider the overall shape, and cut the less desirable one. Remove at ground level or back to the main stem.

Remove up to one third of older inner wood to rejuvenate the plant. This allows more light to reach into the plant and promote new growth.

Step back and study the shape and size.

Cut back plants by up to one third to control size and shape. Some plants can handle much more severe pruning than others. Pruning also depends on the time of year. Make cuts about $1/3$ inch above a bud or set of buds. Examine the branch you are cutting. Select and cut above a single bud that grows outward, to promote a more open look. Cut at an angle with the highest point on the same side as the remaining bud.

Alternatively, for branches with opposite buds cut about $1/3$ inch above the bud set. Make this cut level.

"If I could give but one piece of gardening advice it would be to spend time on the front end creating deep, healthy, well-drained soil with as much organic matter as possible."

5

It's All About the Soil

Soil, Soil, Soil!

If I could only give one piece of advice . . . *spend time improving the soil!* You should know that ideal garden soil is more than just dirt. To me, dirt *becomes* ideal soil when it is improved for conditions favorable to promoting maximum root growth, moisture retention, and drainage. Healthy soil contains almost equal parts of sand, silt, and clay, which are the main components of soil. These tiny fragments of rock or minerals make up nearly half the material in the soil. The other half is composed of air, water, and a bit of organic matter.

Once I have great soil, I can never again think of it as just "dirt." On its own, unimproved "dirt" can provide favorable growing conditions for a great variety of plant material. However, to achieve ideal conditions in our own yard and extend the plant palette, it usually takes some effort on our part.

Three More Dirty Words

Understanding *texture, structure,* and *tilth* should help clear up one of the "dirtier" mysteries of gardening.

- *Texture:* Let's start with soil texture. Texture refers to the relative particle size of sand, silt, and clay. When these three are proportionate, the soil is said to have "good texture." Another term used to describe the same concept is "loamy." Soil that is considered loamy has ideal texture and is generally the best type for any garden. Gardeners covet loamy soil.

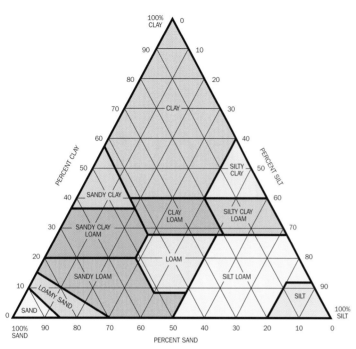

Ideal soil includes a mixture of equal parts of sand, silt, and clay.

• *Structure:* Structure refers to how soil binds together and the shape that the soil takes based on its physical and chemical properties. Simply put, structure is how the sand, silt, and clay hold together. Good structure is evident when the soil holds together if squeezed but breaks apart or crumbles easily when disturbed.

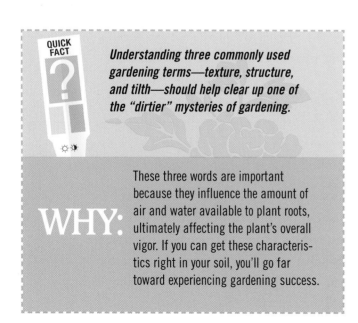

QUICK FACT

Understanding three commonly used gardening terms—texture, structure, and tilth—should help clear up one of the "dirtier" mysteries of gardening.

WHY: These three words are important because they influence the amount of air and water available to plant roots, ultimately affecting the plant's overall vigor. If you can get these characteristics right in your soil, you'll go far toward experiencing gardening success.

• *Tilth:* When a soil has good tilth, it drains well, but not *too* well. It is loose enough to allow for adequate drainage, yet dense enough to retain moisture long enough for plant roots to utilize it. This is why garden soil should contain neither too much sand nor clay.

The Jar Test

Find a jar with a tight fitting lid such as a mayonnaise or mason jar and fill it about halfway with soil from your yard or garden. Add water to the jar until it is almost full. Secure the lid and shake the jar vigorously. Set the jar aside and let the contents settle for several hours. It may take overnight to several days. What you will find is that the soil has separated into three distinct layers.

The first layer is sand. Because it is the heaviest, it settles to the bottom. The second layer is silt. Silt is a combination of sedimentary materials that are smaller than sand and larger than clay. The third layer is clay. It is the finest and lightest of the three most solid components of soil.

Conducting a jar test like this is a great way to observe visually how your native soil is made up. You can easily see if your soil is loose and sandy or dense and full of clay. It also gives you a clue on how you need to approach amending it to give it ideal texture, structure, and tilth.

Few parts of the country have ideal soil conditions naturally. Most of the time, soil is either too heavy with clay (such as in the area of the country where I garden) or too loose with sand (usually associated with coastal and desert areas).

Amending the Soil

Regardless of the soil texture, structure, or tilth, you can change what you already have. Call it a soil makeover. The ultimate goal for amending the soil is for it to pass what I call the "squeeze test." If you were to squeeze a handful of ideal garden soil, it would bind together and hold its shape. However, it would also be loose enough so that by running your fingers through it, the lump would crumble

Clay soil benefits from adding gritty organic matter such as composted bark, wood chips, shredded leaves, or compost.

or break apart easily. Adding organic material like compost, humus, composted manure, leaf mulch, peat moss, etc., will greatly improve soil so it will easily pass the

test. The key is to know from which extreme you are starting.

- *Sandy or loose soil:* Soil that is too loose or sandy will not bind together if you pick it up in your hand and try to squeeze it. Most likely, it will run through your fingers with very little effort if any on your part. For soils that are too loose or sandy, the goal is to increase its water holding capacity. Sphagnum peat moss has been the amendment of choice for improving sandy conditions and is readily available around the country.

Another amendment that is popular as an alternative to peat moss is coir. This is the husk of coconut shells and performs in much the same way as peat moss. Sandy soil benefits from adding plenty of organic material. Incorporating composted particles of different sizes and textures creates air pockets and allows moisture to be retained and slowly released to plant's roots without saturating the soil.

- *Dense or compacted soil:* Soil that is too dense or compacted will easily bind together if you pick it up and squeeze it. It will look like a lump of clay. Also, it will not crumble apart when the clump is disturbed with your fingers. If a soil is too dense, it will drain poorly—retaining too much water so that the plant potentially drowns. The soil particles are bonded together so tightly that there is little room for air and only tiny openings for root growth.

Your job is to loosen it up by adding gritty organic material such as composted bark, wood chips, composted manure, shredded leaves, or compost. However, this is a time where you

Amended soil ready for planting.

Great soil gives you the best chance for the best garden.

would not add sphagnum peat moss or coir. These are very good at retaining moisture, but that is not the objective of amending heavy soil.

Conversely, dense soil when completely dry can keep water from penetrating the surface—causing run-off so the water can't soak down to plants' roots. In this case it's not a matter of the plant drowning. Instead, the plant can die from lack of water.

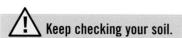 **Keep checking your soil.**

All organic material continues to break down over time. Monitor your soil regularly, and amend often with the appropriate material to maintain the best growing environment. Whether soil is too compacted or too loose, it will benefit from the periodic and consistent addition of organic matter.

Soil Testing

Whenever I'm diagnosing someone's plant problem, my first question is usually, "Have you done a soil test?" The answer is almost always, "No,"—which is a shame, because many plant problems can be easily diagnosed and rectified by knowing the condition of their soil.

• *A soil test will reveal the pH level of the soil:* The pH is a relative range, from 0-14.0, which measures the acidity or alkalinity. A pH reading of 7.0 therefore is "neutral". A reading below 7.0 indicates acidic soil (sometimes referred to as "sour"), while readings above 7.0 are alkaline (sometimes referred to as "sweet"). Most plants grow best in a range of 6.0-7.0.

• *Plants need a certain amount of nutrients to thrive:* Many of these are found naturally in native soil. However, there are major and minor, as well as micronutrients, that are all used by plants in various quantities. A quality soil analysis will indicate the levels of these nutrients.

• *The soil pH should be within an appropriate range:* Knowing both the pH and nutrient levels is important. Many times, gardeners will add additional fertilizer in an

COMMON ACID-LOVING PLANTS	
Azalea/Rhododendron	*Rhododendron* species
Hemlock	*Tsuga canadensis*
Blueberries	*Vaccinium*
Holly	*Ilex* species
Juniper	*Juniperus* species

COMMON ALKALINE-LOVING PLANTS	
Boxwood	*Buxus sempervirens*
Firethorn	*Pyracantha*
Lilac	*Syringa*
Cherry	*Prunus*
Spirea	*Spiraea*

QUICK FACT

Don't worry if you find that the soil pH reading for your garden is outside the preferred range for what you are trying to grow. You can change the pH.

HOW: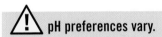

You can make an acidic soil more alkaline (raise the pH) by adding lime. You can lower the pH of an alkaline or slightly acidic soil by adding sulfur, iron sulphate, or even peat moss. A soil test will provide the information you need to make these adjustments.

effort to correct some sort of problem with their lawn or garden. But what they don't realize is that—even with all the nutrients a plant could want—unless the soil pH is within the proper range, some of those nutrients are locked up and unavailable for use by the plants.

pH preferences vary.

Plants and turf grasses have different preferred ranges for ideal soil pH. One level or reading is not practical to provide the ideal conditions for every plant. However, there is an acceptable range that is suitable for most plants. If it is impractical to create multiple zones of pH, then work to achieve a range of between 6.0 and 7.0. This will create a slightly acidic to neutral range which is suitable to a very large number of trees, lawns, shrubs, flowers, and edibles.

Where Can You Get a Soil Test?

Soil tests are available from a number of sources. You can purchase do-it-yourself kits from a garden center, online, or through mail order sources. They are usually simple and come with a color chart for comparison. It's not the most scientific approach, and if you're color-blind you can forget about it! *None compare in quality or accuracy to the results you get through your county extension service.* For the money, it is the best value, in my opinion.

From Joe

I am often asked questions about what type of lime to use. You may have dealt with this problem yourself:

"I need to raise the pH by adding lime. I'm not sure what type of lime to add. The garden center carries several types including powder and dolomitic lime. What's the difference and which type is best?"

The basic ingredient of lime for garden use is ground **limestone.**

Agricultural lime is a white powder. It is ground limestone and a good source of calcium. It is cheaper than pelletized lime and a good option to add to soil that you are tilling in. It is faster acting in this powdered form. However, it is very messy because it is so powdery and light. It is not the best option for a mechanical spreader. I like to use this type when I scoop it out and sprinkle it onto my vegetable beds, turning it in with a spading fork.

Dolomitic lime is a popular choice in garden centers and for good reason. It is sold in pellatized form, so it's easy to use in a spreader and less messy. I like that! Next, it has the added benefit of **calcium** and **magnesium,** two essential nutrients for healthy plant growth. It is the most common form of lime added to lawns.

A soil analysis conducted by the extension service is inexpensive and thorough. The report includes a reading of the soil pH, and it details the major and minor nutrient levels. One of the best features of this report is the suggested amounts and type of nutrients to add to your existing soil to bring it into optimal levels for growing the plants or crops you have specified. Gathering soil for this type of test is easy, as you'll see in the project at the end of this chapter.

Compost: The #1 Ingredient

There is no store-bought product better for improving the soil in your garden than compost, and I believe it's the single most important ingredient we can add to our gardens. Even better, compost is free and we can make as much of it as we want! It helps add life and fertility to the soil, improving drainage while allowing the soil to retain

There's nothing magic to knowing when compost is ready to add to the soil. You can easily judge for yourself.

HOW:

You'll know compost is ready when the compost ingredients are unrecognizable and there is no odor. The compost should smell rich and earthy and it should look like crumbly, rich, dark soil.

sufficient moisture.

Compost creates good soil structure, a critical element in allowing nutrients and water to be absorbed, and roots to spread. Compost is considered "living soil." A small sample of compost has billions of beneficial bacteria and fungi that perform many important roles. These microbes help break down other organic nutrients into a soluble form that can used by plant roots.

Composting occurs in nature constantly. Plant and animal waste breaks down naturally into soil-like particles over time, with no involvement from us. The simplest compost piles at home are just that—piles of yard waste and kitchen scraps. There are no fancy systems, containers, bins, or compartments necessary to facilitate the process. Although a simple pile will suffice to make perfectly usable compost, more elaborate systems can be built or purchased to contain the mix, and help speed up the decomposition process.

You'll know the compost is ready by its texture and earthy smell.

Make Your Own Compost

There are a few essential elements necessary for compost to occur. They are water, air, heat, carbon (brown matter, like dead leaves and twigs), and nitrogen (green material, such as grass clippings and vegetable and salad scraps).

To make a compost pile, you don't need anything fancy. A simple accumulation of green waste (10-25 percent), and brown waste (75-90 percent), will get you going. Every week or so, try to mix up the pile, so you introduce oxygen to help speed up the decomposition process. Add a sprinkling of water, enough to give the pile the moistness of a damp sponge, and you will be well on your way to making compost. Depending on the variables, you should be able to have usable compost within four months to one year.

You can add many items to your compost pile or bin. Almost anything from the yard or garden can be used. In addition I keep a small galvanized can with a tight-fitting lid under my sink. After every meal, all the usable scraps go into the can and at the end of the day I make a trip to the compost pile to empty the contents. By the way, don't

forget the coffee grounds. They make a great addition. It may not seem like a lot from day to day but believe me, it really adds up over time!

There are some ingredients to avoid when composting:

• *Diseased plants:* Disease pathogens may not be killed in the composting process, and you can end up reintroducing them into your soil.

• *Weeds that have bloomed:* Weed seeds are notorious for persisting for a very long time, and many are able to survive through the composting process, only to be spread to other areas of your garden as you add new compost.

• *Meat and dairy products:* They attract a variety of outdoor pests, and they can harbor many types of non-beneficial bacteria and disease.

• *Limbs thicker than a pencil:* Although not problematic, they'll take longer to break down unless you shred them first.

How to Create a Simple Compost Bin at Home:

• Form a ring of wire several feet around and 3 or 4 feet

A simple compost bin can be created from a ring of welded wire.

tall. Staking it in place is optional but will help keep it secure.

• Simply add yard and kitchen waste to the bin and to speed up the decomposition process, mix it together periodically and sprinkle it with water.

• The more often you do both, the quicker you should have usable compost.

Compost is the single most important amendment we can add to our gardens.

project **How** to **Conduct** a **Jar Test**

A great way to get a graphic visual on the make-up of your soil structure and texture is to do what I call the "jar test". The results will allow you to see the relative proportions of sand, silt, and clay in your soil.

Obtain a clean jar, such as a mason or mayonnaise jar. Make sure it has a tight fitting lid.

Add soil from your garden so that it fills the jar about halfway.

Fill the jar with water and secure the lid.

Shake vigorously to mix the contents.

Place on a table or shelf. Once the contents have settled, you will see the proportion of sand, silt, and clay in your garden soil.

The bottom layer is sand. It is the largest of the three particles and will sink to the bottom first. Next is silt. It makes up the middle layer. It is smaller and lighter than sand. The top layer is clay. It is fine and light and therefore settles in last. Equal amounts of each are ideal. At a minimum, you'll have a good idea of what you need do to do to improve your soil.

project # How to Take a Soil Test

You will need:
- ❏ a clean trowel or scoop
- ❏ a clean bucket or bowl
- ❏ a sample bag
- ❏ a pan or shallow tray

The basic technique for collecting a representative soil sample is to gather soil from random parts of the total area you would like tested. This may be a small raised vegetable bed, a large plot used for cut flowers, or an entire lawn.

Here are the steps for taking a basic soil sample that can be delivered to your county extension service:

Use a scoop, trowel, shovel or spoon—but whatever you choose, make sure it is clean so that no foreign matter is being introduced into the sample.

Gather a representative sample for the area of your garden or landscape that you would like to have tested. Ten to twelve small scoops would make a good sample population. Place each scoop into a clean large bucket or bowl.

Once you've collected a dozen or so random samples, **mix them together** to create one large representation of the area.

Once mixed, **spread the total sample out on a pan or shallow tray** so it will dry out. This is also a good time to remove rocks and foreign debris.

When dry, **combine about 2 cups of the aggregate soil** into the sample bag. Many county extension services have bags specially made for this and will be happy to send those to you along with specific instructions.

Close the bag tightly and deliver or mail the sample (along with a check) to your local extension office. **Important:** Note what you plan to grow in the area from which you took your soil sample.

This sample and information allow for the technician to determine which pH level and nutrients are necessary to provide the optimum benefit to your plants (vegetables, turf, flowers, blueberries, etc).

Within a couple of weeks, you will receive a detailed report that outlines all the important information you can use to bring the soil into the ideal range for what you want to grow. It will include instructions on what and how much to add to adjust the pH and nutrients to proper levels.

"Although I was taken aback by the lush color in this dramatic garden, I recognize it is equally gratifying and perhaps more challenging to create a tasteful garden of only one or a few colors."

6

Color in the Garden

A Rainbow of Choices

Most people, I believe, think the beauty of a garden is determined by the quantity and variety of flowers packed into a given space. Although I agree gardens of this type are often breathtaking, gardens of only one or a few colors can be equally beautiful.

If you are unsure which plants to mix with each other to get colors that are complementary or related, then find a "color wheel" from an art supply store. These wheels do a great job of letting you see what colors are opposite or related and which work well together. It's also an easy and inexpensive way to experiment and design your garden before ever buying the first plant.

It is a well-known fact that colors are effective at creating moods. Cool colors calm and hot colors excite. By studying the color wheel you are able to choose colors that create the mood you prefer or you want others to experience.

Every color conceivable in nature is composed of various quantities of the primary colors; red, yellow, and blue. Numerous combinations can be derived by juxtaposing colors next to, or opposite each other, on the color wheel.

Without getting complicated, cool colors are primarily in the blue, green, and purple range; hot colors encompass reds, yellows, and oranges. Of course there are many color combinations in between, but if you want a portion of your landscape to jump forward and be seen immediately,

(1) Cool colors tend to recede. (2) Hot colors excite. (2) Opposites attract.

choose a palette of hot colors. Depth can be created in small gardens by using cool colors which recede into the background.

A virtually unlimited selection of annual and perennial plants can be used to provide just about every color under the rainbow. Annuals are the most popular choice for adding a bold punch of color to a flower bed or border because they perform all season long. They are readily available from places like garden centers, grocery stores, and drug stores. Many are also easy to grow from seed. Annuals go from seed to plant to flower, and then to seed again and finally die—all in usually just a matter of months. Perennials too are famous for providing color in the bed or border. But unlike annuals, perennials last from season to season, even though their time in bloom is usually only a few weeks.

The Difference Between Annuals and Perennials

• *Annuals: An annual is a plant that grows from seed, then flowers, produces seed, and dies all in one season.* When I go to a nursery or garden center, what always draws me in is the sea of beautiful flowers calling my name from the parking lot. Most of what we see from the pavement is the seductive beauty of annuals.

The variety of annuals to choose from seems mind boggling, and more are coming on the market all the time. They are a great addition to the landscape and provide a

punch of color right where you need it. Classic examples of annuals include pansies, petunias, and marigolds.

A comment I often hear regarding annuals is that people get tired of replacing them year after year. Today, there are more demands on our time than ever before. Trends indicate that many of us are seeking ways to spend less of it in the garden while still enjoying the benefit of a colorful landscape. The usual solution for those not wanting to replant annuals is to go with flowering perennials.

• *Perennials: A perennial is a plant that lives from year to year whether it is evergreen or dies back to its roots and returns the following year.* Although the flowers of the plant aren't any less dramatic than annuals, they often bloom for only a few weeks. However, these plants persist for more than one season and therefore perform longer in the garden. I say, "Go with both!" Each plays an important role in the landscape.

One trick to getting more color from a perennial display is to arrange beds so that just as one perennial is completing

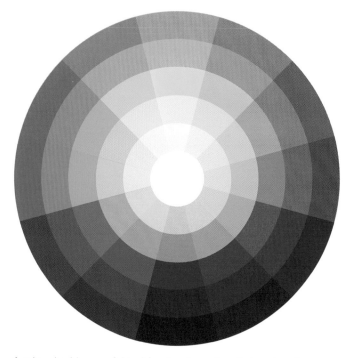

A color wheel is a useful tool for choosing colors that work well together.

that same bed. Once late-season daffodils have finished blooming and are in decline with their not so attractive foliage, the daylilies are there to fill in, literally. Color from the same bed now continues from early spring through late summer with a similar form. The best part is that the display continues the following year and for years to come with little additional work.

Perennials like hosta and ferns are often selected more for their foliage. This benefit is important because perennial flower time can be short, such as that of tulips or daffodils.

 Now let me throw you a curveball.

Sometimes *annuals* re-seed so freely, we often think of them as *perennials*. And, sometimes *perennials* that aren't cold hardy are used as *annuals* in other parts of the country. These are usually referred to as "tender perennials." *Biennials* on the other hand are plants that form leaves in the first year, bloom the second year, produce seed and then die. One of the most familiar biennial plants is *Digitalis* or foxglove.

Perennials are a good longer-term solution for providing not only great color, but also great foliage.

its bloom cycle, another is beginning. For example, daffodils can be purchased as early-, mid- and late-season bloomers. To further extend the display, add daylilies to

Growing Annuals

You get a lot of color bang for your buck with annuals. There are plants for nearly every season and plenty of colors from which to choose. Annuals are readily available and easy to care for, especially when given their ideal growing situations. Various annuals can thrive in moist, well-drained soil to near desert conditions.

Frequently the sea of color at nurseries calls seductively to me from the parking lot.

Perennials are long-lived but short-flowering and reasonably low maintenance because they don't have to be planted each year.

Routine Maintenance for Annuals Includes:

• *Fertilizing:* For a nutrient boost, you can add a slow release fertilizer into the soil at the time of planting. Be sure to use the appropriate amounts as specified on the package label for season-long feeding. You can also apply a liquid fertilizer to your plants. These products are generally faster acting, but you will need to feed your plants more often throughout the season.

• *Deadheading:* Promote new flowering simply by plucking spent blooms off the stems every few days. It is not necessary to deadhead every annual, but in many cases it can lead to a healthier, bushier plant. For annuals like pansies, this extra step will reward you with a longer season of blooms.

• *Removal of plants at the end of the season:* You will know when annuals are ready to be removed because they will look "tired" and in decline. But the beauty of annuals is that there is usually another one ready to take its place. There is something to be said for change in the garden. It marks a new season and the opportunity to try new plants and combinations.

Growing Perennials

Unlike annuals, perennials are not removed from the garden at the end of the growing season. They may die back to the ground, but they come back the following year

ANNUALS FOR SHADE	
Browallia	*Browallia speciosa*
Coleus	*Coleus* hybrids
Forget-me-not	*Myosotis*
Foxglove	*Digitalis* (bi-annual)
Impatiens, Busy Lizzy	*Impatiens walleriana*
Johnny Jump-up	*Viola cornuta*
Lobelia	*Lobelia erinus*
Love-in-a-mist	*Nigella damascena*
Money Plant	*Lunaria annua* (bi-annual)
Tobacco plant	*Nicotiana*
Wishbone flower	*Torenia fournieri*
Wax Begonia	*Begonia semperflorens*

ANNUALS FOR SUN	
Geranium	*Pelargonium*
Ageratum	*Ageratum houstonianum*
Cosmos	*Cosmos bipinnatus*
Four O'clock	*Mirabilis jalapa*
Love-lies-bleeding	*Amaranthus caudatus*
Marigold	*Tagetes*
Pansy	*Viola x wittrockiana*
Petunia	*Petunia* hybrids
Poppy	*Papaver* species
Verbena	*Verbena* hybrids
Zinnia	*Zinnia elegans*

Crowded perennials will begin to perform less which signals their need to be divided.

bigger and better than before. They are long lived but compared to annuals they are short-flowering. Perennials are reasonably low maintenance because they don't have to be planted each year.

Routine Maintenance for Perennials Includes:

• *Fertilizing:* Perennials are typically fertilized in spring and fall but not throughout the growing season. Too much fertilizer will result in lush foliage growth at the expense of flowers.

• *Deadheading:* Removing the blooms from perennials will in some cases give a secondary although less spectacular bloom period. Other times, once the flower is removed it will not bloom again until the following year.

Spent flowers are usually removed at the end of the blooming season to tidy up the plant.

• *Dividing:* This is one of my favorite things about perennials. Since they continue to multiply over time, there is ample opportunity to divide the plants, allowing an easy and inexpensive way to add plants to your own garden or give them away.

Perennials can grow so much below ground it is often to their advantage for you to divide them every three to five years. Otherwise they become too crowded, and the roots don't have as much room to spread out. The consequence of this is the plants may bloom less from season to season or simply not look as good overall from one season to the next. In fact, this is a good indication that it is time to divide your plants.

 Dividing perennials is not a big deal.

Don't let the occasional need to divide perennials stop you from considering adding a plant that intrigues you. The worst case scenario is that you will eventually have plenty to share. If the idea of periodic division is not appealing to you, invite your gardening friends over and allow them to dig their own plants!

PERENNIALS FOR SUN		ZONE*
Autumn Sage	*Salvia greggii*	3-9
Agastache	*Agastache*	5-9
Aster	*Aster oblongifolius*	5-9
Balloon Flower	*Platycodon grandiflorus*	3-8
Bearded Iris	*Iris germanica*	3-8
Black-eyed Susan	*Rudbeckia fulgida*	3-9
Daylily	*Hemerocallis*	3-9
Lantana	*Lantana camara*	8a-11
Phlox	*Phlox paniculata*	3-9
Purple coneflower	*Echinacea*	3-9
Yarrow	*Achillea*	3-9
*hardiness zone varies with cultivar and variety		

(1) Using a variety of textures and shades of green adds visual interest without focusing on flowers. (2) As a general rule six to eight hours of direct sunlight is need for these sun lovers. (3) Color in the shade is provided by the flowers of these deep purple hellebores as well as the foliage that persists all year.

PERENNIALS FOR SHADE		ZONE*
Coral Bells	Heuchera	4-8a
Bergenia	Bergenia	4-8
Bugleweed	Ajuga reptans	4-9
Chinese Ground Orchid	Bletilla striata	5-9
Christmas Rose	Helleborus orientalis	4-9
Columbine	Aquilegia	3-8
Epimedium	Epimedium grandiflorum	4-8
	Epimedium fargesii	4-8
	Epimedium diphyllum	5-8
Ferns	Various	2-8
Hosta	Hosta	3-8
Spiderwort	Tradescantia	4a-9b
Toad Lily	Tricyrtis formosana	6-9
	Tricyrtis hirta	4-8

*hardiness zone varies with cultivar and variety

Color Is More Than Flowers

Flowering trees are a welcome addition to the landscape and add interest vertically. If color is an important element in your landscape design, consider adding trees and shrubs that flower or have complementary foliage colors.

Although plants in flower are most commonly what we think of in a beautiful garden, color is present in other ways as well, and often in a more lasting way. Veteran gardeners and garden designers will say that they look to other attributes of the plant first, before they select it based on flower color. Bark tones of brown, grey, green, and orange can be just as vivid and colorful in winter as a flower display in summer. Bold colors and contrasting hues can also be seen in the foliage of many plants and trees.

Japanese maples are a classic example of a tree with up to four seasons of interest. You don't buy one for flowers but rather the attention it provides from spring through fall with changing hues of green, yellow, red, and orange. Then in winter many Japanese maples have spectacular structure simply in their branching.

- *Green is a color:* One example which provides seem-

Beautiful foliage and the intricate branch structure of Japanese maples add interest to the garden without regard to flowers.

White flowers and light foliage show up well in dim light.

sun. It takes a lot of energy for a plant or tree to make flowers and fruit. They get that energy from the sun. For *these* plants and trees, the more sun they get, the better they'll perform. As a general rule, six to eight hours of direct sunlight is needed for them to look and perform at their best.

•*Color in shade:* Yes, you can have color in shade, although not in the way you might think. Although there are many plants and trees that flower in partial shade (and some even in fairly deeper shade), the choices are far less than options for full sun. This is especially where your focus on flowers should be secondary.

Consider a white garden, for example. It may not draw the initial "oohs" and "aahs" until you realize how spectacular

ingly limitless choices is the green color palette. Try looking for different shades of green that work well together in a similar environment. A common example is to blend the many shades of green found in hostas. These range from the yellow-greens of chartreuse to smoky shades of deep blue-green. Add to this any number of other plants which have different textures or forms, such as ferns. Then, add a third plant with yet another shape or form such as helle-bores or epimediums, still showcasing the green shades in the foliage. The result is a combination of plants that works and grows well together, adds visual interest, contrast, and variety, yet places no real emphasis on flower.

• *Color in sun:* When you think about it, almost every brightly colored display of flower beds and borders, and the most brilliant canopy of trees in bloom, are in full

FLOWERING SHRUBS		BLOOM TIME	ZONE*
Witchhazel	*Hamamelis* x *intermedia*	Early Spring	5-8
Forsythia	*Forsythia* x *intermedia*	Spring	5-8
Flowering Quince	*Chaenomeles speciosa*	Spring	4-9
Winter Honeysuckle	*Lonicera fragrantissima*	Spring	4-9
Azaleas	*Rhododendron*	Spring	4-8
Rhododendrons	*Rhododendron*	Spring	4-8
Pearlbush	*Exochorda racemosa*	Late Spring	4-8
Fothergilla	*Fothergilla gardenii*	Late Spring	4-9
Scotch Broom	*Cytisus scoparius*	Late Spring	5-8
Mockorange	*Philadelphus coronarius*	Late Spring	4-8
Butterflybush	*Buddleia davidii*	Summer	5-9
Smokebush	*Cotinus coggygria*	Summer	4-8
Hydrangeas	*Hydrangea*	Summer	6-9
Rose-of-Sharon	*Hibiscus syriacus*	Summer	5-9
Chaste Tree	*Vitex agnus-castus*	Summer	6-9

*hardiness zone varies with cultivar and variety

FLOWERING TREES		ZONE*	FLOWERING TREES		ZONE*
Allegheny Serviceberry	*Amelanchier laevis*	4-8	Japanese Snowbell	*Styrax japonicus*	5-8
American Mountain Ash	*Sorbus americana*	2-5	Japanese Stewartia	*Stewartia pseudocamellia*	4-7
American Yellowwood	*Cladrastis kentukea*	4-8	Korean Stewartia	*Stewartia koreana*	5-7
Amur Chokecherry	*Prunus maackii*	2-6	Kousa Dogwood	*Cornus kousa*	5-8
Basswood	*Tilia americana*	2-9	Loebner Magnolia	*Magnolia x loebneri*	4-8
Bigleaf Magnolia	*Magnolia macrophylla*	5-8	*Malus* Cultivars	*Malus*	4-8
Callery Pear	*Pyrus calleryana*	5-9	Mazzard Cherry	*Prunus avium*	3-8
Carolina Silverbell	*Halesia tetraptera*	5-9	Mimosa	*Albizia julibrissin*	6-9
Chinese Chestnut	*Castanea mollissima*	4-9	Myrobalan Plum	*Prunus cerasifera*	2-8
Chinese Stewartia	*Stewartia sinensis*	5-7	Northern or Western Catalpa	*Catalpa speciosa*	4-8
Common Horsechestnut	*Aesculus hippocastanum*	3-7	Okame Cherry	*Prunus x incam* 'Okame'	5-8
Common Pear	*Pyrus communis*	4-9	Peach	*Prunus persica*	5-9
Cornelian Cherry Dogwood	*Cornus mas*	4-8	Pendant Silver Linden	*Tilia petiolaris*	5-7
Devil's-Walking Stick	*Aralia spinosa*	4-9	Red Buckeye	*Aesculus pavia*	4-8
Downy Serviceberry	*Amelanchier arborea*	4-9	Red Horsechestnut	*Aesculus x carnea*	4-7
Eastern Redbud	*Cercis canadensis*	4-9	Sargent Cherry	*Prunus sargentii*	4-7
English Hawthorn	*Crataegus laevigata*	4-7	Sargent Crabapple	*Malus sargentii*	4-8
European Mountain Ash	*Sorbus aucuparia*	3-7	Saucer Magnolia	*Magnolia x soulangiana*	5-9
Flowering Dogwood	*Cornus florida*	5-9	Southern Catalpa	*Catalpa bignonioides*	5-9
Fragrant Snowbell	*Styrax obassia*	4-8	Star Magnolia	*Magnolia stellata*	4-8
Glossy Hawthorn	*Crataegus nitida*	4-7	Sweetbay Magnolia	*Magnolia virginiana*	5-9
Golden Chain Tree	*Laburnum x watereri*	5-7	Washington Hawthorn	*Crataegus phaenopyrum*	3-8
Golden Rain Tree	*Koelreuteria paniculata*	5-8	White Fringetree	*Chionanthus viginicus*	4-9
Higan Cherry	*Prunus subhirtella*	4-9	Yellowhorn	*Xanthoceras sorbifolium*	3-7
Japanese Flowering Crabapple	*Malus floribunda*	4-8	Yoshino Cherry	*Prunus x yedoensis*	5-8
Japanese Pagoda Tree	*Sophora japonica*	4-7	Yulan Magnolia	*Magnolia denudata*	4-8
*hardiness zone varies with cultivar and variety			*hardiness zone varies with cultivar and variety		

it is at night or even on a cloudy day. I have a friend who employs lots of white in her shady garden. White is a color that stands out exceptionally well in dim light, and it can be achieved in a variety of ways. My friend works during the day, and yet she is still able to enjoy her garden in the evening because the plants with white and light-colored foliage are always there to greet her.

I have a rather deeply shaded back yard myself. From my family room window, I can see the beds of white impatiens tucked among the ferns and shrubs, several hundred feet away. Impatiens are a great low-growing annual to brighten up any shade garden. Similarly, I use the perennials hosta, pulmonaria, and a white striped form of liriope 'Silver Dragon' for enlivening shady areas. From there, as I move up into shrubs, I love to use hydrangeas. Two white varieties that work well for my back yard include 'Annabelle' and oakleaf.

As you study a garden of only one or very few colors, you begin to appreciate the subtleties and sophistication that working with fewer colors requires.

To change the color of hydrangeas you'll need to change the soil pH.

during the growing season should produce blue flowers by the next summer.

Conversely, if you have blue flowers on your hydrangeas, you can have pink flowers next season by adding a cup of dolomitic lime or ground limestone around the root zone of each plant several times during the year. However, current plant breeding has developed more color stable varieties

Fooling Mother Nature

White isn't the only color for shade. I've just mentioned hydrangeas. They are probably my favorite of all shade tolerant plants. In addition to some great white varieties, hydrangeas come in amazing shades of blue, pink, and purple. What's more, they grow in most parts of the country, and you can change the color from pink to blue or vice versa on many of the varieties by adjusting the soil pH.

If you have alkaline soil, they'll tend towards the pink color range. One tablespoon of aluminum sulfate per gallon of water applied to the root zone several times

JOE'S SHADY FAVORITES	
Annabelle Hydrangea	*Hydrangea arborescens*
Hosta	*Hosta* sp.
Impatiens	*Impatiens walleriana*
Liriope	*Liriope spicata* 'Silver Dragon'
Lungwort	*Pulmonaria*
Oakleaf Hydrangea	*Hydrangea quercifolia*
Viburnum	*Viburnum* sp.
Variegated Solomon's Seal	*Polygonatum multiflorum* 'Variegatum'
Camellia	*Camellia* sp.

GREAT PERENNIALS PLANTS FOR SHADE		ZONE*
Monk's Hood	*Aconitum* spp.	2-9
Barrenwort	*Epimedium*	4-10
Bleeding Heart	*Dicentra* spp.	3-9
Columbine	*Aquilegia* spp.	3-10
Coral Bells	*Heuchera* spp.	3-10
Cranesbill Geranium	*Geranium* spp.	4-9
Daylily	*Hemerocallis* spp.	3-9
False Spiraea	*Astilbe*	4-8
Foxglove	*Digitalis* spp.	4-10
Globe Thistle	*Echinops ritro*	3-10
Hardy Ageratum	*Eupatorium coelestinum*	6-10
Honesty	*Lunaria redeviva*	6-9
Jack-in-the-pulpit	*Arisaema* spp.	4-9
Lady's Mantle	*Alchemilla mollis*	3-9
Lungwort	*Pulmonaria* spp.	3-10
Campion	*Lychnis*	3-10
Obedient Plant	*Physostegia virginiana*	3-10
Spiderwort	*Tradescantia x andersoniana*	5-10
Stinking Hellebore	*Helleborus foetidus*	3-10
Veronica	*Veronica* spp.	3-10
Virginia Bluebells	*Mertensia virginica*	3-10
Windflower	*Anemone*	6-10

*hardiness zone varies with cultivar and variety

You can change the color from pink to blue or vice versa on many varieties of hydrangeas to suit your preferences.

HOW:

Hydrangeas that bloom pink generally can be changed to blue by adding aluminum sulfate to the soil. Make sure to thoroughly water the root zone before applying. Too much aluminum sulfate around the plant can burn the roots. To turn blue hydrangeas pink, add lime around the root zone, several times during the year.

Continue this process yearly, otherwise the natural pH conditions for your area will ultimately dictate the flower color.

Tips for Buying Annuals and Perennials

The allure of those beautiful annuals as we drive by the nursery or home improvement store can be too much to resist. We probably didn't even have flowers on our shopping list. Now I'm as weak as the next guy when it comes to impulse buying, and I'm an admitted plantaholic. But, before any new flowers or plants go home to my garden, they must pass a tough inspection.

Fortunately for me, many happy gardeners buy up all the annuals in full bloom, the ones with the most blooms currently on display. I on the other hand, use these flowers as a guide, but proceed to purchase the plants that have yet to bloom, or are just starting to bud. These are the plants that will look great a few weeks from now in my garden, when the others may have already fizzled out.

- *It's okay to purchase annuals without blooms.*

Now I realize *annuals* are easy plants to grow, and they're usually very productive for the few weeks or months that they are on display. But when I plant these beauties, I want them to direct their energy into establishment. It

that are not as sensitive to pH fluctuations. For example, some pink varieties stay pink from year to year. However, true white hydrangeas cannot be changed by adjusting the soil pH. 'Annabelle' will always be white no matter what type of soil you have.

If your yard or landscape setting is in shade, you can still have a beautiful, inviting garden and even some color. But, you should also appreciate the colors and textures of foliage. The many hues of green can give you a great place to start. Look for burgundy, chartreuse, white, and silver tones as well. Add different foliage textures and shapes for combinations.

Bleeding Heart is colorful in bloom but its foliage also adds a lacy texture to the shady garden.

When planting, I'll opt for disbudding an annual in full bloom (removing all the current flowers and buds), or I'll plant annuals yet to bloom.

WHY:

Annuals especially have one mission in life: to produce seed. In order to make seeds, it needs flowers. After flowering, they have completed their life cycle. So, when old flowers are removed the cycle starts over and new flowers are produced.

takes a lot of energy to put out flowers, and I prefer that energy to go into making a bigger, stronger root system first, rather than trying to spread plant resources in too many directions. So I'll opt for disbudding an annual in full bloom (removing all the current flowers and buds), or I'll plant annuals yet to bloom. Don't worry, disbudding a plant sends a signal that it has not yet completed its life's purpose, and it will continue to flower. But by the time they bloom again, they're well established in my beds or containers and looking good for all to see.

• *Consider perennial foliage as well as blooms.*

When purchasing *perennials*, it is so much more fun to see the plants in bloom. You know what you are bringing home, and let's face it, we all enjoy that immediate gratification only flowers in bloom can provide. But perennials are not considered to be as prolific in flowering all season as annuals. Like annuals, a perennials' primary purpose in blooming is to produce seed. *Unlike* annuals though, deadheading perennials may produce a secondary but less dramatic flush of flowers, or sometimes the plant may not flower again until the following year. When shopping for perennials, I am more inclined to look at foliage attributes and purchase plants in bud so that I can enjoy the blooms to come.

• *Look for signs of pests and diseases.*

Check for pests when purchasing new plants. The last thing you want to do is bring more pests home! Be sure to look all around the plants, especially *under the leaves* where most pests like to hide. Look for signs of discolored leaves, holes, or the appearance that they've been chewed.

Also look for signs of disease such as discolored or spotted leaves. In some cases a plant may have simply had too much water or light, but disease symptoms can show the same signs. Assuming I have enough selections to choose from, the plants that show stress don't come home with me. Although it may be a very correctable

Removing buds from annuals prior to planting allows energy to be directed to the roots for quicker establishment, a bushier plant, and more blooms.

Steer clear of root bound plants such as this one on the left; they have likely been in the pot for too long.

problem, why take the chance?

- *Choose a plant with compact form.*

The next inspection point comes with the general form of the plant. Is it short, stocky, and full looking? Or is it tall and leggy and kind of gangly? Compact form indicates that a plant has matured under the best conditions, and it's a much better choice than trying to rehabilitate a plant that has suffered.

- *Check for healthy roots.*

They should be firm and white, not brown and mushy. Are they fully developed, without being root bound? Root bound plants can become stunted, and without some help from you at planting time, may never break the cycle. The plant will simply languish at best.

- *Believe me, it's worth it.*

This sounds like a tough test for little annuals and perennials, and I admit, most of these problems can be corrected with some knowledge. Use these same techniques when shopping for trees and shrubs. Since you're spending good money, then being a bit more selective at the point of purchase will pay big dividends in your garden later on.

I'm always sure to look under the leaves for signs of pests and disease.

You will need:
- ❏ digging spade or fork
- ❏ water
- ❏ tarp
- ❏ organic fertilizer
- ❏ mulch

project Dividing Perennials

Most perennials grow best when divided every three to five years. You'll likely recognize the ones that are ready. Their performance begins to suffer as the plants become crowded. They will flower less and outgrow their space.

In general, it is best to divide spring and summer blooming perennials in the fall, and fall blooming plants in the spring. Be sure to divide plants on a cool or cloudy day. It's always a good idea to thoroughly water the plants you will be dividing the day before to ensure that they are adequately hydrated, especially when it has been hot and dry.

1. Dig the clump from the ground. Allow for adequate room (about 6 to 8 inches) around the outside of the clump if possible. If the clump is very large or heavy you may try to take it out in sections using a sharp spade.

2. Remove the clump from the ground and place on a firm surface. Placing on a tarp will make cleanup easier.

3. Wash off soil and clean out dead and tattered leaf debris. Removing the soil makes dividing the clump easier to see and work with. Sometimes, I will simply slice into the clump without washing away

dirt. I usually take this approach when I have a sharp spade and good spacing in the clump to drive my blade. It's faster and so far my plants have recovered nicely.

4. Divide the clump into multiple sections and replant at the same level they were growing in the ground.

5. Firm in soil around the new plants and water thoroughly. If available, add compost and liquid organic fertilizer to get the plants off to a fast start.

6. Add mulch to retain moisture and moderate soil temperatures.

"I'll always include an ample area for lawn in my garden. That year-round carpet of green provides a cooling look, a resting place for the eye, an area for my family to play and entertain, and is the tread that connects my garden rooms."

7

Creating a Great Looking Lawn

Start with the Right Conditions

All great-looking, healthy lawns have a few things in common. First, they get plenty of sunlight. Although it is true that some grass types are more shade tolerant than others, all *prefer* full sun. "Shade tolerant" is an often-misunderstood term. It really only means there is *some* tolerance to shade, not a preference for it. Don't be discouraged if your lawn appears to be hopelessly shaded. In many cases, a few simple changes might be all that is needed to transform a thin, sparse stand of grass into a thriving lawn. However, if you find yourself in a situation where it's not possible to limb up or remove trees to provide extra sunlight, you might want to consider alternatives to grass. These will be covered later in this chapter.

The Right Conditions for Turf Establishment

- A site with plenty of sunlight (six hours or more is best)

- Loose soil that allows for deep root development

- Access to water and supplemental irrigation

- Proper pH and nutrient balance

This chapter will teach you how to achieve all of these conditions.

How Much Sunlight Does Your Lawn Get?

The first step in assessing the potential for successful turf establishment is to see how much sunlight actually reaches the ground. Although you can

There are many turf choices across the U.S. Pictured is the demonstration garden at The University of Georgia Experiment Station in Griffin.

get by with less, ideally you should have at least 6 hours of direct sunlight and more is better for top performance. Many yards easily pass this first test because there are no obstructions. Other yards that are currently in shade can have significantly increased sun exposure at ground level by limbing up existing trees.

Certain situations may not lend themselves to a healthy lawn without actually removing trees. Tree removal can be an expensive undertaking, and you will need to decide just how important having a lawn is compared to keeping the trees and choosing a grass alternative.

Do You Know Your Soil?

Another important consideration for establishing a healthy lawn is the condition of the soil. It should be loose enough for grass roots to work their way deeply and into the soil. When trying to establish a new lawn, it is disappointing to

COMMON WARM-SEASON TURFGRASS ACROSS THE U.S.					
TYPE	PLANTING METHOD	LIGHT	MOWING HEIGHT	WHEN TO FERTILIZE	UNIQUE CHARACTERISTICS/ COMMENTS
Zoysiagrass Lower half of US	Sod or Plugs	Full Sun (some shade tolerance)	1/2 - 1 1/2 in.	Late Spring Late Summer	Deep green, compact look; spreads slowly; lush carpet-like look
Bermudagrass Lower third of US especially SE	Seed (Common bermuda-grass, aggressive, invasive) Sod-Hybrid	Full Sun	1 - 2 in. 1/2-1 1/2 in.	Mid Spring Early Summer Late Summer	Common bermudagrass—very aggressive, not good for lawns; spreads by rhizomes Hybrid—dense turf in full sun; common on golf courses and sports fields; excellent lawn
St. Augustine Lower SE US	Sod or plugs	Full Sun to Part Shade	2 - 3 in.	Spring Summer Fall	Best warm-season grass for part shade; grows well in sandy and alkaline soil; does well in coastal areas; spreads rapidly
Centipede SE part of US	Seed, Sod or Plugs	Full Sun to Light Shade	1/2 - 1 1/2 in.	Late Spring Mid Summer	The "Lazy Man's Grass'; greenish yellow look; prefers low pH (4.5-5.5); needs low-nitrogen fertilizer; do not use lime; low maintenance

TYPE	PLANTING METHOD	LIGHT	MOWING HEIGHT	WHEN TO FERTILIZE	UNIQUE CHARACTERISTICS/ COMMENTS
Kentucky Bluegrass Top half of US and most of SW except extreme SW; best adapted to northern states and higher elevations of southern states	Seed or Sod	Full Sun in cooler climates to part shade in warmer climates	2 - 3 in.	Spring and Fall	Preferred choice for cool-season grass; easy to grow if conditions are right; great color and texture; blends well with other cool-season grasses
Perennial Ryegrass Top half of US, all but SE portion of California	Seed or Sod	Full Sun	2 - 3 in.	Spring and Fall	In the South, used to overseed dormant warm-season grass in the fall; dies out in the heat; good wear tolerance; best adapted to coastal regions; not tolerant of extremes in temperatures, or drought; blends well with other cool-season turf to improve wear
Fescue All of California and the top half of the US from Nevada to central Georgia	Seed or Sod	Full Sun to Part Shade	2 - 3 in.	Spring and Fall	Many varieties; blends well with other cool-season grasses; best choice of shade-tolerant, cool-season turf grass

COMMON COOL-SEASON TURFGRASS ACROSS THE U.S.

see little to no germination or to have new sod die. Creating soil conditions hospitable to germination and root development may require tilling and mixing in organic soil amendments such as compost, peat moss or topsoil, ideally to a depth of 6 inches.

 Do a soil test.

An often overlooked step, yet one of great importance, is to complete a soil test. The results from a soil test will provide the information needed to properly amend the soil to bring it into the right pH range for optimal turf establishment and growth. Even with perfect growing conditions, without the proper pH, no lawn will be at its best. The complete steps for taking soil samples and conducting a soil test are provided in this book in chapter 5.

What Type of Grass Should You Choose?

No matter where you live, turf grass falls into two main categories: warm- and cool-season types. Warm-season grasses perform best in the hotter months of summer and

in the warmer regions of the country. In cooler climates, warm-season grasses go dormant, turning tan when temperatures drop. Cool-season grasses, in contrast, often struggle in the warmest parts of the country. They prefer the cool months of fall and spring when they look their best and are actively growing.

• *Warm-Season Grass:* Many people enjoy the golf course look of a green carpeted lawn that warm-season grasses offer. When healthy, this type of grass grows rapidly and must be maintained at the proper height. Warm-season grasses typically change from deep green to a tan, straw-like appearance when dormant in cooler climates.

• *Cool-Season Grass:* Cool-season lawns, if cared for properly, will hold their rich green color year round. Generally, this type of grass requires more maintenance and a fall overhaul each year. For many, the evergreen appearance cool-season grasses offer is the deciding factor in selecting them.

The extra maintenance with cool-season lawns usually

Kill existing weeds within the lawn with a "selective" weed killer, labeled for use with your type of grass.

WHY: These products are designed to kill only certain weeds without killing your grass. However the wrong product has the potential to kill your grass, too. Be sure to read the label so you will know if it is safe to use on your grass type.

includes raking out and removing dead grass and over-seeding in the fall or spring. In addition, it requires an increased watering regime until new seed germinates.

Should You Renovate or Replace?

The question of whether or not to replace turf, rather than attempt to improve existing lawns usually pertains to cool-season grasses that have declined over the summer months. A general rule is to replace lawns and start over when 50 percent or more of the grass has died or has been replaced by weeds.

• *Replacing* a lawn means to kill *all existing vegetation,* typically with a non-selective herbicide that contains glyphosate. You may even need to repeat this process a second time for really stubborn problems. About seven days after all grass and weeds have died, seeds can be sown or turf installed.

• *Renovation* means to work with your existing grass if at least 50 percent or more of the total lawn area is represented by healthy living grass. In this case, prior to over-seeding, kill existing weeds within the lawn with a "selective" weed killer, labeled for use with your type of grass.

There are many branded weed killing products on the market, but if you read the "active ingredient" found on their labels you'll find there are only a few chemicals used for this purpose. Herbicide formulations vary, and

some will kill certain types of grass as well as weeds. Check the instructions on the herbicide label to see how long you must wait before it is safe to apply grass seed or sod to the area.

Is it Better to Use Sod or Seed?

Grass seed is not an option for certain turf varieties. Particularly various types of warm-season hybrid grasses such as zoysiagrass and bermudagrass. In those cases, sod is your only option. Your local county extension service should be able to provide details on seed availability for the variety of grass you desire.

In some cases, both sod and seed are available. For many, the decision of which to use is simply a matter of cost. Sod provides an instant lawn and saves a great deal of time. Installation is simple, although labor intensive. However, once installed, consistent watering is all that is required for establishment. The downside of course is cost. Compared to the price of a bag of grass seed, the equivalent amount of sod required to cover the same area can cost several thousand dollars. But for many, the benefit of an instant

Sod provides an instant lawn and saves a great deal of time.

STEPS FOR SEEDING A LAWN

WHAT TO DO	WHY THIS IS IMPORTANT
Conduct a soil test. Assess the site.	Different grasses have different unique nutrient requirements to perform their best. Create a blank slate and eliminate current weeds, compaction problems, nutrient deficiencies and grading issues now while there is nothing to damage and while you have unlimited access.
Kill existing weeds. Use a non-selective herbicide to kill all vegetation. Wait 7 days before sowing seeds.	Some weeds will persist and return if not eliminated now. If seeds are sown too early, herbicide may not have completely dissipated and could affect germination.
Incorporate organic material and compost into the soil to a depth of 6 inches.	Adding several inches of organic material will loosen the soil surface for germination and create long-term benefits by enriching the soil.
Rake out dead weeds and grass.	A cleaner smoother surface allows for better seed to soil contact.
Smooth and level the grade.	If you don't do it now while it's easiest, you'll regret it later. This also eliminates low spots that can collect water and cause problems.
Add lime and fertilizer at the recommended rates based on the soil test results.	Now that the soil is loose, it's the optimal time to apply these important elements. They will work into the soil more easily.
Sow certified grass seed. Stay with the suggested application rate and resist spreading too thickly.	Certified seed is under strict standards to maintain purity. Seed lots must also meet specified standards. Certified seed is free of prohibited noxious weed seeds. It must pass stringent inspection and laboratory testing before it can be sold as certified seed. Heavy applications can reduce air circulation and sunlight leading to decline and disease.
Rake or roll seed into the soil.	This provides good seed to soil contact. A water-filled roller presses seed into the soil and smoothes the surface.
Lightly cover with straw.	Keeps the seed protected, moist, and out of sight of birds. Moist seed will germinate more successfully.
Water in thoroughly.	Seed must stay moist in order to germinate. Apply several brief waterings each day until germination occurs.
Continue to water.	Newly germinated seeds should continue to be watered to encourage establishment. Then phase back slowly to 1 inch per week, including rainfall.

STEPS FOR INSTALLING SOD

WHAT TO DO	WHY THIS IS IMPORTANT
Conduct a soil test.	Different grasses have different unique nutrient requirements to perform their best.
Research and select the most appropriate sod for your unique situation.	Factors you should consider: shade tolerance, foot traffic, drought tolerance, and disease resistance.
Contact nurseries and sod farms in your area to confirm availability and delivery details.	Depending on the type of sod, it may be available only certain times of the year. Growers that ship to your area may not carry the variety you are looking for.
Make sure sod is "Certified."	Certified sod is pure. The seed must be examined and tested before it can be planted. The soil itself must be examined prior to planting to make certain it contains no noxious weeds, insects or diseases. Problems must be corrected before fields are planted. Fields must be maintained to pass further inspections before final certification.
Prepare site. Add organic material such as compost, aged manure, or leaf mold and till to a depth depth of 6 inches. Soil surface should then be smooth, weed-free, and loose.	Loose soil, complete with organic amendments will create the great growing environment needed for quick and long-term establishment. It's what gets new turf off to a fast start as roots take hold. There is no better time to get the grading smooth and level. Many weeds not eliminated now will be back.
Lay sod in rows, staggering seams from row to row, as in a brick pattern.	Staggered seams blend better.
Pull seams tightly together as you work from section to section.	Tight seams eliminate gaps and establish a solid mat more quickly.
Don't discard small scraps too early.	Smaller pieces are easier to work with. They accomodate curved areas and are easy to work around sprinkler heads.

lawn is worth the cost.

When available, grass seed is an inexpensive and simple alternative to establishing a healthy lawn. The work is not difficult, but does require several steps and some diligence in watering. In a few short months though, the results can be as satisfying as the sod alternative.

When Should You Start Your Lawn?

Here is the simplest way to know when to start a new or renovation lawn project: *Begin when the type of grass you are working with is actively growing.* For cool-season grasses, this is usually early to mid-fall or early spring. Late spring to early summer is the best time for starting warm-season grass.

A renovated or replaced cool-season lawn establishes best for the long term when completed in the fall, especially if by seed. Success rates for strong turf establishment by seed in spring are not as high. The root system usually has not had adequate time to mature sufficiently before the demands of summer.

Fertilizing Guidelines

Throughout the book, I've suggested it is better to use less fertilizer rather than more. What is true for plants, trees, and flowers is also true for grass. In fact, some of the most common diseases of all turf are

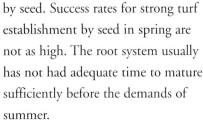

(1) The first step in a lawn renovation is to kill all the vegetation. Then it's time to till up. (2) A water filled roller does a great job of smoothing out the bumps and ensuring good seed to soil contact. (3) Two weeks later, there are good signs of early germination. By spring this lawn will be well established.

GRASS TYPE	WHEN TO FERTILIZE
Fescue	Spring and fall
Kentucky Bluegrass	Spring and fall
Bermudagrass	Mid spring, early summer, late summer to early fall
Centipede	Late spring and mid summer
St. Augustine	Late spring to early summer and late summer to early fall
Zoysia	Late spring and late summer

made worse by excessive nitrogen—the fertilizer component most responsible for green color and rapid growth.

Turf problems are often the result of fertilizers applied too late in the growing season. No plant, including grass, should be encouraged to grow by the use of fertilizer as it is trying to slow down and move into its dormant season. This potentially stressful scenario could lead to a weakened plant (a direct consequence) and promote the potential for pests and disease (a secondary consequence).

In the best scenario, healthy soil—enriched with compost and organic material on a regular basis—may never require supplemental fertilization. However, most home lawns benefit from systematic, judicious applications of nutrients, always applied during the active growth cycle.

Some grass types are light feeders and can decline with excess fertilizer. Others are heavier feeders and benefit from applications that are more frequent. Notice I said *frequent* applications—not *heavier* applications.

There are many fertilizers on the market labeled for lawns and turf. Some are engineered to give newly seeded lawns a boost. Others are marketed for established turf. Yet, others include an herbicide to kill broadleaf weeds while feeding the grass.

To truly know which formulation is best for your specific area, doing a soil test will provide the important information needed to apply the most appropriate nutrients.

Sowing grass seed is an inexpensive way to establish a great looking lawn.

Weed Control

No matter how hard you try, weeds are here to stay, and you can never completely eliminate them from your lawn. They find their way into your grass from wind, birds, neighbors, pets, and other wildlife. Furthermore, weeds aren't necessarily all bad, especially when you keep them from going to seed with proper mowing. Weeds attract beneficial insects, add nutrients to the soil, and create biodiversity. For those hoping to eliminate weeds from the lawn completely, a few ongoing steps will be required to get you closer to your goal.

There are many herbicides available to effectively manage weeds in turf. These products are classified into two broad categories.

Pre-emergent and Post-emergent Herbicides.

• *Pre-emergent weed control:* These products are designed to inhibit the growth of weed seedlings. The key to using this product effectively is the timing of the application. Weed seeds germinate at different times based on temperature. Therefore, the pre-emergent product must be in

place before these temperatures arrive.

• *An organic pre-emergent alternative:* Some products were not originally developed for how we use them today. Such is the case with "corn gluten," patented in 1991 as a natural pre-emergence herbicide. As it was being tested for another reason entirely, it was observed that it had a non-selective inhibitory effect on the germination of grasses. Further testing revealed that the corn gluten had the same effect on germinating weed seeds. And since corn gluten has a 10 percent nitrogen content by weight, it also makes an excellent natural fertilizer for established plants with a mature root system.

Corn gluten has gained popularity as a natural alternative to synthetic pre-emergence herbicides. However, timing of the application of corn gluten is critical and should be disbursed four to six weeks prior to seed germination. First

QUICK FACT ?

A renovated or replaced cool-season lawn establishes best for the long term if you plant in Fall, especially if using seed.

WHY:

Grass roots have half a year or more to establish a healthy root system, before the stresses of summer arrive. Cool-season lawns started by seed in the spring will establish but usually require a lot of extra care.

Fall is the best time to fertilize a fescue lawn.

season weeds.

- *Post-emergent weed control:* The second type of chemical control kills weeds after they have germinated. These herbicides are referred to as "post-emergent." They are used to kill broad-leaf weeds.

 Choose the right product.

Be sure to read the package label whenever using chemicals. Some post-emergent products are only designed to work with certain grass types. Using a product not made for your grass type could inadvertently kill the grass as well. Read my personal story later in this chapter.

year reduction of targeted weed populations has about a 50–60 percent success rate. Two to three years of repeated applications are necessary to match the effectiveness of synthetic counterparts. Corn gluten's success is due to its high nitrogen, which increases a lawn's density.

Although corn gluten may be more expensive to use as a weed and feed, a growing number of gardeners and landscapers are happy to pay the higher price for a more environmentally friendly alternative.

Just like many plants, lawn weeds can be either annual or perennial. Annual weeds are further classified as cool or warm-season types. For this reason, pre-emergent should be applied in the late summer or early fall for cool-season annual weeds and again in mid to late winter for warm-

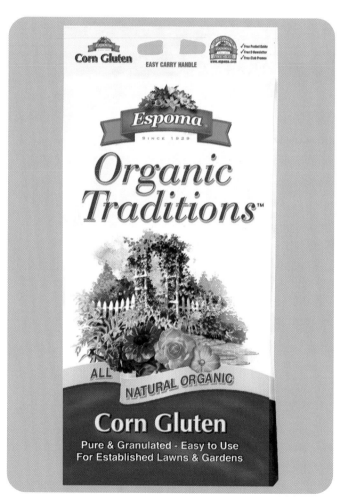

Corn gluten has been found to be a safe and effective non-selective pre-emergent with the added benefit of nitrogen.

Vinegar with 20 percent acidity is useful as a safe and effective organic non-selective weed control.

• ***Organic post-emergent alternatives:*** Organic solutions to post-emergent weed control are all "non-selective"—that is, they kill weeds and anything else these products come in contact with. For the most part, all are effective at burning down top growth. However, long term control varies depending on the weed and the extent of the root system. In my experience, deep "tap-rooted" weeds are difficult to control with one application. Multiple applications may be necessary.

Boiling water is effective at killing annual weeds, and with repeated use will kill a number of perennial weeds as well. Even though the water is not actually "boiling" at the moment you apply it to the weeds, hot water will still work. Use care in handling hot water, and pour the water from just a few inches above the plant.

There are ready-to-use products on the market that incorporate

one or more of the following ingredients which are also non-selective, organic, post-emergent weed eliminators. Look for products containing:

• Vinegar–(20 percent concentration)
• Clove Oil
• Thyme Oil
• Citric Acid

Cultivation by hand or tools is still the most effective "selective" method because you decide which plants are weeds.

 Labels contain important information.

• Apply herbicides early in the morning or late in the day. Conditions are usually calm at this time. Any wind at all can carry the fine mist onto non-targeted plants and damage them.

• Hot temperatures and direct sun can intensify the killing action of even "selective" herbicides—so much so that it can kill the grass, which otherwise would not be affected.

• It is important to give newly seeded lawns ample time to mature before applying any post-emergent. It is necessary to wait six weeks after grass seed germination.

Irrigation

One of the most common mistakes when it comes to the long-term health of lawns is the amount of water they receive. With the ease and convenience of automatic irrigation systems, many homeowners set their systems to

CONTROLLING WEEDS WITH CHEMICALS			
ANNUALS WEEDS	WHAT TO USE	WHEN	WHY
Cool-season weeds	Pre-emergent	Late summer or early fall	Needs to be in place before germination
Cool-season weeds	Post-emergent	During active growth	Pre-emergents are ineffective against weeds that have already germinated
Warm-season weeds	Pre-emergent	Mid-winter or early spring	Needs to be in place before germination
Warm-season weeds	Post-emergent	During active growth	Pre-emergents are ineffective against weeds that have already germinated

Sometimes it's best to leave well enough alone! Read how Joe ruined this perfectly good lawn.

water every day or every other day. This creates problems at several levels. First, lawns don't need more than 1 inch of water per week, including any rainfall. Anything in excess is unnecessary and a waste of valuable resources.

Second, when grass roots become accustomed to accessing water near the soil surface, they have no need to send roots more deeply into the soil. This problem occurs when a light but steady water

From Joe

Personal experience is the best teacher! One glorious spring season, many years ago, I had a nearly perfect looking lawn. In fact, to most eyes, it WAS perfect. But to me, I saw a few stray weeds barely noticeable to even the most discerning eye. However, in my ignorance and in pursuit of a totally weed free lawn, I opted to apply one more treatment of post-emergent weed killer.

Off to the garden center I went, focused and determined to eliminate these few remaining stragglers. I hurriedly marched into the store, made my purchase and within a few minutes, I was back home, applying this product to my lawn and feeling smug that I was in control, NOT the weeds!

In a matter of minutes, my mission was complete. Now all I had to do was wait a day or two to enjoy the results of a totally weed free lawn.

The next day, just as a child anticipating the bounty of presents on Christmas morning, I headed out to the back yard to see if I could notice the effects of my anti-weed assault. That's when it hit me. My formerly near perfect looking lawn was now marred with yellowish criss-crossing stripes (hmmm . . . about the width of a chemical spreader) running all through my lawn. It looked like someone had been doing figure 8's all over it!

Then I realized that someone was me! In my haste to treat the lawn, I had purchased the wrong chemical. What I bought was not to be used on fescue grass and it clearly said so on the label. The problem was, I hadn't bothered to read it! The morals of this story are obvious.

First, leave well enough alone! When we strive for perfection, we get greedy and make mistakes. No one would have ever noticed those weeds except me. I should have left them alone. The lawn had never looked better.

The other lesson (and most important) is to be sure and read the label! I didn't know then nearly as much as I know now, but I learned the hard way how important the label information really is. Hopefully my mistake can be a lesson that saves you from a similar experience or worse.

For a truly no-maintenance lawn this homeowner chose artificial turf!

lawns growing under this method of irrigation.

Turf Management

• *Mowing:* All grass varieties have a preferred height at which they look and grow their best, although some of the same care and maintenance guidelines apply to all varieties. For example, when mowing, avoid cutting more than one-third of the grass blade. Removing more can create stress and increase the chance of secondary problems such as diseases and pests. Another contributor to turf stress for all turf types is mowing with a dull blade. Sharp blades make a clean cut while dull blades tear grass and expose it to additional problems.

• *Disease Control:* Turf grass is susceptible to a number of diseases. Most can be prevented or controlled with products. However, simply following sound turf management

supply is interrupted for several days or more. Shallow grass roots will dry out rapidly and the lawn can quickly show signs of stress. Lawns under stressful conditions are weaker and more likely to be affected by pests and disease, or die out more quickly.

Infrequent, deep watering once or twice a week is a much better way to encourage grass roots to grow deeper for moisture. Extended periods of drought are far less damaging to

QUICK FACT

Avoid creating ruts in the ground from the mower.

HOW:

Vary the cutting pattern each time the lawn is mowed. For example, one time work north to south. Next time, try east to west. Then try alternating diagonal patterns from corner to corner. By applying this principle, you can mow four times before repeating a direction.

TURF MANAGEMENT PRINCIPLES FOR A HEALTHY DISEASE-FREE LAWN
1. Choose turf varieties proven to thrive in your area and your growing conditions.
2. Conduct a soil test and follow the recommendations on the report.
3. Top-dress the soil with compost or organic material often.
4. Provide plenty of sunlight (six or more hours is best).
5. Always cut with a sharp blade.
6. Only remove 1/3 of the grass blade or less when cutting.
7. Practice grasscycling.
8. Water deeply but infrequently (one inch per week).
9. Aerate the lawn once each year to increase air circulation for roots and relieve compaction - use a "core aerator."
10. Alternate the directions of the cuts each time you mow to reduce rut impact.

Even the finest gardens struggle with grass in shady areas. Notice how the grass is thick and green in the sunnier area beyond the stone.

(1) Dwarf mondo grass makes a nice looking, low maintenance lawn alternative. (2) The burgundy and green leaves of Ajuga make an attractive ground cover. (3) Creeping thyme is a good ground cover choice for the sun.

principles can prevent most diseases.

- *Grasscycling:* Most lawn mowers today are designed to cut grass blades into very small pieces. So small in fact, that if left in the lawn, the grass breaks down quickly and returns valuable nutrients to the soil. This term is referred to as "grasscycling". Studies indicate that grasscycling reduces the need for supplemental nitrogen by 30 percent.

Additionally, regular and consistent grasscycling does not contribute to thatch buildup nor does it increase weed populations. An added benefit is that it improves the quality of the soil and keeps the grass cuttings out of landfills.

Lawn Alternatives

Try as you might, sometimes you just have to acknowledge that not every yard was meant to grow turf. This is usually the case with yards that are densely shaded. Although there are grass types that will tolerate some shade, no variety will flourish. Unless you can significantly increase the amount of light reaching the ground, grass will not thrive in this type of environment. In these situations, you are better served to cut your losses and look for alternatives.

There are a few options to try when attempting to grow grass in shade. First, make sure you are using a shade tolerant variety. Next, limb up as many trees as you can to bring light to the ground. You may want to consult with a professional arborist for advice on which trees to prune. Also, allow grass to grow higher between mowings.

In other cases, you may simply decide to have smaller grass areas, or even a no-mow yard. Fortunately, there are great grass alternatives for sun or shade.

ALTERNATIVES FOR SUN OR SHADE		LIGHT	ZONE*
Dwarf Mondo Grass	*Ophiopogon japonica*	Light shade-full shade	6a – 10b
Bugleweed	*Ajuga reptans*	Part Shade to Shade	3-11
Bunchberry	*Cornus canadensis*	Light Shade	3-6
Creeping Sedum	*Sedum* sp.	Sun	3-9
Creeping Thyme	*Thymus surpyllum*	Sun	4-9
Japanese Spurge	*Pachysandra terminalis*	Part Shade to Shade	4-8
Monkey Grass	*Liriope muscari*	Sun to Shade	7-11
Periwinkle	*Vinca minor*	Sun to Part Shade	4-8
Three Toothed Cinquifoil	*Potentilla tridentate*	Sun	2-10

This garden is always a favorite of mine to visit throughout the seasons. It is not only peaceful but inspirational as well. The breathtaking fall color of these trees and shrubs can be just as stunning in your own garden setting. **"**

Tree and Shrub Basics

Options for Planting and Growing

With so many innovations in plant breeding today, trees and shrubs can thrive in all kinds of environments—from moist shade to dry full sun, from tight to wide open spaces, and in every type of soil. I'm not saying every tree or shrub will grow in every environment, but there now are plenty of selections for your particular growing conditions.

Besides being beautiful to look at, trees are the workhorses of our environment. Filtering air pollutants and absorbing carbon dioxide (CO_2), trees return oxygen to the air. The shade of a large tree creates a drop in temperature, sometimes by as much as 20 degrees F. Trees act as sound barriers, capture and slow water runoff, and retain soil. Trees even affect us psychologically. We are happier in cities with trees. So keep in mind that, although trees have ornamental attributes, they serve a greater purpose in the long run.

Shrubs clean the air also, but to a lesser degree. Shrubs can be purely ornamental, provide screening and security, or accomplish all three at the same time. They are part of the middle layer that makes our landscapes appear more natural.

When selecting trees and shrubs, it pays to do your homework beforehand. Become familiar with your own environment. Ask yourself why you want that particular tree or shrub. How much sunlight do you get? What type of irrigation and what type of soil conditions exist in your area? Proper selection of plant material for your growing conditions is the

To avoid a pruning nightmare, be sure you know the full potential of your plant at maturity.

key to easy establishment, lower maintenance and subsequent survival.

How Large Will Your Tree or Shrub Be?

Whenever you see a tree or shrub for sale in the nursery, be sure you understand its full potential when planted in the landscape. So many of us are guilty of either not reading the plant tag or assuming we will be able to tame

the plant into submission once we get it home. It rarely works that way.

When you read the tag on a tree or plant in the nursery and it describes the height and width of that plant, it assumes a mature plant growing in ideal conditions. Although we don't always plant in the best conditions, don't underestimate the future size of those trees and plants that look so cute in the nursery.

When shopping for just the right plant for your landscape or container, be aware of one term that can lead to a lot of misunderstanding. The term "dwarf" naturally leads one to make the assumption that it stays small. Often times we think of "dwarf" as "miniature." In reality it simply means

Dwarf or miniature plants simply take longer to attain their full mature size which may be only slightly smaller than the non-dwarf variety.

Understory trees like this redbud tolerate some shade and do a wonderful job of filling in the middle level of our vistas.

benefit from added sunlight if you can provide it.

One effective way of allowing more light to reach the area where you would like trees to grow is to limb up neighboring trees that block sunlight. Short of removing the mature trees completely, this is the best way to increase the amount of light available to trees and shrubs below.

Trees that grow well under the shaded canopy of taller trees are referred to as understory trees. You are likely to see these growing naturally in woodland settings. They include dogwoods, redbuds, silverbells, and other native trees that may suffer in full sun. However, these trees do require a certain amount of sunlight to bloom and look their best.

Understory trees are beautiful in nature and a great addition to any landscape. They give a layered look and do a wonderful job of filling in the middle level of our vistas. They fill a void and offer the perfect solution to that area of your yard that needs trees but is neither full sun nor full shade.

it will grow slower and will not attain the same full size at maturity of its non-dwarf cousin. For instance, a full grown hemlock may grow to 50 feet. A "dwarf" version of the same may at maturity grow to 45 feet. That's not a substantial difference.

Terms on a plant label can sometimes be confusing. Although there are no industry standards, here is what the American Conifer Society has some guidelines.

Sometimes we plant too closely together, wanting the instant impact of a mature landscape. Unfortunately the consequence is plants and trees that are too crowded languish their entire lives, often succumbing to pests and diseases. Other times, the plant is sited poorly. For instance it may have been planted in shade when it really needed full sun to thrive.

How Much Sun or Shade Do They Need?

Most trees and shrubs do best in full sun, some grow well in partial shade. Some like being under the canopy of tall open trees, and a few will adapt in shadier situations. Trying to find trees or shrubs that grow well in deep shade can be a bit more challenging. Even when you do, they

SIZE TERMINOLOGY GUIDELINES**		
CATEGORY*	GROWTH PER YEAR[1]	APPROX. SIZE AT 10 YEARS[2]
Miniature	Less than 1 inch	Less than 1 foot
Dwarf	1 to 6 inches	1 to 6 feet
Intermediate	6 to 12 inches	6 to 15 feet
Large	12 inches	12 feet

**American Conifer Society guidelines
[1]Size may vary due to cultural, climatic and geographical region
[2]Refers to growth in any direction

SHADE-TOLERANT TREES		ZONE*
Amur Maple	*Acer ginnala*	3-8
American Beech	*Fagus grandifolia*	4-9
American Hornbeam	*Carpinus caroliniana*	3-9
Bigleaf Magnolia	*Magnolia macrophylla*	5-8
Eastern Redbud	*Cercis canadensis*	4-9
Flowering Dogwood	*Cornus florida*	5-9
Fragrant Snowbell	*Styrax obassia*	5-8
Fraser Magnolia	*Magnolia fraseri*	5-8
Japanese Maple	*Acer palmatum*	5-8
Kousa Dogwood	*Cornus kousa*	5-8
Ohio Buckeye	*Aesculus glabra*	3-7
Red Mulberry	*Morus rubra*	5-9
White Fringetree	*Chionanthus virginicus*	4-9

hardiness zone varies with cultivar and variety

 Don't crowd your trees.

Whenever two or more trees are growing very close together, they are competing with each other for light, water and nutrients. Although they might look okay, you may want to consider selectively removing one or more of the competing trees. In time this will reduce the competition and allow the remaining tree(s) to prosper.

Deciduous vs. Evergreen: What's the Difference?

• *Deciduous* trees and shrubs shed their leaves as winter approaches, transferring energy resources from above ground into the roots. These are most often found north of the subtropical zones of central Florida.

Consider planting evergreen trees along with deciduous types to provide greater visual interest.

QUICK FACT ?

A common design technique for combining deciduous and evergreen trees is to provide a backdrop of evergreens and place deciduous trees in the foreground.

WHY: The deciduous trees will stand out even more against the dark backdrop of the evergreen trees, especially when their leaves fill with color in the spring or fall.

• *Evergreen* trees or shrubs maintain their foliage for the entire year. They also retain their leaf color. Evergreens are most often associated with needled conifers such as spruce, pines, junipers, and hemlocks, but there are many broad-leaved evergreens such as azaleas, camellias, pieris and many hollies. These trees and shrubs are not only beautiful, with some providing seasonal blossoms or colorful fruits, but they offer an excellent way to create privacy and screening in any home landscape.

When thinking about what to plant in your landscape,

Colorful winter berries brighten our day and provide a necessary food source for birds and other wildlife.

the birds don't get to them first! But if they do, that's all the better. Little enlivens the garden more than the interaction of birds in the landscape, and shrubs provide a necessary winter food source. There are many selections of trees and shrubs which provide colorful fruit that last throughout the winter season. In fact, for some shrubs it's their best ornamental quality.

consider combining evergreens and deciduous types because together they create greater visual interest. Remember: You can use the common design technique of providing a backdrop of evergreen trees and place deciduous trees in the foreground.

Bark, Texture, and Berries for Year-round Interest

While planning your landscape and garden, appreciating the subtle differences in plants and trees can add many choices to your design for year-round interest. Look for trees and shrubs that offer more than just eye-catching summer or fall foliage.

A tree or large shrub with attractive bark color or texture can keep the garden interesting in even the bleakest months of winter. Against a backdrop of snow or grey skies, exfoliating bark with cinnamon shades, mixed with oranges, rust or gray, can command attention.

Just as a variety of bark textures add interest to a dull winter landscape, nothing lights up a dreary winter day like the bright red berries of a deciduous holly. That is, if

TREES WITH INTERESTING BARK		ZONE*
American Hop Hornbeam	*Ostrya virginiana*	4-9
American Hornbeam	*Carpinus caroliniana*	3-9
American Sycamore	*Platanus occidentalis*	4-9
Amur Corktree	*Phellodendron amurense*	4-7
Carolina Silverbell	*Halesia carolina*	5-8
Common Hackberry	*Celtis occidentalis*	3-9
Common Horsechestnut	*Aesculus hippocastanum*	3-7
Cucumber Tree Magnolia	*Magnolia acuminata*	4-8
Dawn Redwood	*Metasequoia glyptostroboides*	5-8
Japanese Maple	*Acer palmatum*	5-8
Japanese Stewartia	*Stewartia pseudocamellia*	5-7
Lacebark Elm	*Ulmus parvifolia*	5-9
Oriental Cherry	*Prunus serrulata*	5-8
Paperbark Maple	*Acer griseum*	4-8
Trident Maple	*Acer buergerianum*	5-8
River Birch	*Betula nigra*	4-9
Shagbark Hickory	*Carya ovata*	4-9
Yellow Birch	*Betula alleghaniensis*	3-7

hardiness zone varies with cultivar and variety

When planting, dig a hole two to three times the diameter of the root ball but no deeper.

Planting & Transplanting Your Selections

Don't be too hasty when planting. Attention to some simple steps can be very important to the future health of your new tree or shrub.

• *Preparing the hole:* For any tree or shrub that you are preparing to plant, be sure to water it well first. Then dig a hole at least two to three times the width of the rootball or container. The wider the better. However, only dig as deep as the tree was growing in the ground, or in its container. For trees never plant deeper than where the flair at the trunk enters the soil.

• *General Planting Steps:* Once the tree is placed into the planting hole at the proper level, keep the native soil on-hand. Remove any rocks, and break apart any clumps that are in the excavated soil. Then back-fill this thoroughly broken up earth until the hole is filled half way. Add water to settle it and eliminate any air pockets. Add soil until it just covers the rootball which should be level with, or slightly higher than the existing grade. Water again to settle the soil.

What's Wrong with Digging Too Deeply?

Even if you were to backfill with soil to make up for it, the risk is that the earth will settle and the tree or shrub will ultimately end up growing too deep, subjecting it to many possible problems, including the risk of suffocation or drowning.

A better option would be to *plant it slightly higher* than the existing soil level. This will help prevent the roots from sitting in a pool of water and keep the tree flair clear of accumulated soil. Keep in mind, when the root ball is situated slightly above grade, mulch becomes even more important to shield the roots from exposure and help retain moisture.

Breaking News on Amending Soil

I realize I've made this point before but it bears repeating. I have *not* mentioned the need to amend the soil *in* your planting hole for a reason. This is because the most current studies have found that, in general, properly selected trees and shrubs establish more quickly when exposed simply to the native soil. Loosening the soil allows water to drain and an exchange of oxygen and gas to take place. Those items are critical to healthy growth—more so than adding soil amendments.

Envision a planting hole that is heavily amended with compost and light soil. As the roots of a newly planted tree or shrub expand into their new surroundings, they find the conditions quite favorable. That is, until they reach the edge of the hole where the native soil begins and the amended soil ends. Roots often will not press

QUICK FACT
?

When preparing to plant, dig a hole at least two to three times the width of the root ball or container but no deeper.

WHY: Roots need a hospitable environment to grow and expand. A planting hole no wider than the container from which it came can inhibit root growth. If soil is looser around the roots, they will have an easier time expanding and establishing.

forward into the native soil. Instead they continue to grow as if in a container and wrap themselves around each other, until they are so intertwined and girdled, growth becomes stunted. In extreme cases this may kill the plant.

 NOT amending soil is a radical idea.

If you've gardened long enough, this goes against every-thing you've learned in the past and how you've planted previously. Even with prior success in planting the "old way," many recent studies have validated the reasons to *not* amend the native soil.

What is "Balled and Burlaped?"

Balled and burlaped trees and shrubs are commonly referred to as "B&B". They are dug from the ground and the root ball is wrapped in burlap and contained by string or wire. This is how you find these trees ready for sale in the nursery.

The advantage is that you are able to purchase a very large plant. Its size is not limited to the size of a container. The disadvantage is that only a portion of the total root zone is retained when it is dug from the ground in preparation for sale. Consequently, B&B plants can be harder to establish when transplanting in your landscape due to the reduced root mass. However, do not let this be a deterrent to purchasing this type. With proper planting techniques, it should establish well in the landscape.

Before planting, it is important to pull away the top part of the burlap, near the trunk flare, making sure nothing is wrapped around the trunk(s) itself. A tree or shrub that is encumbered at the base (such as with string, wire, burlap, etc.) can have its growth constricted or "girdled," cutting off the flow of water and nutrients through the plant.

As a tree or shrub matures, it can become stunted or stressed. Abrasions in the tissue can result as the trunk expands. Exposed tissue is an open invitation for many types of pests and diseases.

This B&B tree was placed in a container but should be planted according to B&B guidelines.

(See the planting project at the end of this chapter.)

Containerized Plants and Trees

Containerized plants in most cases have lived their entire life in a pot, so the total root system is complete. Notice I said *in most cases*. For larger specimens, you may find that what appears to be a container plant is actually a balled and burlapped tree which has been placed in a container. By the time you purchase it, the roots may have grown through the burlap. In this case, follow instructions for planting a balled and burlapped tree, rather than treating it like a typical container plant.

The advantage to planting container trees and shrubs is that the entire root system is intact, so establishment is a fairly simple process. However, you still have a few important steps to ensure sure these plants get off to a good start (see the planting project at the end of this chapter).

Bare-root Plants and Trees

Sometimes trees and shrubs are sold with nothing but sphagnum moss, peat moss, or sawdust around their roots. This is done while the plant is dormant. It's an economical way to order plants without the added weight (and added shipping cost) of the soil. The roots will stay relatively moist for a short period of time but it is important that you soak the roots in a bucket of water immediately upon receiving them.

Don't wait too long to get the plants into the ground. Having the planting hole prepared in advance is usually the best procedure. If the ground is too frozen to plant right away dig a shallow trench and lay the plants in it with soil covering the root zone. This is called "heeling in" and will allow them to survive until they can be planted properly. If the plants are small, you could also place them in a container with potting soil until you are ready to plant.

Although an economical choice, be aware that bare root plants will only survive a short time without being planted, heeled in or potted up.

When Should You Plant?

In many parts of the country, trees and shrubs can be planted all year long. But, no matter where you live, *fall is the very best time.* The cooler air is kind to plants and especially to ones that have just lost a major portion of their roots from being dug up. Fall planting is also kind to foliage because there is minimal pest activity. In addition, soil temperatures are still warm, creating an excellent environment for the production of new root growth.

Another benefit to fall planting is that most plants and trees are entering a period of dormancy. Rather than continuing to transfer energy into new foliage and growth above ground, plants are now transferring energy into their roots and storing nutrients and resources for the cool months ahead. The fact that roots continue to grow through fall and winter is the primary advantage to fall planting. By spring, the result should be a well-established root system and a plant that can handle the upcoming demands of summer.

Early spring is also a good time to plant or transplant trees and shrubs. I consider it the second best season because they still have some time to grow and establish new roots below ground to support new top growth that will be coming on as the temperatures warm up.

QUICK FACT

Fall is the best time for planting trees and shrubs.

WHY: The fact that roots continue to grow through fall and winter is the **primary** advantage of fall planting. By spring, the result should be a well-established root system and a plant that can handle the upcoming demands of summer.

Care and Maintenance

Once your plants are safely in the ground it is critical to provide adequate water until the plants become established. This is especially important for spring planting since there is less establishment time before hot weather arrives. However more trees and shrubs are killed by *over-watering* rather than under watering.

How Long Does it Take for a Shrub or Tree to Become Established?

That depends on a number of things, such as the time of year when you plant it. Roots continue to grow throughout the year, although not as rapidly in winter as in spring and summer. It also depends on the plant itself, and the natural rate of that plant's growth. The size of the rootball that you start with will have a tremendous bearing on establishment. For example, bareroot trees and shrubs typically lack small feeder roots needed for development.

Next, the type of soil, the nutrient content, and finally, the amount of moisture in the ground affects how long it takes for roots to take hold and grow. It can take a year or more before you can safely say that a plant and tree has become established.

You can plant any time as long as the ground is not frozen. Summer is hardest on plants, so be sure to keep the soil moist.

 Water in winter too.

When planting in winter, don't ignore watering. Winter air is very dry, and so is the soil. Roots need moisture to establish no matter what time of year it is.

Tips for Establishment:
- *Mulch:* Using mulch is very important for retaining moisture and for the establishment of newly planted trees and shrubs. It insulates the soil from evaporation, temperature extremes and protects the plants from soil borne pathogens.

(1) Sometimes temporary support is necessary, but the tree should be allowed some movement and protection from direct contact with the wire. (2) These restraints should have been removed months ago—this is called girdling and jeopardizes the life of the tree. (3) Protection from sunscald reduces the chance of bark splitting which allows pest or disease problems to manifest themselves.

Mulch is sold in many forms such as shredded bark of some sort. But, it can also be shredded leaves, peanut shells, grass clippings, pine or wheat straw, etc. It doesn't matter so much *what* it is, rather the fact that you *use* it that is important.

- *Staking:* Sometimes it is necessary to support a tree temporarily after planting. This is often the case when the tree is top heavy or has a leaf canopy that can catch the wind and topple the tree before it is rooted in and established. Also when newly planted trees have a very small root system or with bare root trees, the need for staking may be required.

If you find it necessary to stake your trees, there are a few rules that should be followed:

Don't make the guy-lines too tight. You are not trying to prevent the tree from moving in the wind. Rather, you are simply trying to keep the tree supported and upright. Allowing for some side-to-side give is desirable and actually helps the tree become stronger and establish more quickly.

Remove the guy-lines after just a few months. Otherwise, the lines can cut into the tree, damaging it or even cutting off its entire food and water supply.

Provide protection around the wire. Do this where it comes in contact with the trunk. The wire or strap will easily cut into the tender bark and should be avoided. A section of rubber garden hose makes a quick solution.

Protection from sunscald: Trees can be susceptible to sunscald, especially young trees with tender bark. This most often occurs on the west and south side of the trunk, where sun exposure is strongest. Sunscald causes bark to split allowing an entry point for pests and diseases. There is material you can purchase for protection that will allow the trunk to breathe, yet protect it from the damaging effects of the sun's rays. Ask at your garden center.

Shopping Tips

Avoid purchasing trees and shrubs that show bark or limb damage or splitting. These problems can invite pests and diseases or stress the plant enough to keep it from establishing quickly. Check the container for good root development and to be sure it is not root bound. Roots generally should be light-colored and intact. If they are dark brown to black, break apart easily, or have a bad odor, find another tree. Be sure to inspect the foliage as well for any signs of pests or disease.

QUICK FACT

It is important that you keep an eye on trees and shrubs for at least the first year and provide supplemental water when necessary.

HOW:

For a few weeks, watering every other day may be necessary. The key is to make sure the soil is moist but not soggy! Gradually reduce watering to every third or fourth day. By the second month, watering once a week should be all that is required. However, continue to monitor the plant to prevent over- or underwatering.

Plant in the fall when temperatures are cool, the soil is warm, and pest activity is minimal, allowing for less stressful establishment.

Planting project
and **Transplanting**
Trees and **Shrubs**

You will need:
- ❏ shovel
- ❏ access to water
- ❏ mulch

You might need:
- ❏ wire cutters
- ❏ scissors
- ❏ pliers

Whether planting or transplanting, make sure the plant is well watered. You may want to apply water the night before digging up or water the container or root ball before placing it in the ground.

For any tree or shrub, dig a hole two to three times the width of the root ball or container. However, only dig as deep as the tree or shrub was growing in the ground if transplanting and no deeper than it was growing in the container. An even better choice would be to plant it slightly higher than the existing soil level.

Loosen the soil. Remove any rocks and break apart any clumps that are in the excavated soil.

Place the tree. Position it in the planting hole and check to make sure it is sitting at the proper height. Remember, it is better to plant slightly high.

Return native soil halfway. Add back the thoroughly broken up native soil until the hole is filled half way.

Add water and more soil. Use water to eliminate any air pockets and to hydrate the roots. Add the remaining

soil until the hole is filled and level with the existing grade, and add water again to settle the soil. Add any remaining soil only to the settled areas. Be careful not to overfill.

Cover with mulch. Cover the soil with about 3 inches of natural mulch, covering at least the area of the root zone. Keep mulch two to three inches away from the trunk or stem otherwise this can create an avenue for pests and disease.

Special Considerations

Balled & Burlaped Plantings

Remove as much binding materials as possible. Once the root ball is placed in the hole, cut or remove as much of the string that is wrapped around the base as possible. Remove any nails. Cut or bend the wire cage away (if included)—at least the top third. Cut or pull back the burlap as much as you can without damaging the roots. You may need pliers to remove the nails that secure the excess burlap to the root ball.

As a final step make sure the root ball is well hydrated.

Containerized Plants and Trees

Water the container. Make sure the roots are thoroughly saturated before placing in the new planting hole. Sometimes it is easier to place it in a bucket of water for several minutes to several hours just before planting.

Make sure the roots are not pot bound. If they are, loosen them with your fingers or score the roots with pruners or a knife to break up the tight circular pattern. Note: The order of soaking and scoring is not as important as simply doing both.

Although I love all aspects of vegetable gardening, there is no better feeling than the day I am able to harvest the fruits of my labor.

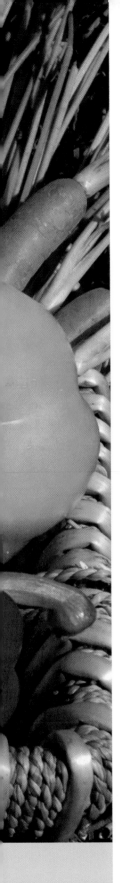

9

The **Edible Garden**

From Planting to Harvest

The Importance of Sunlight

The best vegetable gardens have a few things in common, and one of the most important is plenty of direct sunlight. For a vegetable garden to really be at its best and produce the most abundant fruit, eight hours or more of full sun each day is essential. Although vegetable plants can produce fruit in less sun, the quality, quantity, and overall productivity of the plants will be diminished.

To give yourself the best chance of success with your vegetable garden, find the sunniest spot in your yard and start there. Even if the sunniest spot in your yard only gets a few hours of direct sun each day like mine, try it anyway. You won't get the results of a full sun garden, but it's fun to try and you might be pleasantly surprised.

Options for Watering

Vegetable plants benefit from soil that is consistently moist but not wet. A general rule of thumb is to provide an inch of water per week. Realistically, providing this water only once per week would likely result in soil that does dry out between waterings. Therefore, I prefer to water using soaker hoses, set to turn on and off with automatic timers. Supplying water every two to three days, so that a total of an inch is delivered each week works well for me.

How you water is just as important as how much you water. Too little or

In a site that does not get full sun, try leafy vegetables like spinach, lettuce, cabbage collards, and kale. I've actually even grown tomatoes with marginal success in about four hours of direct sun followed by dappled light the rest of the day.

WHY:

It takes a lot of energy for a plant to produce fruit. The fuel for that energy comes from the sun. It starts the process and keeps it going. The reason leafy and non-fruit producing vegetables do better in less light is that they don't need it to make fruit. Quite often, the leaves of leafy crops such as cabbage, lettuce, kale, etc., have large surfaces that are better able to capture enough of the sun's energy to keep growing.

too much water can be equally damaging in the garden. Similarly, water that stays on the plant foliage too long can create problems of its own, such as the increased risk of plant disease.

For these reasons, I like to control how, when, and how much water is getting to my vegetable plants. My favorite method of watering my garden, as I mentioned, is to use soaker hoses. Soaker hoses are porous and allow water to seep out slowly. This is advantageous for several reasons. First, because the water seeps out slowly, roots have time to absorb it. Secondly, a slow drip does an excellent job of saturating the soil all around the plant, rather than quickly running

through the bed before all of the roots have time to take in the moisture.

Soaker hoses also deliver the water right where it is most efficient—at the soil surface. There is little if any evaporation, and the foliage stays dryer. Dry foliage is a key element to a disease-free garden.

Soaker hoses are also inexpensive, readily available and easy to work with. If you find that the length you have is too long for your garden or bed, then cut it off at the proper length and fold the edge over by crimping it and secure it with a zip tie.

Autopilot in the Garden

Adding a battery operated timer to control when the water comes on and off is an easy way to ensure your plants are being watered at the right time and getting the right amount of water. They are one of the greatest time savers in the garden! Imagine being able to go on vacation for a week or longer and not having to worry about your plants drying out. Conversely, worries of overwatering are eliminated as well.

Soaker hoses are my favorite way of watering the vegetable garden.

In a large vegetable garden, individual soaker hoses can be impractical. In this case, an overhead irrigation head, such as an impulse sprinkler mounted on a tripod, can do a great job of watering a large area efficiently. In fact, this is often how I would water my large gardens on the set of *Fresh from the Garden*. But I always made sure to water very early in the morning. I'd set the timer to turn the water on around 4 A.M. and off by 6 A.M. This way, I'd be sure to provide the best chance of drying the foliage quickly as the sun comes up. Wet foliage is a major contributor to plant disease.

Another favorite watering method of mine is to use a watering wand. These are great for delivering water right at the soil level and it's easy to control the flow. Although hand watering is more time consuming, using a wand can make this important task much more efficient.

Great results can still be achieved even when you're away from home by using timers to control when the water comes on and off.

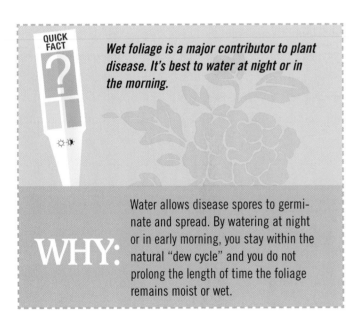

QUICK FACT

Wet foliage is a major contributor to plant disease. It's best to water at night or in the morning.

WHY: Water allows disease spores to germinate and spread. By watering at night or in early morning, you stay within the natural "dew cycle" and you do not prolong the length of time the foliage remains moist or wet.

Convenience Matters

No matter how perfect the garden site, if it is not conveniently located, you'll likely find many reasons not to make it out and into the garden. Frequent if not daily strolls are important because they keep you in touch with what's going on. Gardens are dynamic, especially vegetable gardens! Each day can bring new discoveries, including pests, diseases, and ripening fruit. Frequent visits to the garden can contribute greatly to your overall experience and certainly help prevent adverse conditions from getting out of hand.

One of the most important ways to keep a vegetable garden healthy and productive is to stay proactive and keep on top of any potential problems. The best way to do that is to visit it often. Having the garden conveniently located makes that easier!

I like to use organic amendments to create the ideal soil for my garden beds.

Soil Preparation

I think in all of gardening, I love soil as much as what grows in it. That's because I know how important healthy soil is to growing vigorous, productive, pest- and disease-free plants. In real estate, the mantra of selling success is "location, location, location!" Without a great location, you have nothing! In gardening, my manta is "soil, soil, soil!"

Soil is more than just dirt or a place where roots live. It's the warehouse for nutrients, minerals, oxygen, and moisture. It's also habitat to billions of beneficial bacteria, fungi, and other microorganisms that not only improve plant health, but fight off disease as well. Soil is a home

to earthworms, insects, and nematodes, that do lots of good work underground—including aerating the soil and adding nutrients.

Ideal Soil for Vegetables

Ideal vegetable garden soil should be rich in organic matter, such as compost and aged manure. It is soil that retains moisture, yet drains well enough so that water is never standing. It holds together when squeezed and breaks apart easily when disturbed. Another important component to ideal garden soil for vegetables is to have the proper pH. Amending the garden to create the best growing environment for vegetables is essential. For complete details on why proper pH is important and suggestions for soil amending, please refer to chapter 5.

Planting Environment

When I talk about creating the best planting and growing environment for vegetables, soil preparation is paramount. Next in importance is creating the best physical space for the roots to spread deep and wide. The biggest impediment to plants growing tall and wide is the physical limitations of the roots underground. Providing the room for roots to expand down and out allows for the most vigorous plants possible. And that happens by providing

QUICK FACT

The width of your planting bed is very important.

WHY: It has everything to do with convenience and getting the most planting options out of the available space. In a bed that is four feet wide, you can usually plant at least three rows of most crops and still comfortably reach in from either side of the bed to get to the center.

Raised beds allow for easy soil preparation and expansive root growth which contributes to robust plants.

I have my preferred way of providing this environment. In my own garden I love a really deep planting bed. I also like the physical structure of raised beds. So, I make raised beds from wood that are typically 3 or 4 feet wide, 12 feet long, and 12 inches tall. The length is not as important. Length is more a result of physical limitations and budget. Width, on the other hand, I do consider to be very important.

deep and wide beds or rows.

It's not important that the soil be contained within a physical boundary but simply that the roots are provided with the best opportunity for expansion.

The height of the raised bed is one dimension with which I've become spoiled. After having such success with beds that are 12 inches deep, I can't see going any less deep in the future. However, it is not necessary that your beds be this deep. Many vegetable plants can thrive in beds half as deep. I've simply become accustomed to the good results I've achieved over and over again with deeper beds.

Another way to create raised beds is simply to mound up soil to the desired depth. It is important though to angle the sides out, reducing the effects of erosion.

Raised beds contained within physical boundaries are more permanent and resistant to the effects of erosion. To me, they are

Raised beds don't necessarily need physical boundaries.

PLANTING CHART FOR WARM-SEASON VEGETABLES			
CROP	DAYS TO MATURITY	START SEED INDOORS PRIOR TO PLANTING	PLANT OUT
Bean, bush	50-60	3-4 weeks	After last frost
Bean, pole	65-75	3-4 weeks	After last frost
Bean, lima	65-75	3-4 weeks	1-2 weeks after last frost
Cantaloupe	80-90	3-4 weeks	2 weeks after last frost
Corn	80-100	2-4 weeks	0-2 weeks after last frost
Cucumber	60-65	3-4 weeks	1-2 weeks after last frost
Eggplant	75-90	8-10 weeks	2-3 weeks after last frost
Okra	55-60	4-6 weeks	2-3 weeks after last frost
Pepper	65-80	6-8 weeks	2-3 weeks after last frost
Pumpkin	75-100	3-4 weeks	2 weeks after last frost
Soybeans	75-100	NA	Sow directly after frost
Squash, bush	50-55	3-4 weeks	2 weeks after last frost
Squash, winter	85-90	3-4 weeks	2 weeks after last frost
Tomato	70-85	6-8 weeks	1-2 weeks after last frost
Watermelon	80-90	3-4 weeks	2 weeks after last frost

much easier to maintain from season to season because the physical boundaries hold the soil in. All that is required of me between planting seasons is to add some amendments to freshen up the soil.

The downside to a raised bed with physical structures is that it is more difficult to move them should you decide to do so in the future. However, this has never deterred me from using structured raised beds.

The choices in materials used for building them are many. They can be made of wood, wood composite, stone, bricks, recycled concrete, cinder blocks or anything that will keep the soil from spilling out.

Wood is easy to work with, readily available, and consistent in size. There are different types of wood that can be used for raised beds. Some are more resistant to rot, such as cedar and redwood. This should be taken into consideration as you think about how long you may be using these beds.

Other materials such as stone, bricks, and concrete may be readily available but not so uniform in shape. They can also be heavy to work with and awkward to move.

However, it still may be the best choice for your situation and that is what matters.

What to Plant and When

Vegetable plants are considered annuals for the most part. They complete their life cycle in one season. And like most annuals, they have a preferred growing season. Vegetables are classified as either warm- or cool-season plants, depending on the time of year that they prefer to grow.

Warm-season crops are typically planted after the risk of frost has passed for your area. Examples of warm-season crops are tomatoes, peppers, beans, squash, cucumbers, and melons.

Cool-season crops are usually planted in late winter to early spring and sometimes again in late summer for a

Warm-season plants such as tomatoes are planted after the risk of frost has passed.

Cool-season crops like these onions are planted in late winter to early spring.

harvest prior to a hard freeze. Examples include carrots, beets, peas, spinach, lettuce, cabbage, collards, kale, and mustard. Some cool-season crops, such as brussels sprouts, actually taste better after a chilling frost.

Extending the Season

If you're not ready to give up on the gardening season yet, or you simply can't wait any longer to get started, there are a couple of tricks that will allow you to gain a few extra weeks on either side of the growing season.

It may be as easy as looking for varieties that are considered "cold hardy." They have a higher tolerance to colder temperatures than some of their less hardy cousins and may be all

that is required to buy some extra time for your plants.

In many parts of the country, simply covering soil with black plastic will suffice to provide the growing environment roots need to remain viable and productive as temperatures drop. As a surface covering, black plastic is very effective at trapping and retaining heat. It is readily available in home improvement centers. It's inexpensive, and easy to install and remove at the end of the growing season.

Frost and freezing temperatures can make the difference between a plant surviving or not. By keeping frost off the leaves or keeping the temperature around the plants even a few degrees warmer, cold-sensitive plants may survive and continue to produce for a little longer.

One technique I often use includes applying a thick layer of mulch around the base of all my plants. Not only does it keep the roots warmer, it also helps to maintain the soil temperatures at a more even level.

Physical barriers are another effective way to capture and retain a few extra degrees of heat while keeping season-ending frost off the plants. Floating row covers are typically made of lightweight spunbound material. The material is so light that it can actually be laid directly on the plants, so that it appears to *float*.

Row covers are designed to allow in light, water, and air but provide a protective barrier against frost and pests. When the sides are secured around the bed completely, several extra degrees of warmth can be retained. This extra warmth could make the difference in survival for marginally hardy plants.

Insulation, plastic, blankets, buckets and the like can all serve to add critical protection on frosty nights. It's most important to be sure the covering extends all the way to the ground. This step protects the foliage and ensures that warmth from the soil is trapped—the essential component for protecting your plants.

PLANTING CHART FOR COOL-SEASON VEGETABLES			
CROP	DAYS TO MATURITY	START SEED INDOORS PRIOR TO PLANTING	PLANT OUT
Beet	55-65	4-6 weeks	2 weeks before last frost
Broccoli	60-80	6-8 weeks	4 weeks before to 2 weeks after last frost date
Brussels Sprouts	85-95	6-8 weeks	4 weeks before to 3 weeks after last frost date
Cabbage	65-80	6-8 weeks	5 weeks before to 2 weeks after last frost
Carrot	70-80	NA	Sow outside 4-6 weeks before last frost
Cauliflower	55-60	6-8 weeks	4 weeks before to 2 weeks after last frost date
Collards	55-70	6-8 weeks	4 weeks before to 2 weeks after last frost date
Celery	120	10 weeks	3 weeks before to 4 weeks after last frost date
Kale	50-70	6-8 weeks	5 weeks before to 2 weeks after last frost date
Lettuce	60-85	4-6 weeks	2 weeks before to 3 weeks after last frost
Mustard	40-50	4-6 weeks	4 weeks before last frost
Onion	100-120	4-6 weeks	6 weeks before to 2 weeks after last frost
Parsnips	100-120	4-6 weeks	4 weeks before to 4 weeks after last frost date
Peas, garden	60-80	4 weeks	3 weeks before to 4 weeks after last frost
Potato, Irish	70-90	NA	2-4 weeks after last frost
Radish	25-30	NA	Sow outside 4-6 weeks after last frost
Spinach	40-45	4-6 weeks	3-6 weeks after last frost
Swiss Chard	50-60	4-6 weeks	3-4 weeks before last frost
Turnip	45-65	3-4 weeks	4 weeks after last frost

However, with the exception of row covers, whenever an enclosure is placed over your plant(s) at night, be sure to remove it the next morning or at least provide a way for the heat to escape. Otherwise, efforts to save your plants may backfire since too much heat may build up when the sun comes out.

When time and energy permit, container-grown plants offer maximum portability to maneuver plants away from Jack Frost. Having the ability to move plants from the frigid outdoors to a protected shelter and back again can buy you several weeks or more of extended growing time.

I managed to get a jump on the season by planting these melons into soil protected by black plastic with an additional insulating blanket of straw.

Floating row cover material is so light it can be laid directly onto the plants for protection against frost and pests.

Planning Your Garden Layout

When laying out your vegetable garden it's not important to configure the beds so that they are all north and south, or east and west. In the continental United States, the sun is so high overhead during the peak growing season, that direction of the garden rows is not all that important. However, what does matter is how you position the plants within the beds for maximum exposure to the sun.

Harvest Time

After months of hard work and tender care, it's finally time to be rewarded for your patience and dedication. It's harvest time, and you'll never have a better salad, ear of corn, or squash casserole than you will today. But in order

Cold Frames for Protection

Cold frames are another technique for providing additional protection in the early spring or late fall and potentially year-round. Think of a cold frame as a mini greenhouse. The basic premise is a solid, insulating barrier around the plants and a glass or plastic top that allows sunlight in. However, all cold frames should provide a way for excess heat to escape during the day. Otherwise you run the risk of literally cooking your plants. Cold frames can be constructed from wood, cinder blocks, hay bales, and other materials.

You can plant directly into the soil within the cold frame or place seed flats and containers inside. A sufficiently insulated cold frame can extend the growing season, and it can even provide an environment warm enough to allow tender plants to thrive all the way until spring.

There is a season for everything, but it doesn't mean you have to stop gardening just because temperatures fall. Extending the season is an exciting and rewarding endeavor, and it gives you even more time to hone your skills before next spring.

QUICK FACT

Plant your vegetables so that they all get maximum exposure.

HOW: The tallest plants should line the north or west side of the garden so that they do not shade out the shorter plants. Place medium sized plants in front of (to the south) of the tallest plants or to the east. The smallest plants would then go in front of the medium plants or to the east of them.

Be sure to allow excess heat to escape during the day when using cold frames to extend the season.

to have the best tasting, freshest fruit, knowing when and how to pick it is just as important as knowing how to grow it.

As a rule of thumb, it is almost always better to harvest your fruits and vegetables a little early rather than a little late. Fruit that is overly mature can have a different flavor and texture than what you're used to. And many times, allowing all the fruit to stay on a plant until the peak of ripeness can cause your plant to shut down production of other buds. For the best results, read the back of your seed package or your seedling card, and mark you calendar for the expected date of maturity. Then begin checking your plants about a week before that date. And remember, the more you harvest, the more you'll have.

⚠ **Taste it fresh!**

If you want to experience what fresh vegetables really taste like, eat them right off the vine or plant. Nothing tastes better! Sugar snap peas, corn and tomatoes are my favorite right off the plant. (A reminder, be sure to wash your harvest first if your garden is not chemical-free.)

Knowing when and how to harvest your vegetables is just as important as knowing how to grow them.

Crop Rotation

From season to season, move crops of the same family to a different location within the garden. There are many pests and diseases that lurk in the soil, constantly working to build up populations from year to year. Once

they find a preferred food source or host they will take up residence and stay indefinitely.

Their food sources happen to be plants within a particular family. For example, tomatoes, peppers, eggplants, and potatoes are all members of the nightshade family. They will attract the same pests and diseases. Moving those host plants to different locations in the garden breaks the cycle that allows pests and diseases to persist.

Garden Clean Up

Another way to reduce problems in any garden is to practice good sanitation. Weeds, rotting, diseased leaves or plants, and surrounding mulch should be removed from your garden. This debris should be destroyed, not composted. (Note that unlike mulch around diseased plants, mulch around *healthy* plants can be turned back into the soil to decompose and improve organic content.) Diseases and pests will attempt to overwinter in many parts of your garden. Because weeds and rotting leaves are some of their favorite places to live, many problems can be greatly reduced by eliminating their food and shelter sources when possible.

A clean garden is a healthy garden. The more you can do to keep it that way—not only during the season, but especially between seasons—the more likely you are to have the best possible start at each new gardening year.

WHEN TO HARVEST VEGETABLES	
VEGETABLE	**OPTIMUM TIME TO HARVEST**
Asparagus	When spears are 6 to 8 in. tall and pencil thin. Limit harvest period to 6 to 8 weeks.
Beans, pole	Pick when the pods are turgid and the seeds are just visible.
Beans, snap	Pick when the pods are turgid, before you see the seeds bulging.
Beets	Harvest when shoulders protrude from soil line, eat greens as you thin rows.
Broccoli	While florets are dark green and not yet open.
Brussels Sprouts	Harvest when the bottom up when sprouts are 1 in. diameter. Remove lowest leaves to improve sprout size. Frost improves flavor, but harvest before hard freeze.
Cabbage	When heads are hard, leaves tight. Over maturing may cause splitting.
Carrots	Harvest at 1 to 2 in. thickness. Light frost improves flavor. May be left in ground when mature.
Cauliflower	Harvest when head are firm and curds are still smooth.
Corn	When silks are dry and brown. Pierced kernel bleeds milky.
Cucumber	High glossy skin, harvest when slightly immature. Yellow indicates over-ripeness.
Eggplant	Firm, shiny and slightly immature. Dull color indicates over-ripeness.
Kale	Leave should be dark green and firm. Flavor improves in cooler weather.
Kohlrabi	When bulb has reached 2 to 3 in. in diameter.
Lettuce (Head)	Harvest entire plant when heads are firm and good sized.
Lettuce (Leaf)	Harvest outer leaves continuously once about 4 in. in height.
Okra	When pods are 2 to 3 in. long and snap easily. They get tough quickly so harvest often.
Onions	When tops are yellow and $3/4$ have fallen over. Earlier if preferred.
Parsnips	Harvest in late fall after moderate freezes, or mulch heavily for winter harvest.
Peas, English	Peas are bright green, small to medium size. Taste to determine sweetness.
Pepper, Hot	Harvest when needed. Young peppers are hotter.
Pepper, Sweet	When fruits are firm and full sized. May be harvested when red, yellow or orange.
Potato, Irish	New potatoes two weeks after flowering or when tops begin to die back for full size.
Pumpkins	Fruit skin will be hard and impervious to scratching. Leave 2-in. stem attached.
Radishes	When tops are $1/2$ to 1 in. in diameter. They will be tough if left too long.
Soybeans	When pods are thick and bright green.
Spinach	When leaves reach attainable size. Cut out as needed.
Squash, Summer	Pick when young and skin can be easily penetrated with fingernail.
Squash, Winter	When skin is impervious to scratching. Leave 1 in. of stem attached.
Sweet Potato	Harvest in fall before frost and freezing temperatures.
Swiss Chard	Harvest continuously, breaking off outside leaves. Allow center to grow.
Tomato	When fully red but firm. Use immediately. Picked green, they will still ripen.
Watermelon	White spot on bottom will become deep yellow. Tendril turns brown and curly.

Head problems off at the pass by practicing good sanitation.

Vegetables and Flowers from Seed

Starting vegetables and flowers from seed is a great activity, especially when you just can't wait any longer to get your hands dirty before spring. It's an inexpensive project, lots of fun for the whole family, and the choice of seed available from multiple sources far exceeds the varieties and types of plants you can find locally.

It usually takes six to eight weeks for plants started from seed to be ready for outdoor planting. When you start seeds indoors, you have better control over the environment and can time your plantings to ensure they are not subjected to freezing conditions, which would kill tender seedlings.

Seed trays may be purchased, but common household items, such as small cups or bowls, are just as effective. I like the plastic containers you get at the grocery store or from a take-out restaurant. They have a clear plastic lid—perfect for watching your progress and keeping moisture in. Just be sure whatever container you choose has holes for drainage.

When planting, use a seed starting mix that is "soil-less."

Homemade recipes vary, but I buy ready-made versions at any garden center. These mixes are light and sterile. They are usually made up of a combination of peat moss, perlite, and vermiculite. Avoid using garden soil. It is too heavy for tender seedlings, plus soil contains disease

Starting vegetables from seed gives me the opportunity to be involved in the earliest stages.

Using a folded piece of paper is an easy way to control seed disbursement.

the seeds need to germinate. However, not all seeds have the same germination requirements, so it's best to refer to instructions on the seed packet or elsewhere for specific details.

Next, cover the tray with a plastic lid that allows light through but holds moisture in. Plastic bags also work well. With adequate moisture, condensation will develop inside this tent or cover.

pathogens, which can kill your plants.

When sowing seeds, pre-moisten the mix so the seeds are not disturbed by water after planting. It should be about the dampness of a wet sponge. Assuming the container or tray stays covered, the mix should hold all the moisture

Supplemental lighting is important for best growth. A simple shop light consisting of two 40-watt florescent bulbs is perfect and very inexpensive. Place your tray or containers under the lights. Position the lights just above the container cover. The lights should stay on for about sixteen hours each day. This is easily accomplished with an electric timer.

Keep an eye on the seeds daily. As soon as you notice them sprouting, remove the cover. Too much trapped moisture could cause plants to rot. Placing a small fan nearby to keep air moving across the soil will help keep new seedlings disease free.

Finally, continue to add water as needed to keep the soil moist but not wet. Once the cover has been

Condensation will form when the soil-less medium is adequately moistened. Keep lights within inches of the seedlings.

Use a pair of scissors to easily thin crowded seedlings.

removed, soil will dry out more quickly. Since supplemental water will be necessary, drainage is important. Continue to raise your light, keeping it to within an inch or two from the tops of your sprouts. In about six weeks, the seedlings will be ready to make the transition into the garden.

Starting seeds indoors is just one more element of gardening that I find addictive, and it's a great activity when not much else is going on outside. As a bonus, your seedlings will eventually reward you with months of vivid colors, fresh produce, and the satisfaction of knowing you had a hand in making it happen.

beds. This is a handy tool that all gardeners should have if they plan on ever sowing seeds again, or laying out seedlings in an evenly spaced row.

An Easy Tool to Simplify Planting

A tool I've seen in use for years on *The Victory Garden* television show is a planting board. I always thought that it would be an excellent tool for my garden, but it took me almost three years, thousands of seeds, and hundreds of seedlings before I finally got around to making one of my own.

Now that I have one, I can't believe I ever lived without it. I use it virtually every time I plant something new in my garden

I found this planting board to be an invaluable tool in the garden.

There are several advantages to this board. First, it provides an easy way to level the soil in the bed before planting. Next, the planting board is a convenient way to make shallow furrows in the soil. Simply place the smooth end of the board into the soil and apply some pressure as you slide it back and forth. The depth of the row is simply a result of how much pressure you apply to the soil.

Then, by virtue of the notches and markings, spacing seeds or transplants is a snap. This is my favorite part of using the board. Simply plant your seedlings or sow your seeds at the desired spacing, cover, and you're finished. If you need to come back later and thin out your plants, the board makes it easy to get the exact spacing you want.

project Making a Planting Board __

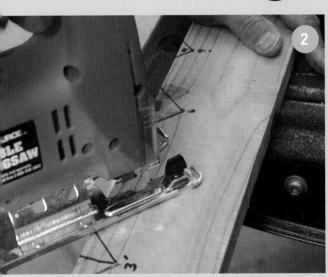

Making this board is easy.

1. Obtain a 1 inch x 4 inch board, 6 feet long.

2. Make marks in board with a permanent marker every 3 inches.

3. Make "V" shaped cuts using a jigsaw and straight edge. The 3-inch and 9-inch marks are 1 inch deep and the 6-inch and 1-foot marks are $1^{1}/_{2}$ inches deep. This gives a quick visual as you sow or plant.

That's all there is to it. The entire job takes less than thirty minutes and I love my new tool. For a couple of dollars and just a few minutes, I now have a tool that I'll use often for years to come. Do yourself a favor and make one too. Just don't wait as long to do it as I did!

You will need:
- ❏ a board 1 inch x 4 inch x 6 feet
- ❏ speed square
- ❏ marking pen
- ❏ jig saw
- ❏ tape measure

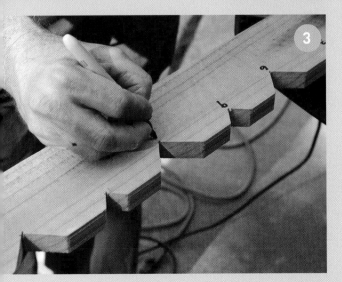

❝Even with the beauty of the countryside, two small strategically placed containers command attention without detracting from the scene beyond. I love the way they echo the similar tones of the hills in the distance.❞

10

Container
Gardening

Instant Gardens

Containers provide instant gardens no matter how much space you have. From the smallest deck or patio, to the largest estate, containers are one of the easiest ways to provide just the right punch of color or drama anywhere you want it. Containers also allow anyone to create a mini garden in minutes.

A container, soil, a single plant, or a combination of plants are all you need to have a great looking container garden. All of this can be easily acquired with one stop at any garden center or nursery.

The Benefits of Using Containers

- *Focal points:* There are many great benefits to gardening with containers. One is being able to draw the eye to it by placing your container in a strategic spot.

- *Mobility:* Containers are an ideal way to experiment with design, color, and placement. Unlike plants in a garden bed, plants in containers can be more easily relocated if you decide you don't like them in a certain setting. This not only reduces the wear and tear on you but will not stress plants from repeated digging up and moving. Getting just the right look and placement couldn't be easier.

Even the plants within the container can be considered mobile. Container plants are easily removed and replaced as they go out of season, as your mood changes, or if you simply want a fresh look.

You can be as fickle as you want without doing any real harm to your landscape. Flowers and shrubs planted in the ground are not as easily moved and may not respond well to being up-rooted.

• *Limited space:* If your outdoor space does not lend itself to a full scale garden, complete with large trees, a lawn, shrubs and flowers, a container garden can be a reality in any size space. Balconies and small patios are good candidates. Even as houses seem to become larger and gardening areas smaller, containers can be the perfect alternative to otherwise permanent landscapes.

One container can be dramatic even in the smallest of areas. Consider just one or two beautifully landscaped pots

This container is in the optimal spot to slow you down and draw your eye upward towards the conservatory beyond.

by the front door or stoop. This is one of the reasons container gardening is so popular with anyone who has limited space. Place several together in a vignette and you have a "potscape": a mini landscape completely designed with containers.

Potscaping is a popular concept since just about any plant, from annuals and perennials to shrubs and trees, become candidates with the proper attention to cultural requirements and design. Pots can be arranged and rearranged much like we do with furniture.

I even know some people with very limited sun who grow vegetables in containers on their small patio. As the sun moves across the sky during the day, they reposition their container to take advantage of as much sun as possible. And with a great deal of success I might add!

Anyone Can Do It

If you have been too intimidated to plant a garden bed, for whatever reason—perhaps from concern about the physical work or the uncertainty of how it would look afterwards—containers provide the perfect solution. They are a cinch to plant and could not be more forgiving. Garden centers stock a variety of soils designed for containers, virtually ensuring success. In addition, there are many plant choices available for both sun and shade and in varying colors, textures, forms, and height. The many options allow you to experiment, be bold and take chances.

Should you tire of that arrangement, once again, it's simply a matter of pulling out the plants you don't like and replacing them with fresher material or different plants for a more updated look.

Containers are a wonderful way for physically challenged individuals to enjoy gardening. By selecting containers that are at wheelchair height or tall enough to tend without bending over, the task of gardening becomes much easier. Granted these could be structures too large

Plants in containers are easily moved to create just the look you are after.

Pick Your Favorite

For years, traditional choices for containers were heavy terra cotta or concrete pots. The sheer weight was enough to keep all but the strongest gardeners away from the larger sizes.

Today, many choices of containers are available that are much lighter, yet they look like ceramic, terra cotta, or concrete. They are made from composite materials that have the strength

to move around, but they provide no less joy to those who really want to get their hands in the dirt. And, the lightweight planting soils are easy to work with, requiring less strength to dig the hole.

and durability of much heavier types. Even when you are up close, until you actually pick one up, it's hard to tell it's not a solid, heavy material. Composite containers are even better designed these days to look exactly like their traditional counterparts.

The benefit, besides the greatly reduced weight and corresponding mobility, is that they're more durable. Unlike the heavier materials, these newer containers hold extreme temperatures better, including alternate freezing and thawing. Traditional containers, in addition to being extremely heavy, often crack in freezing temperatures unless their contents are removed and the pots stored accordingly.

With so many container choices today, it's easy to find one to suit anyone's taste.

A potscape is a mini landscape suitable for any sized area.

These newer materials also offer better moisture retention within the container itself. Terra cotta and concrete are porous materials and tend to draw the moisture away from the soil, drying it out more quickly.

Be Creative

Plant containers can be just about anything that will hold soil and allow water to drain out. I've seen watering cans, buckets, old wheelbarrows, shoes and the like converted into planters. *The key is to allow water to drain from the soil and exit the container.* This requires that anything you use have a hole in the bottom.

For some gardeners, the concept of allowing the plant's roots to breathe is an important aspect of the container. They tend to choose porous types such as terra cotta and concrete. For others, this does not seem to matter as much as choosing containers based on color and design preferences. I don't believe there is a right or wrong answer here, as long as the soil in the container is not compacted and the container allows water to drain well while providing air exchange to the roots.

Prepping the Soil

One of the most important requirements for container

CONTAINER CHOICES TYPE	PROS	CONS
Terra Cotta	Traditional natural look, allows for air exchange	Can crumble or crack in freezing weather, soil dries out more quickly than other choices
Concrete	Traditional natural look, allows for air exchange	Heavy, porous, soil dries more quickly
Wood	Natural, allows for air exchange, holds water well, won't crack in freezing weather	May be heavy, prone to rot, seams may expand in freezing weather
Ceramic	Many color choices, holds water well	Breakable, little air exchange, may crack in freezing temperatures
Composite	Holds water well, lightweight, won't crack or break, many traditional design choices	Some may not look natural, little air exchange
Cast Iron	Traditional look, holds water well, won't crack in freezing temperatures	Heavy, prone to rust, little air exchange
Various Metals	Contemporary look, holds water well, won't crack when frozen, or break	May be heavy, some prone to rust, little air exchange
Plastic	Lightweight, inexpensive, contemporary look, many colors, holds water well, won't crack if frozen	Breakable, little air exchange

This attractive container planting is made wheelchair accessible by changing the length of the chains that support it.

- *Perlite:* This is a lightweight volcanic material that expands from four to twenty times its original volume when heated rapidly. The resulting shape is covered with tiny air chambers. These produce a large surface area which retains moisture and creates space in the soil for CO_2 exchange, drainage, and root development. Perlite is considered sterile and has a neutral pH. You can recognize perlite because it looks like small white BB's.

- *Vermiculite:* Also used for drainage and moisture retention, it is similar to perlite in its use. Many times you will see them mixed together. When it is heated, it has the ability to expand many times its original volume. It is odorless, and sterile. It does not deteriorate, turn moldy, or rot. The pH of vermiculite is essentially neutral.

- *Water retention granules:* As the name implies these granules hold many times their weight in water, slowly making this moisture available to the plant's roots. The polymer-based granules absorb so much water, a little goes a long way. Be careful if adding it to your own soil mix.

I'm never surprised anymore by the creative aspects of container gardening.

plants to look their best is to make sure the soil drains well, and provides the ideal situation for plant roots to grow and expand. For this reason, companies that offer bagged soil products have developed many options. Usually their products consist of sphagnum peat moss as the primary ingredient. The moss provides the required drainage, yet retains moisture without becoming saturated and rotting the roots. In addition, many companies include other amendments such as perlite, vermiculite, water retention granules, and compost or other organic material. A common ingredient in many container mixes is slow release fertilizer, designed to feed your plants for several months. Let's look at some of these amendments for a more thorough explanation of their benefit:

Hypertufa is a lightweight material that allows you to be creative, is easy to make into any shape, and can be left out year-round once properly cured. See how to make a container at the end of this chapter.

An organic option made of cornstarch is reported to be even more effective in releasing the moisture over an extended period.

• *Compost and other organic material:* Products are now available for purchase in bagged form that include organic material such as compost, composted manures, worm castings, and even beneficial bacteria. These "organic lines" are all designed to meet the needs of the organic gardener or simply to provide the benefits of natural amendments.

Plant choices for containers have come a long way, too. Genetically smaller forms of just about any type of plant material make gardening in containers easy, fun, and

rewarding. Plant breeders today offer many varieties of ornamental plants as well as small fruit trees and vegetables designed specifically for container culture. So even the asset of a kitchen garden or fruit orchard right outside your back door is a realistic and manageable goal.

Watering Methods for Containers

One of the biggest challenges of container gardening has always been knowing how to keep containers adequately hydrated.

During the hottest months of the year, it is not uncommon for outdoor containers to need watering several times each day to keep the plants performing their best. This creates a tremendous problem for anyone unable to stick to this regime; especially if you might be away for several days or weeks at a time. A drip irrigation system combined with timers is a great way to ensure that your containers receive the water they need. It also frees you from the responsibility of always having to be around.

Assuming you have the proper soil mix and have chosen the right plants (such as sun-loving plants for a sunny location), containers are relatively maintenance free. The most important detail to keep plants looking their best is

QUICK FACT

Make sure your container plant is getting the proper amount of water.

WHY: The best way to tell if your containers need water is to stick your finger into the soil to the second knuckle. If it comes back up dirty, then the moisture is sufficient. However, if it comes up clean, the soil is dry and needs hydration.

Put your containers on auto-pilot with drip irrigation, timers, and water saving granules that keep up with your watering needs even when you can't.

There Are No Rules!

One of the many beauties of container gardening is that there are no hard and fast rules. Although there are guidelines to help you design a great looking and long-lasting container, your creativity can really come into play. Containers can be planted with a single specimen or a variety of plants with different shapes, sizes, colors, textures, and forms.

to make sure the soil doesn't dry out completely between waterings. If you choose to use water retention granules, the soil should not dry out as quickly. Fortunately, soil container mixes drain so well, there is little risk of overwatering.

With so many unique qualities to the container itself, a single plant may be all that is needed to really create a great combination between pot and plant. Other times, the various colors and tones of the pot can be echoed in the plant material, creating another way to unify the entire ensemble.

Give attention to the physical shape of the container itself. Is it tall and narrow? If so, consider accenting that form with a plant that is also tall and narrow. Or is the pot short and wide? In this case, try more rounded plants that are in scale with the container size.

If you're adding water retention granules to your soil mix, be careful—a little goes a long way!

In this container planting, dark elephant ears are the thriller, while the grass acts as both filler and spiller, accented with creeping jenny.

Thrillers, Fillers, and Spillers: A Classic Container Recipe

With just about any container, a winning combination can be achieved by putting together three layers of plants.

- *Thrillers:* The first layer is the "thriller." It draws attention to itself because it is the tallest and is often dramatic in form, color, and/or texture. If the container will be viewed from all directions, place the thriller in the center. If the pot will be placed against a wall or only viewed from the front and sides, place the thriller in the back of the container.

- *Fillers:* Next add the "filler." This is the middle layer. It is designed to fill in the container and hide the potential

legginess of the thriller. Select plants that complement the thriller in some way. Consider a more subtle complementary plant selection or go for a bold contrast in either color or foliage form.

- *Spillers:* The "spiller" is intended to grow out over the container edge, softening it while cascading down the sides for dramatic visual interest.

With so many plant choices available, it's hard to not create a winning combination using this formula. The sky is the limit!

Other Considerations

Just like plants in the ground, container plants are often susceptible to weeds, insect infestations, and diseases. It pays to be diligent, inspecting your plants often, taking action when necessary. Use the information in the following chapters to guide you through weed-free, disease-free, and insect-free container culture.

 There's no need for rocks and fillers.

Contrary to popular practice—it is *not* a good idea to add several inches of rocks and fillers to the bottom of a container. By doing so, there is less soil area to hold whatever amount of water you've added.

Water will be retained in the soil, and not flow through as you might think. Since this isn't a science book suffice it to say that water binds to the smallest particles. Because of the difference in density of these materials, water tends to stay in the soil around the root zone even after the initial draining period. Although this may sound like a good thing, the consequence is a higher chance of root rot.

A better idea is to use something such as a single stone or pot shard to cover the drain hole. This allows for more soil in the pot and the opportunity for water to pass through the root area lessening the chance for root rot. I like to use a coffee filter because it allows water to drain but retains the soil—keeping the area cleaner under the pot.

project Making a Hypertufa Container

You will need:

- ❏ mould
- ❏ peat moss
- ❏ Portland cement
- ❏ sand, vermiculite, perlite
- ❏ water
- ❏ plastic bags
- ❏ dowels for drain holes
- ❏ gloves
- ❏ container and tool for mixing

Hypertufa is a porous medium created out of peat moss, concrete, and sand that has absorbent qualities similar to tufa rocks from which it gets its name. It is easy to make into any shape, is lightweight, and will not be damaged by freezing temperatures once properly cured.

Combine two parts peat moss, one part Portland cement, and one part sand, vermiculite, or perlite. Mix the dry ingredients well. Add one part water. The mixture should be approximately the consistency of oatmeal.

For your mold, use any object with a shape that appeals to you. Invert the object and cover it with a layer of plastic to make removal easy. Apply a 1- to 1½-inch layer of hypertufa mix to the inverted form. Dowels can be used

to create spaces in the bottom for drainage holes. Try to keep the material evenly distributed, maintaining a consistant thickness. Press firmly, expelling air pockets as you smooth the sides of the container. Work to compact and smooth the material as you go.

Leave your newly created container undisturbed for at least a week in warm weather. Double that time if temperatures are 50 degrees F. or below. For proper curing, keep it from freezing. It will cure better if you are able to spray it with water several times a day. This is especially important in hot weather and will prevent the pot from cracking.

Once this initial curing is complete (after one to two weeks or more) carefully separate the pot from the

form. Your pot is still somewhat fragile and could chip so handle it gently. Remove the dowel(s) and smooth the drainage hole(s). Smooth the rim and roughen the outside of the pot using a wire brush or similar abrasive object. The material is still easily scored at this time.

Leave the pot outside to cure naturally for several weeks. This is to neutralize the alkalinity of the concrete. As a final step to ensure neutral pH, prepare a vinegar/water solution using ¼-cup of vinegar to a gallon of water and immerse the entire pot if possible.

Now you are ready to plant! Keep in mind these pots are very porous. So, if using plants other than rock garden plants (succulents, grasses, etc.), be mindful of their watering needs.

The greatest reward is in seeing the results of the end game: a weed-free bed or yard—even if for only a fleeting moment!

11

Weed Control
and **Prevention**

A Plant out of Place

Weeds have often been defined as simply a plant out of place. More optimistically, I view it as a plant whose virtues have yet to be discovered. Be that as it may, I still discourage their existence in many of my personal situations.

Weeding is a task most people loathe, and is one of the biggest reasons many choose to avoid the hobby of gardening altogether or opt for the condo life! Personally, I enjoy all aspects of gardening, and this even includes the act of weeding. It's the joy in seeing them come out of the soil one by one. It is especially gratifying to conquer the big guys, knowing that I have managed to get even their smallest roots. The greatest reward is in seeing the results of the game: a weed-free bed or yard—even if only for a fleeting moment.

A yard full of weeds can be discouraging for even the most seasoned gardener. I have found that by taking one section at a time, the job is far more manageable and rewarding. Definitely less intimidating!

There are a number of ways to deal with the fact that weeds will always be with us. Whenever time permits (which is not too often), I enjoy the mechanical process of hand pulling. I have some favorite tools that make the task much easier. More on those later. Other times, the weeds are far too great for even a full day of effort. In this case, there are effective chemical controls.

Just like many ornamental plants, weeds are either annual or perennial.

Knowing which you have will help you understand how to control them. Preventing the weeds from going to seed has a great impact on how big a problem you will have in the future.

Even when you proactively manage your landscape and garden successfully, weed seeds will find their way into your yard from other means. Staying on top of the problem by eliminating them before they have a chance to disburse makes your future weeding problems more manageable.

How Will You Know It's a Weed?

I am often asked, "How does one tell good plants from weeds?" My standard humorous *first* answer is "Just tug gently on it. If it comes out easily then it must have been a plant!"

 Know friend from foe.

In reality the first step in dealing with weeds is to know friend from foe. It almost seems obvious, but there are many desirable plants in our landscape that produce seeds and subsequent seedlings. In many cases, we'll want to encourage these seeds to grow into larger plants. This is especially true if you have beds of perennials or naturalized areas of desirable plants in your landscape.

QUICK FACT

Preventing weeds from going to seed will have a great impact on how big a problem you will have in the future.

WHY: Before a weed develops seeds, it has a flower. If you see weeds in flower, eliminate them immediately. One weed can produce thousands of seeds, and many plants have an amazing ability to disburse them. This is one reason they are so prolific and difficult to eliminate completely.

Although this tomato plant is clearly "a plant out of place" I could never bring myself to call it a weed. Rather, I'd nurture it the same way this homeowner did and be rewarded in the end for allowing it to grow right where it started—in the driveway.

Annual and Perennial Weeds

• *Annual weeds:* Weeds that emerge each year only from seed are referred to as "annual weeds." Although they die after just one season, the stage has been set for their return the following year if the flower from the plant has been able to produce and disburse seeds.

A neglected lawn or garden is the primary way annual weeds are allowed to proliferate in subsequent seasons. On the other hand, a proactively managed yard is one where the weeds are kept in check, or at a minimum, the weeds are prevented from going to flower, either by

Don't be too hasty. These are *helleborus* offspring and you may want to encourage them to grow.

grow from mid-spring, to mid fall. There is certainly the opportunity for an overlap of warm- and cool-season plants depending on the variability of the temperatures.

Warm-season weed seeds germinate when soil temperatures reach a certain temperature for a consecutive number of days. The specific details depend on the type of weed. *Cool-season* annual weeds, on the other hand, germinate when soil temperatures drop to a certain level for several days at a time. Again, the specific soil temperature depends on what each weed variety needs to germinate.

mowing them before they get to this stage or by using other means.

Depending on the variety, annual weeds are considered either cool- or warm-season plants. *Cool*-season weeds grow late-fall through early-spring and *warm*-season weeds

• *Perennial weeds:* Just as annual weeds have a preferred growing season, so do perennial weeds. There are warm- and cool-season types. However, unlike annuals, perennial weeds can live from year to year, even though they usually die back to the ground before emerging the following season. And like annual weeds, perennial weeds can spread by seed.

In addition to weeds being classified as annual or perennial, weeds

Dandelion seeds are designed to make effective use of wind (and sometimes the breath of children!) as a disbursement method.

Beware of hitchhiking seeds that can find their way into areas of your garden that you'll wish they hadn't!

Weed Spreading and Controls

To know the many ways weeds can spread is to understand how they become so prolific and have persisted for thousands of years. In fact, it is almost comical to see how some seeds are set to disburse at the first sign of disturbance, like just as you reach down to pull them. It's as if some are actually booby-trapped—set to "explode" their seeds at the slightest touch!

Seven Primary Ways Weed Seeds Can Spread:

1. Gravity

2. Wind (dandelion, milkweed)

3. Hitchhiking on people and animals (seeds can attach themselves and be released elsewhere)

4. Animal waste (from the weeds, seeds and berries animals consume)

5. Explosive (Hairy bittercress)

6. Rhizomes (underground roots that sprout new plants)

7. Stolons (surface runners that spread new growth)

Weeds come in many forms from broadleaf to narrow-bladed and can occupy the same small space.

are also classified as either "broadleaf" or "grass-like." These terms are applied to both annual and perennial varieties.

- *Broadleaf weeds:* Aptly named because unlike grass, these weeds have broad or wider leaves. Their shape is not blade-like. Some broadleaf weeds are wide and obvious, like clover, thistle, and dandelions. Other weeds in this category are very small and narrow (but not blade-like).

- *Narrow bladed or grass-like weeds:* Appropriately named, their shape more closely resembles grass, such as poa annua (annual bluegrass), yellow nutsedge, or wild onion.

Exciting alternatives exist that are more environmentally friendly such as this corn gluten product for pre-emergent weed control.

whether it is a weed or a highly prized perennial or shrub. It is extremely effective for those times when you want to eradicate an entire area of all plant material. There is another category of herbicide called *"pre-emergent"* that controls weeds before they develop.

 Know what you're killing.

Should You Just Pull Them?

As I mentioned earlier in this chapter, there are two primary ways to deal with weeds once you have them. You may choose to either physically pull them, or use chemical controls. Of course, hand pulling or mechanical control is the safest way to make sure that non-targeted plants are not harmed in the weed removal process. It is also the most environmentally friendly way to manage the problem.

Should You Use Chemicals?

The second way to deal with weed control is by using chemicals. Although removing weeds manually is the same whether it is a broadleaf or narrow-bladed weed, eradicating these weeds chemically may require separate products unless your desire is to eliminate an entire area of vegetation.

Chemicals developed for weed removal by the homeowner are considered either "selective" or "non-selective." Probably the best known non-selective active ingredient is glyphosate which is found in many brands. The term "non-selective" applies to the fact that the chemical is designed to kill whatever plant it comes in contact with

Exercise great caution when using a non-selective control. Whatever vegetation the chemical lands on will likely be killed.

Sometimes you will only want to deal with the weeds within a certain area. You should use "selective" herbicides designed to target specific plants, such as broadleaf weeds. When used properly, these products can be highly effective at removing many undesirable weeds without harming the grass. The general category to describe this type of herbicide that kills weeds *after* they emerge is called a

QUICK FACT

I suggest using corn gluten as a good organic pre-emergent alternative against weeds.

WHY: Corn gluten has the added benefit of providing nitrogen to plant roots. Nitrogen is an important nutrient in helping lawns and garden beds look healthy and green.

"post-emergent," because the weeds have already emerged or germinated.

Cautionary Tips:

• Always read the label on selective and non-selective products. You need to know that they will be safe to use on your lawn or within the area where you are trying to control weeds.

• Never spray herbicide chemicals on a windy day. The drift can travel farther than you might think to non-targeted plants and harm or kill them as well.

• When spraying any weed killer on your lawn, keep the water pressure low if applying the chemical through a hose end sprayer. The high pressure alone can create drift that can travel a good distance away.

Pre-emergent Herbicides

If dealing with weeds chemically, you can attempt to control them before they emerge with products referred to as *"pre-emergents."* These chemicals are designed to create a barrier that prevents weed seeds from developing as they germinate. Pre-emergents have no effect on *existing* weeds.

In order to achieve maximum effectiveness, you must apply pre-emergent chemicals at the appropriate time. That is, before soil temperatures reach the ideal range for weeds to sprout.

Organic and Synthetic Options:

Exciting alternatives that are more environmentally safe exist with

Read the label carefully. It will help you select the right product, and give you important information and specific directions.

From Joe

While working on the set of *Fresh from the Garden*, I became aware of a nasty little patch of crabgrass that was becoming quite an eyesore as I entered and left the garden. I wanted to try out a type of organic post- emergent weed control composed of blended plant oils.

Fortunately I recorded the before and after to document my experience. I applied the spray to the weeds right before breaking for lunch. By the time I returned, the crabgrass had already shown visible signs of desiccation. I monitored its effect over the next several days only to find that the crab-grass was making a recovery. A subsequent application of the spray was all that was needed to eliminate this patch for good.

My observation was that some types of weeds were killed using one application while others, such as the crab grass, needed an additional spray or two for effective control.

pre-emergent herbicides. Corn gluten is an effective organic alternative solution. It is derived from a by-product of corn. It has been found to safely and effectively prevent the development of most weeds when used properly and over several consecutive years.

These photos show the effects of an organic post-emergent herbicide after three hours.

Complete control is not achieved with only one application, but studies have shown that repeated use of this product over several years can control most if not all seasonally emerging weeds and can be as effective as synthetic counterparts.

Synthetic pre-emergent products are readily available and very effective. However in all cases when applying chemicals, use caution and follow package label instructions closely.

Post-Emergent Herbicides

For chemical control of weeds which are already present, use products referred to as "post-emergents." These have no effect on preventing weeds from germinating, but they can be very effective in eliminating weeds already present. Post-emergents, as explained earlier, can be selective or non-selective. A *selective* herbicide is what you want to look for to target specific weeds while not killing your lawn or other plants. Unfortunately, selective herbicide products have yet to be developed that can target *all*

broadleaf and grass-like weeds without harming *any* variety of lawn grass. Therefore, most of the consumer herbicide products on the store shelf today were developed for use in eliminating either broadleaf weeds (the most common type of post-emergent weed control) or narrow-leaf weeds.

QUICK FACT

Encouraging a healthy stand of turf is the best non-chemical way of discouraging weed formation in lawns.

WHY:

A thick lawn will provide the shade necessary to discourage many weeds from developing. The effect is the same as a layer of mulch which shades out the weeds. Even if weeds do germinate hopefully the grass is healthy enough to out-compete them for light and nutrients.

Mulch can be an effective and attractive non-chemical weed control.

However, you can now find readily available herbicides that are designed to kill both weed types in an all-in-one type product.

Product labels give you specific directions and important information including what weeds the product is designed to control. They say when to apply, how much to apply, when *not* to use, and give other appropriate warnings. This is always important but especially with products such as the all-in-one type. It's effective at working double duty but it's *not* for every type of lawn and *it says so right on the label.* I learned a lesson like this the hard way. If you missed it, be sure to read my story on this very subject in chapter 7.

Organic Alternatives:

Just as corn gluten is an organic pre-emergent herbicide there are organic alternatives for post-emergent weed control as well. Options include vinegar at a 20 percent concentration, and a variety of products composed of blended plant oils that contain clove, thyme, or citric acid.

Mulch as a Non-Chemical Option

One of the most effective and environmentally friendly weed control techniques available is a natural barrier. A layer of mulch 3 to 4 inches thick is a very effective means of preventing most weeds from germinating.

There are many mulch options from which to choose. I've used just about every type of mulch barrier available, including traditional bark and straw mulch, plastic sheeting, and wet newspapers with additional mulch on top of that. It doesn't matter as much what you choose to use, but rather that you simply use it.

In other cases, mulch is not practical for suppressing the germination of weed seeds. For example, a lawn is not a candidate for a layer of mulch. In this case, encouraging a healthy stand of turf grass is the best non-chemical way of discouraging weed formation.

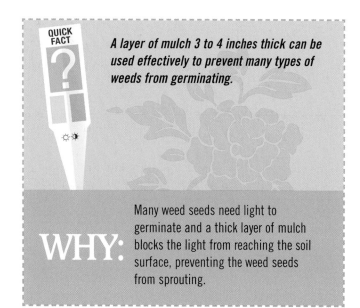

QUICK FACT

A layer of mulch 3 to 4 inches thick can be used effectively to prevent many types of weeds from germinating.

WHY: Many weed seeds need light to germinate and a thick layer of mulch blocks the light from reaching the soil surface, preventing the weed seeds from sprouting.

(1) One of the most effective tools for slicing through and eliminating shallow-rooted weeds is this loop-hoe combination tool. (2) Tools designed to remove tap-rooted weeds are made to plunge deeply into the soil. (3) Tools such as this are effective at removing deep tap-rooted weeds from a standing position.

Tools of the Weed-Fighting Trade

The roots of weeds either grow along or near the surface of the soil and are known as shallow-rooted weeds, or they can develop deep tap roots. One of the most famous tap-rooted weeds may be the dandelion. Leave even a small piece of its root in the soil and soon you'll see a new dandelion growing in its place.

Fortunately there are very effective tools to deal with any type of weed in your garden. Some of the most popular are listed below:

• *D or loop-hoe:* This is one of the most effective tools for slicing through and eliminating shallow-rooted weeds. The back and forth motion allowed by this tool efficiently cuts the roots in a pushing and pulling motion. There are many models on the market from small hand-held versions to long-handled varieties that make this type of weeding or cultivating easy from a standing position.

• *Weeding by hand:* No manmade tools are necessary here, and this is possibly the most personally satisfying way to eliminate weeds from a manageable area of your garden. *Weed right after a good rain.* Even the deepest weeds pull out easily.

• *Tap root extraction tools:* Tap rooted weeds are the hardest to remove without the proper tools. When removing them, be sure to get all of the root. Tools designed for this job are made to plunge or penetrate deeply into the soil, below the tap root. You then pry or pull the tool out of the ground along with the entire root and weed (hopefully!).

Wait! Take another look! This is NOT a bad bug. Before you reach for the pesticide spray, you might be surprised to know that only 3 percent of the bugs in your garden are considered pests. The other 97 percent are either beneficial insects or they do no harm at all.

12

Controlling
Pests

Good Bug, Bad Bug

You might be surprised to know that, of all the bugs and insects in your yard or garden, only about 3 percent are considered pests. The other 97 percent are either beneficial or they do no harm. They are considered beneficial because they prey on insect pests and many play an important role in our environment as pollinators.

The Importance of Pollinators

Thanks to the wonderful work of pollinators like bees or butterflies, beetles, wasps, and even flies for that matter, many of the products we consume and flowers and plants we enjoy are possible. But despite the importance of pollinators, they are taken for granted all too often.

Unfortunately there is an alarming decline in pollinator populations worldwide. Excessive use of pesticides, and an ever-expanding conversion of landscapes for human use are the biggest culprits.

Think about it. It is estimated that over 1,000 types of plants are grown around the world for food, beverages, medicines, condiments, spices, and even fabric. Of these, a large number are pollinated mostly by insects. Indirectly, pollinators ultimately play a role in the majority of what foods we eat and products we consume. I can't imagine living in a world without coffee or chocolate!

Pollinators are vital to creating and maintaining the ecosystems that many animals rely on for food and shelter. They facilitate the reproduc-

From Joe

One time when we were taping a show on organic gardening for *Fresh from the Garden,* we incorporated a segment on using beneficial insects to control pests. We invited an entomologist from The University of Georgia to be our guest on the show.

Prior to her arrival, we ordered 100 lady beetles and a praying mantis egg sack. The sack contained hundreds of future baby praying mantis which would grow up and hopefully patrol our garden along with the already mature beetles. Our plan was to introduce these insects into the garden as a way to demonstrate the use of beneficial insects as an organic pest control method.

Our guest reminded us that if we introduced both beneficial species, we would likely see a rapid decline in our lady beetle population, once the praying mantises hatched and matured. That is because the mantises are non-selective predators. Although they are very effective at eating many garden pests, they are also proficient at munching on just about anything that moves, including lady beetles and other beneficials.

We opted to forego the use of the mantis egg sack and rely on the work of the lady beetles instead. Regarding the fate of that unused egg sack, I've often wondered what ever happened to it. I accidentally left it in the home of the person's house we were using to tape the show. I doubt she ever found it until after those babies hatched. By then we were long gone. I would have liked to have seen what happened!

Use pesticides only when necessary and then only late in the day or evening.

WHY: At that time most pollinators have retired for the day. Pesticide use in the evening will minimize the chance of pollinators coming in contact with it, especially those pesticides that kill on contact.

tion of a vast majority of the world's flowering plants. At a local level, you can positively influence their existence in your own environment. Provide a diverse assortment of flowering plants to encourage native pollinators in your landscape. *Use pesticides only when necessary and then only late in the day or evening.*

Look for alternative ways to deal with pest and disease issues before reaching for the quick fix that often comes at a price. Learn about and practice IPM (Integrated Pest Management). The actions you take in and around your garden can either reduce or promote the population of pollinators in your landscape. Hopefully it's the latter.

The good guys

Just as pests are attracted to their favorite plants, beneficial insects are attracted to their favorites, too. If you want more beneficial insects to reside in your garden, discover what they like, and plant accordingly. In addition, they have preferred nesting sites. The more you can learn about what attracts them to your garden, the more good bugs you'll have and the fewer bad bugs.

Integrated Pest Management (IPM)

Integrated Pest Management (IPM) is a method we can

If you want to attract more beneficial insects to your garden, discover what plants they like.

Typically viewed as a beneficial insect, it is unfortunate to note that the praying mantis is a non-selective predator.

been crossed. In many ways, IPM appears similar to organic gardening. The biggest difference is that with IPM, synthetic pesticides *are* an acceptable method of treatment in the final steps or as a last resort. In fact, the use of all tactics—biological, cultural, and mechanical—are employed *prior to using pesticides.*

The first step in IPM is to ***properly identify the pest.*** Second, ***understand its life cycle*** and behavioral patterns so the most environmentally friendly treatment method may be applied first. Third, ***monitor activity.*** Is the pest population isolated to a small area or a certain crop, or is it taking over? Is the damage getting worse? Is the damage within an acceptable tolerance level? Are there any beneficial insect populations? If so, the problem will likely correct itself.

The ***fourth*** step in IPM is to determine your acceptable threshold level; how much damage are you willing to

use to do our part for protecting beneficial insects. It approaches pest control using a combination of treatments. The idea is to start with the least toxic steps first. By identifying a pest and understanding its life cycle and habits, we can effectively use non-chemical, preventive strategies in the initial stages.

When IPM practices are employed, the positive results are many:

- healthier plants

- less application of chemicals

- less runoff

- higher survival rates for beneficial insects and pollinators

- better long-term control of pest populations.

With the IPM method, a certain amount of pest damage is acceptable, and it is up to the individual gardener to determine when controls are needed. As a result, a more extreme approach to treatment does not take place until a threshold of tolerance has

SOME BENEFICIAL INSECTS	WHAT THEY CONTROL
Ladybug	Aphids, other soft-bodied bugs
Lacewing larvae	Aphids, thrips, scales, moth eggs, small caterpillars, mites
Hover Flies	Aphids
Ground beetles	Slugs, snails cutworms, root maggots
Parasitic Wasps	Eggs of garden pests
Spiders	Many kinds of insects
Tachinid Flies	Cutworms, armyworms, tent caterpillars, cabbage loopers, gypsy moths, sawflies, Japanese beetles, squash bugs and sowbugs
Other Predatory Bugs (Pirate bugs, ambush bugs, and assassin bugs)	Tomato hornworms, thrips, spider mites, many insect's eggs, leafhopper nymphs, corn earworms and other small caterpillars

IPM is a method of pest control that uses the least toxic steps first before resorting to chemical control.

accept before control measures are required—which is the *fifth* step.

Controlling Pest Problems Using IPM Methods

• *Cultural:* Look for plant varieties that are pest- and disease-resistant and do well in your area. This helps to create an inhospitable environment for pests. Healthy plants are better able to resist pests when they are growing vigorously. The best candidate is one that is growing in the proper environment. Conversely, plants that are struggling due to poor placement are much more susceptible to pest attacks.

Don't give pests a reason to stick around. For instance, in the vegetable garden, crop rotation is a good method. By relocating their favorite food source family from one season to the next, pests are starved out, or they simply move on. For instance do not plant tomatoes, potatoes, eggplant, or peppers, all of which are in the same family, in the same location in consecutive seasons.

• *Physical:* This includes creating barriers to prevent pests from getting to your plants. Row covers are a good example. Another would be the use of collars around the stems of tender seedlings to protect them from cutworms.

• *Sanitation:* Keeping your garden free of debris and infested plant material will help keep plant diseases and insect pests at bay. Disease-free plants are tougher and better able to resist and withstand damage, which could be inflicted by certain pests. You can even monitor pest activities in your garden using trapping techniques like glue coated yellow cards.

• *Biological:* Insects such as lady beetles, lacewings, and praying mantis often come to mind as natural predators in the garden. Other less often considered or less familiar controls for the home gardener include predatory parasites such as some mites, beetles, and the eggs of certain wasps, as well as subterranean dwellers like beneficial nematodes.

• *Chemical:* These control options are usually regarded as *the last line of defense* in dealing with pests in an IPM envi-

The fourth step in IPM is to determine the level of damage you are willing to accept.

You can monitor pest activities in your garden using trapping techniques like this yellow sticky card.

ronment because they can harm beneficial insects as well. Chemicals at this phase can include conventional synthetic pesticides, which act as direct toxins, inorganic pesticides (such as lime sulfur), botanicals (such as pyrethrin, rotenone, and neem oil), biological controls (such as *Bacillus thuringiensis*), down to less toxic horticultural oils and insecticidal soaps.

The final step is to evaluate your results. IPM is not an instant fix, but it is an effective one. Results will improve over time as you learn appropriate control techniques for your garden. The outcome will be a healthier garden, with less time and money spent dealing with pests.

Insect Life Cycles

Insects go through various stages during their short existence on earth. Depending on what insect you are trying to control, it will be more vulnerable to certain control methods at specific points in its life cycle. For instance, during the early stages of life, a pest may have a soft body, which is unprotected from the dehydrating effects of insecticidal soaps. However, as it matures, a hard, protective outer shell may develop which is effective at repelling the very same control method that would have killed it just a few weeks earlier.

Investigating the life cycle of a pest gives you the opportunity to more effectively control populations by first using the least toxic methods. When the appropriate stage is missed, effective population control methods require a more *non-selective* approach and one that is much more likely to cause harm to beneficial insects as well.

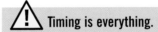
⚠ **Timing is everything.**

This is a great example of the early and later life stages of bean beetles. Control is much easier before the hard outer shell has formed.

Spray too early in the day and you risk the lives of beneficial pollinators such as this beautiful monarch butterfly.

If you resort to spraying non-selective insecticides, do so only after the beneficial insects and pollinators have retired for the day. It is best to spray as late as possible, preferably in the evening. Otherwise, you risk killing beneficial insects hard at work. They are active all throughout the day but especially in the early to mid-morning when many flowers are just opening up.

Methods of Control

As explained in the section on IPM, there are a number of measures that can be taken to prevent many pests from entering your garden. However, when the time comes to deal with a problem, several methods are available.

- *Barriers:* Of the methods listed here, physical barriers are a great strategy for excluding pests. Barriers are completely effective and harmless to beneficials, pets, people, and the environment. For instance they are an effective way to prevent moths from laying eggs on your plants that will hatch into foliage destroying caterpillars. The key when using barriers is to have them in place *before* a problem is apparent.

Row covers are a classic example of a physical barrier designed to manage pests. The typical fabric is made of very lightweight spunbound polyester that allows air, light, and water through but keeps pests out.

- *Biological controls:* This method of pest control is

From a small netted dome to entire row covers, barriers are a safe way of effectively excluding pests.

You may have to look twice, not only to see this tomato horn worm but also to recognize that this is a pepper plant.

when plant tissue is ingested.

Plants take up the systemic insecticide primarily through their roots and absorb it through the tissue. When the pest insect eats the plant tissue, it ingests the active ingredient contained within.

However, be aware that because beneficial pollinators, such as butterflies, start out as foliage-eating larvae, some systemic insecticides will kill them as well. This insecticide is not transferred to the plant's flower pollen, so adult pollinating insects such as butterflies and bees are not affected.

preferred by many, especially organic gardeners. Biological controls use naturally occurring bacteria, for example, which have been determined to be toxic to some specific pests. When applied to plants and ingested by the targeted pest, it is very effective.

A common example is Bt (*Bacillus thuringiensis*) that can be purchased as a powder or liquid and can be dusted or sprayed on plants. Bt targets many tissue eating caterpillars such as the cabbage worm or the tomato hornworm. Once ingested, the bacterium disrupts the feeding cycle of the larvae and it dies within a couple of days. However, Bt is target specific so *certain versions of it may be needed*, based on the larvae to be controlled.

Biological controls are not available for all pests. If you have a specific pest you would like to manage biologically, your county extension service is a good source of information.

• *Systemic:* Although *non-selective*, systemic insecticides are effective at targeting chewing pests rather than beneficials. The active ingredients are contained within the plant tissue, not on its surface. The insecticide becomes lethal

Systemic insecticides are used to control chewing and sucking insects such as caterpillars and these aphids.

Non-selective insecticides come as powders or dusts, soil drenches, and sprays. It is largely up to the individual which delivery method is best.

As I mentioned before, pests have specific plant preferences. Selectively treating only certain plants rather than the entire garden will go a long way to protecting our beneficial insects. Non-selective insecticides come in a variety of application methods.

• **Soil drench:** Drenches are used largely to manage harmful pests in the soil, such as certain varieties of nematodes. But since drenches are also taken up by the roots, they can be used as an insecticide against pests that chew on plant tissue. Systemic insecticides as mentioned earlier are an example.

• **Powder:** Some insecticides can be disbursed as a dry powder. They are useful as a way to see what surface area of the plants are covered and are able to provide excellent coverage due to the fine, light powder of most products. It adheres well if the foliage is made damp before applying.

The disadvantage of using powder is that because it is so light and fine, it will drift very easily with the wind. Since the powder is prone to washing off with rain or irrigation, reapplication will likely be necessary for effective control.

• **Spray:** Most insecticides are designed for you to mix with water or are available as a **ready to use** spray. In either case, applying these to the plants in liquid form is the most common method. Most sprays (if not systemic) are made to control insects on contact and break down quickly in exposed conditions.

Others will have a residual effect beyond the initial application, potentially lasting many days. Each product and

active ingredient is different, so it is essential to review the product label and instructions for safe and effective application. These premixed solutions are convenient but more expensive on a price-per-ounce basis.

 Be careful with pesticides.

Be sure to wear a mask when using insecticidal dusts. Breathing or ingesting this powder can be harmful. Because they have such light properties apply them only on a non-windy day.

Whenever mixing chemicals, never mix more than you'll need for that specific application. Chemicals should always be stored in their original container and clearly marked. Never store pesticides or harmful chemicals in generic containers such as a milk jug, coffee cup, or soda bottle. Sadly, many fatalities of adults and children have been the result of an improperly stored chemical product.

Organic Control Methods

The most proactive step you can take in controlling pests in *every* situation should be to create the most hospitable

Biodiversity utilizes a variety of plant material which allows natural checks and balances to control many pest problems for you.

growing environment for your plants.

Maintaining a healthy garden is the single best pest control treatment there is, organic or otherwise. Strive to create biodiversity with your plant selections. The variety of plants and resulting natural checks and balances allow beneficial insects to do most of your pest control for you.

Although beneficial insects are incredibly effective at helping manage pest problems, you'll likely need to have some level of tolerance for a certain amount of pest damage. Organic methods typically are not as fast acting, and yet, over time can be every bit as effective as synthetic controls.

With any pest control treatment, you must first identify the offending pest and target a control method that affects only that pest whenever possible. There are a number of organic options available, and some are more specific to certain pests. Many organic pest control products are extracted from natural plant material which break down quickly in the environment with little to no residual damage. There are some very effective natural pest control treatments available. Here are some of the more popular options:

- *Insecticidal oil:* Insecticidal oils work by suffocation. The oil coats the insects with a horticultural grade, ultra-fine, petroleum-based liquid. The fine coating cuts off their oxygen supply. This method of control has been around for a long time. It is primarily successful in killing the eggs and immature stages of insects. These products are very effective because they provide good coverage but break down quickly. However, these oils can and do affect beneficial insects if direct contact is made.

Oils are often used to control aphids, adelgids, scales, spider mites, mealy bugs, psylla, and other insects. These oils are capable of harming the foliage of your plants and trees, so be sure to read the directions that come with the packaging.

⚠️ Start with a small area.

Avoid spraying these oils on a hot day, typically if the temperature is over 85 degrees F. It's best to test a small area of your plants first, as the oil may burn the foliage.

After a few days, look for any damage from the oil before commencing with a larger application. If no damage is apparent, then continue spraying, coating the top and bottom of all leaf surfaces.

- *Diatomaceous earth (DE):* Diatomaceous earth is the fossilized silica shells of algae. Although these shells are microscopic, they're covered with sharp projections that cut and penetrate the cuticle of an insect. This causes the pest to leak vital body fluids. The result is dehydration and death. The unique aspect of diatomaceous earth is that it is not a poison that causes the damage, but rather the physical abrasiveness of the dust.

DE is effective against soft-bodied pests including aphids, trips, whiteflies, caterpillars, root maggots, slugs, and snails. However, DE is non-selective and will potentially kill beneficial insects as well.

Apply DE to the soil for ground dwelling pests, and to the foliage for other pests. DE adheres best to moist foliage, so application is best early in the morning, when leaves are wet from dew, or after a rain. Be sure to use "natural-grade" vs. "pool-grade" DE which contains additional chemicals, that can be harmful to humans and animals if

What I like best about DE is that is not a poison. Sharp projections cut into soft-bodied pests causing dehydration.

inhaled. *Wear a dust mask whenever working with any dusting agent.*

• *Insecticidal soaps:* Insecticidal soaps utilize salts and fatty acids to target many soft-bodied pests including aphids, whiteflies, mealy bugs, earwigs, thrips, and scales. They penetrate the soft outer area of these and other pests, causing damage to the cell membranes which begin to breakdown, resulting ultimately in dehydration and starvation.

These soaps can be phytotoxic (poisonous) to certain plants, so be sure to test a small area before applying on a larger scale. The other downside is that soaps can be toxic to beneficial insects, so use them sparingly, as with any pesticide. Insecticidal soaps have not shown to be toxic to humans and other animals.

• *Neem oil:* Neem is a broad-spectrum insecticide, acting as a poison, repellent, and feeding deterrent. In addition, it also sterilizes certain insect species, and it slows or stops the growth cycle of others. Neem comes from many parts of the neem tree, which is native to India. It is applied as a foliar spray or soil drench and is used to kill a wide range of pests, including aphids, thrips, loopers, whiteflies, and mealy bugs.

One unique aspect of this biological agent is its systemic properties. Plants take up the neem extracts through foliage and roots, where it remains present in the tissue. As a result, neem is also effective against leaf miners, which are usually not affected by other non-systemic foliar sprays.

Generally, neem must be ingested to be toxic. Although it breaks down quickly, it should be sprayed only when necessary, and only on plants known to be affected by the pests you want to control.

• *Pyrethrin:* Some products include pyrethrin, which is a *contact* insecticide (meaning it must be sprayed directly on the insect) that attacks the nervous system. The active ingredient is extracted from Pyrethrum daisies. They are considered broad-spectrum and are used to control many types of insects. One of the benefits to pyrethrin is that it breaks down quickly. Note that there is a synthetic version called *pyrethroid* which is even more toxic to insects and persists longer in the environment.

Exercise caution when using pyrethrin products as they are moderately toxic to mammals and highly toxic to fish. Don't apply them around ponds and waterways. Remember this is a non-selective insecticide.

• *Rotenone:* This broad spectrum insecticide occurs naturally in over sixty-five species of plants. Although once a popular organic pesticide, it is no longer recommended in organic gardens for a number of reasons. Because it is

A slimy mucous trail is a clear indication slugs have been quietly munching away at your tender young plants.

I have a friend from India who uses only neem oil and drip irrigation to keep her roses in peak condition.

non-selective, beneficials are killed on contact as well. In addition, rotenone is very toxic to fish, birds, and swine, and moderately toxic to most animals and people.

Snails and Slugs

You don't often see them, but you know they're out there: slugs and snails. From the last frost of spring to the colder days of autumn, they're quietly munching away at many of your favorite plants. For the most part, they are the same creatures. Snails are differentiated by their outer shell. However, both are equally destructive.

Damage caused by these creatures is evidenced by irregular holes with smooth edges in leaves and flowers. Their food of choice tends to be the young, tender tissue of seedlings and herbaceous plants. Although other pests enjoy the same food, a shiny mucous trail will confirm snails or slugs likely caused the damage. Their slimy bodies would quickly dry out in the heat and light of a clear day so snails and slugs hide in shady areas, underneath boards,

Share my quality beer with snails and slugs? I don't *think* so...perhaps my level of tolerance for their damage just increased!

flowerpots and rocks doing their damage under the cover of darkness or on cloudy days.

Snail and Slug Control

There are non-chemical techniques that, although popular, are only marginally effective.

• *Hand picking*: It's a highly effective first line of defense (at least for the ones you are able to find).

• *Inverted melon rinds:* Placing a few slices under the cover of shade may produce a bounty.

• *Beer:* Bury a bowl of beer into the soil so the lip is at ground level. The little lushes are attracted to the beer, crawl into the bowl and drown.

• *Copper strips:* Place copper strips around your plant(s) as a perimeter protection. There is an unpleasant reaction when the mucous layer of the slug or snail encounters the copper.

Controlling snails and slugs is easy with chemical methods. The most widely available slug and snail chemical solution is Metaldehyde. Although effective, it also is attractive and ***highly toxic*** especially to dogs and cats and other wildlife.

 Be careful with Metaldehyde.

Products formulated with Metaldehyde as the active ingredient should not be used anywhere near the presence of children or animals.

Thankfully, there is an alternate product that is effective against snails and slugs, yet safe for use around children and animals. The active ingredient is ***iron phosphate***. Excess granules break down in the soil without any negative consequences.

Mammal Pests

I could write an entire book on dealing with non-insect pests. Any time the word "pest" is mentioned, most of us think of insects. And rightfully so. But keep in mind not all pests have six legs and three body parts. For many of you, those kinds of pests are the least of your worries. Small critters can be quite destructive.

• *Voles:* Take for example the tiny vole. It looks rather harmless, similar to a small mouse with a short stubby tail. But to a gardener or any person who values their plants, voles are major pests!

Voles have a voracious appetite and will munch on roots, shoots, and vegetation under the cover of mulch or darkness. In short order, they can destroy your prized hosta, a favorite azalea, or any number of other woody ornamental plants or trees by severing it from its roots, or consuming the entire root system.

Effective control can be difficult. I am not one to suggest non-selective poisons, questionable repellants or gimmicky gadgets as a way to control these or any other animals. We too often fail to consider the consequence to non-targeted animals including ground feeding birds. Save your money, and get a cat instead! They're the best vole hunters. I should know. My cat Booty feels compelled to let me know she's been hard at work. She even delivers them to my feet!

If getting a cat is not in your pest control plan, then consider the first line of defense in controlling voles to be habitat modification. By exposing voles to predators and eliminating their nesting sites, they are less likely to take up residence around your plants.

Pull mulch away from the base of your plant by several inches at least. Eliminating their protective cover will send them looking elsewhere for their next meal and make them susceptible to predators such as owls, hawks, snakes, and other mammals.

Voles are vegetarians, doing most of their damage to plant roots like this nandina.

- • *Moles:* Another subterranean creature is the dreaded mole. They are rarely seen but are a common pest throughout North America. These little guys look similar to a mouse but they have very large and powerful forelimbs. They use these limbs to "swim" through the soil, tunneling up to 18 feet per hour!

The constant tunneling near the surface in search of their next meal leaves plenty of raised mounds above ground. The tunneling can displace roots from the soil, causing grass to dry out and die. Unlike the vole, they do not eat vegetation but rely on a carnivo-

Large forelimbs allow moles to "swim" through the earth in search of earthworms, grubs, and insects.

Garden destruction comes in some cute and cuddly packaging.

rous pallete of earthworms, grubs, and insects for survival.

Control methods range from lethal trapping, which is effective but cumbersome, to baits and repellents which are only marginally effective. One repellent which gets mixed reviews that skew towards the positive is castor oil. You can buy it premixed or make your own. Recipes vary, but the basics are to mix about three ounces to a gallon of water. Spray it on your lawn, and let the rain or sprinkler wash it into the soil.

Personally, I don't do anything other than stamp the raised areas back down with my foot to reestablish root contact with the soil. Eventually the moles disappear, the grass recovers, and all is well. It's easy, safe, and cheap. I like that.

- *Rabbits:* As cute as they are, rabbits can be quite destructive in the garden. Sadly for them they have many predators and are easy targets. Most rabbits don't live to see their first birthday, and only the really lucky ones survive three years in the wild.

Habitat modification is an appropriate first line of defense. Rabbits depend on the safety and security provided by shrubs, tall grasses, and other objects. Removing these and keeping grass cut low around as much of your property as possible may be all that is necessary. Rabbits will oftentimes seek to live and feed elsewhere.

When habitat modification is not an option, physical barriers in certain areas may be best.

Squirrels are so tenacious and crafty that a complete physical barrier may be the only answer.

⚠ Do the right thing.

If you are considering trapping any animal and releasing it somewhere else, check with your local authorities. Some municipalities have laws that make it illegal to do so. Also consider that rabbits are prolific breeders. Trapping and relocation always runs the risk that you are taking the mother away from a nest of dependant babies. Please consider timing as you think about control options.

My preferred and most effective measure for dealing with pests of all shapes and sizes is to create a physical barrier. An effective barrier for rabbits is a fence about 24 to 36 inches tall, secured around the perimeter of the area you are trying to protect. You can use wire of any sort but be sure the openings are small enough that they can't climb through. Whatever wire you select, bury it at least 6 inches below ground. Rabbits are very good at digging.

There are many repellents on the market designed to dissuade rabbits (and other animals for that matter) from munching on your plants. Usually the repellents are very hot and spicy, or they have a strong odor like moth balls.

You may also try to use live traps in your garden. These humane traps can be purchased at hardware and home improvement stores. Bait them with corn cobs, apples, or even other rabbit droppings. Rabbits spend their entire lives within just a few acres. If you are successful at trapping them, they should be relocated to a protected area. Rabbits depend on dense cover for protection, such as blackberry thickets, tall grasses, and piled up limbs or sticks.

- *Squirrels:* Squirrels may be the toughest critters to keep out of your garden. In fact, short of a total physical barrier, it's nearly impossible! Some gardeners build cages around and *over* their prized plants and edibles as a way to ensure they grow undisturbed. Other gardeners place nylon bird netting over fruit trees and shrubs.

Although live trapping is effective for catching squirrels, I'm not a fan of this method. Relocation is possible if local laws allow for this. Squirrels should be relocated at least three miles from where they were trapped. It even helps if a physical barrier such as a river stands between your property and the release area. *Be aware that relocation is not always the most humane thing for an unwanted squirrel.* Also, female squirrels give birth to three or four babies once or sometimes twice a year in early spring and possibly in the fall. Trapping and relocating the mother when there is a litter of babies back in the nest seals the babies' fate as well.

- *Deer:* Oh deer! They are more of a problem than ever. Urban sprawl and encroachment on their habitat has made

them less fearful of human presence. Furthermore, they are looking to our gardens as their primary food source in many cases. As populations increase and natural habitats decrease, the challenge to keep deer out of urban gardens is becoming an even greater problem.

So what to do? There are three primary ways that are commonly used to repel deer: *physical barriers, scare tactics,* and *repellents.*

1. Using a physical barrier: This method of deer control is often not practical or possible due to the scope of what is necessary to keep them out. From a standing position, deer can clear a fence or object that is 10 feet tall or more.

Ironically though, deer are fearful of jumping over an object where they cannot see their landing zone (even if it is much shorter), nor will they jump over wide barriers, such as a thick hedge or a fence

that has a row of wires angled outward.

These methods make building or planting a deer-resistant physical barrier more manageable. Still, the size of the garden or property can preclude physical barriers as an option.

2. Scare tactics: A more manageable option, using commercial products and home remedies can be somewhat effective. The biggest limitation, no matter how effective it is initially, is that the deer can become acclimated or accustomed to the "scare device" and resume their normal feeding habits. It is only a matter of time before scare tactics alone will not be enough.

3. Using repellents: Deer repellents that create an offensive taste and smell are an effective method of keeping deer from devouring your plants. A common example of an offensive repellent is putrescent whole egg solids. It is the main ingredient of many commercially available deer and animal repellents, but it can also be homemade. (At my house it happens naturally . . . leave the breakfast dishes in the sink for a few days and presto! No deer for miles.)

Love hostas? So do deer, as shown by their leftovers!

Using ten-foot-tall plastic mesh fencing has proven to give some homeowners relief from the ravages of deer.

combination of deterrents simultaneously to achieve the most effective, long-term results.

Other taste repellents including mint oil, garlic oil, and capsaicin can be effective for limited periods. These products should be reapplied after rain or irrigation to maintain their effectiveness.

Some people place decoy plants around their property as a way to distract deer to a more tasteful, less valuable plant. And there is some merit to this strategy. Just know that, no matter what you do or plant, if the deer are hungry enough and they can get to your plants, there is always the chance they will graze.

Deer will likely be the most challenging and destructive pest many home and commercial gardeners face. They'll take out your prized plants without a second thought and come back for more.

Stay proactive and use multiple strategies that incorporate a combination of physical exclusion, scare tactics, and repellents. Home remedies abound, and no one will think you are tacky when you hang bars of green soap in panty hose along the edge of your garden. If it works for you, that's a great place to start.

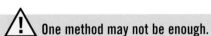 **One method may not be enough.**

It should be noted that when deer are hungry enough, even the most effective repellents or scare tactics or the most unappetizing plants will not stop them. It is best to use a

The electronic eye on this spray device "sees" the author as he really is—a pest!

"To keep my garden looking healthy and productive, I patrol for signs of problems in the very early stages. Since I enjoy being in the garden every day it is easy to do."

Controlling
Disease

Bad Things Happen to Good Plants

Plant diseases can be difficult to diagnose because symptoms for different problems can manifest themselves in similar ways. When a plant is diseased, it is because of a bacteria, fungus, or virus. A better understanding of common diseases will be your best defense for fighting them.

You should understand that a plant may become diseased even though a neighboring plant of a different species never shows the first sign of a problem. Also, it is possible that one year, all your plants of a certain type may become infected with a disease such as powdery mildew (a fungus), and yet the following year, they may be perfectly fine.

In order for a disease to develop on any plant, there must be three components present at the same time. Moreover, even when all the conditions are present, a sufficient amount of time is needed for the pathogen to become active.

Collectively, these three components are referred to as the *disease triangle:*

1. There must be a susceptible host plant.

2. The pathogen must be capable of causing a disease on that plant.

3. Environmental conditions must be favorable for the disease to develop.

Bacteria Good and Bad

Not all bacteria are bad for plants and soil. In fact, most are beneficial, and there are millions! However, there are approximately 200 types of

One indication of a bacterial infection is foliar spotting and subsequent "shot holes" left by dead leaf cells.

bacteria that cause diseases in plants. They are mostly active in warm and humid environments, so this is when you'll see the most evidence of their presence.

There are several symptoms that can indicate a bacterial infection. One is *leaf spotting.* In this case, the bacterium that attacks the plants produces a toxic chemical that kills plant cells. The plant then reacts defensively by killing off the surrounding cells, thereby isolating the infected ones. In some cases, these dead cell areas drop out, creating what looks like holes that have been "shot" into the leaves hence, the term "shot hole" disease.

In some cases bacterial infections manifest themselves as large misshapen growths such as this azalea leaf gall.

Wilting is another common symptom. Bacteria clog the plant's ability to deliver water and nutrients to the rest of the plant. Eventually the foliage begins to wilt or droop. This process can occur rapidly, and within one day, you may see a dramatic decline in your plants. Other symptoms are *cankers* and *soft rot.* These cause sunken areas produced by dead plant tissue.

Another tell-tale sign of a common bacterial infection is the appearance of *burned leaves* and *branch tips.* This appropriately named "fire blight" disease is best known for affecting apple trees. In other cases, abnormal growth is the symptom—manifested as galls. Plants respond to these bacterial invasions by producing a rapid abundance of new cells. This is often evident by *unusually large, misshapen growths* somewhere on the plant or root. You have likely seen larger than normal, thickened, and light colored leaves on azaleas and camellias. This is an example of leaf gall.

Bacteria can spread in several ways, including insects, splashing water, other diseased plants, or tools. They enter plants through tiny openings either caused by damage or cuts, but also through natural openings in the plant itself.

 Sterilize your tools.

Whenever cutting or pruning *infected* plants, it is a good idea to sterilize your tools between each cut. Because infections can spread through tools, spraying the blade with a 10 percent solution of bleach and water will keep the blades from transferring diseases with the next cut.

Once plants are affected, control can be difficult. In all cases, it is best to remove infected parts or whole plants immediately from the garden. Do not add these parts to your compost pile.

Bacteria are best managed on a preventative basis, treating plants before damage is even present. Copper-based sprays provide some help, but they are not a cure. Good cultural practices are the key to minimizing the risk of bacterial infection. This includes providing adequate air circulation, keeping the foliage as dry as possible, using mulch as a barrier, sanitizing equipment, and removing or burning affected plant material.

Fungi Is No Fun

Actually, more fungi are good for the garden than bad. But, unlike bacteria, there are thousands of fungi that are harmful. For this reason, you are likely to encounter fungal problems most often. Because they are present in the soil and above ground, symptoms of fungal attack can be present in both areas. Subterranean symptoms include *rotting, abnormal swelling, or dead roots*. At the soil level, new *seedling stems rot and flop over*. Above the soil line, plants can display *leaf spots, mildews* (white or gray powdery patches on foliage), *rusts* (rust colored blemishes on foliage), and *wilting*.

Fungal spores are very small and light, and they can travel great distances through the air to infect other plants or trees. They are also spread by water, animals, insects, and people. A good way to prevent fungi from attacking your plants is to buy disease resistant varieties whenever possible. Other ways include minimizing the amount of time water stays on foliage. See more about water control later in this chapter.

 Disease *resistant*—not disease *proof.*

Disease "resistant" simply means that the plant shows characteristics of resistance to certain diseases. Don't be fooled into thinking it is immune to disease.

To control fungal outbreaks, as with bacteria, remove all infected plant parts or the entire plant. You may also choose to apply a fungicide. There are many products available for treatment, organically (copper, sulfur, baking soda, and potassium bicarbonate) or with

Mildew is a very common fungal problem, as seen on the leaves of this columbine.

synthetic products which are labeled as fungicides, fungus control, or disease control. These treatments are best at preventing the germination of new fungal spores, so applications before outbreaks occur will provide the most effective control.

Viruses

Even viruses on occasion can be beneficial by creating unique variegations in plant foliage, but, for the most part, they are bad news in the garden. They can persist for many years before they ever appear as a problem. When they do, they often show up in one of a few primary ways. First, *plant foliage may appear yellow,* or it may *exhibit mosaic patches of yellow, light green, or white.* Next, the plant may appear *stunted.* In addition, they are often *misshapen.* Specifically, the leaves may be *rolled, swollen, or puckered* or they may be *abnormally narrow.*

Not every virus is bad. Some cause variegations in plant foliage that are nurtured to create new unique varieties like this spotted ligularia.

Unlike bacteria and fungi, viruses are not spread by water or wind. Instead, they must physically enter the plant. One of the most common carriers of viruses is insects. Insects feed on infected plants then transmit the viruses to healthy plants when they feed again. Other ways viruses are spread include plant propagation, contact by humans, and infected seed.

Unfortunately, once infected, there are no chemical treatments for controlling or eliminating a virus. When detected, you should remove all suspected plants. Although this can seem like a drastic measure, it is the most effective way to reduce continued spread. It is difficult to prevent viruses from entering your garden and affecting your plants. Your best control measures are to follow IPM practices. As an example, look for virus-resistant cultivars, provide physical barriers (such as floating row covers), and practice good sanitation.

Proactive Gardening

The best way to prevent a pest or disease outbreak or to keep your garden or landscape in top shape is simply to apply some fundamental steps—all designed to keep prob-

Taking steps to prevent future problems and ensure a healthy garden is what I like to call "proactive" gardening.

lems like pests and diseases from ever becoming an issue in the first place.

There are certainly plenty of chemicals that can be applied after the fact to deal with pest problems or control plant diseases. But at what price? I credit my success to starting off with a healthy garden and maintaining vigilance along the way. As my personal story in this section attests, the better option is to follow the steps of *proactive* gardening:

• *Start with Great Soil*

I've been accused of having "TV soil" (perfect soil . . . the kind of soil you only see on television gardening shows like mine) in my garden set for *Fresh from the Garden*. It's

true. I do have nearly perfect soil—by design. My plants must not only survive, they must *thrive*. I know my best chance of making that happen is to provide them with the optimum growing environment. The focus is to create the best structure and drainage possible and fill the growing beds with plenty of compost and manure. Those steps alone are essential to building the foundation for a healthy, problem-free garden.

• *Right Plant, Right Place (Have I Mentioned that Yet?)*

As the host of a television gardening show, I have the opportunity to visit some pretty incredible gardens around the country. As expected, they are always impeccable in every way: lush, clean, organized, and of course free of any

Here on the set of *Fresh from the Garden*, Jon Milavec gives our viewers a good look at true TV soil!

185

signs of pests or diseases.

For several years my first question to the gardener was, "How do you keep everything looking so good?" I eventually stopped asking, for I always got the same answer: *"Right plant, right place."* Don't force plants to grow where they were not meant to grow. Pay attention to a plant's need for sun or shade and provide the right environment. Know a plant's preference for soil moisture and soil nutrients and the rest should be a no-brainer. Any plant should thrive if given the right conditions.

What they were saying in four words really said it all. Beyond that, it was just a matter of paying attention to sound gardening practices and some general housekeeping.

As we've learned, one of the biggest contributors to plant problems is stress. Plants become stressed quickly when they are not planted in the appropriate place.

For example, plants can become unhealthy and subject to stress and other problems when they are planted too closely to each other. Consequently, they lack the proper light and air circulation. A plant that does not get sufficient light for its needs will not be able to produce enough food energy to thrive. It's the same as you and me not having access to nutritious food. Eventually something has to give, and our immune system breaks down.

Placing plants too close together also reduces the air flow around them.

Plant material that shows early signs of disease shouldn't remain long in your garden; remove affected parts or the entire plant. Seen here are: (1) spot anthracnose, (2) phytophthora, (3) bean rust.

The right plant in the right place rewards us with lush foliage, colorful flowers, or delicious fruit.

Proper air circulation helps dry out the plant surfaces and reduces the potential for disease pathogens to take hold.

Weeds are a haven for disease-carrying pests. The only thing I want to see growing in my garden are the plants I intended to be there. This means I always have an eye towards the ground, scouting for weeds. They don't stay around long in my garden. If a plant shows early signs of a disease problem, I remove the infected parts, or in some cases, the entire plant.

 You don't have to be fanatical.

Just be proactive about sanitation. Gardening is supposed to be relaxing and fun. Don't stress about having a perfectly clean garden.

As vital as water is to the life of the garden, it is also a major facilitator in the spread of plant disease.

mulched were significantly larger, fuller, and weeks ahead of the same plants in the unmulched portion. Mulch is very important in helping to keep soil-borne diseases from splashing onto plant foliage, keeping soil temperatures even, and preventing competitive weeds from germinating, therefore creating a healthier environment for plants to grow. It is also a great way to improve the soil by incorporating it into your beds at the end of the growing season.

• *Control Water*

As vital as water is to the life of the garden, it can also be responsible for its demise. Water is a major facilitator of the spread of plant disease at and above the soil line.

Whenever you irrigate your plants, apply the water at the soil level if possible and very early in the day. This allows foliage to dry out quickly, should it become wet.

By minimizing the amount of moisture that remains on the foliage, you reduce the chance of spreading diseases. This is best accomplished by using drip irrigation systems whenever possible. Another technique is to water early in the day so foliage that does get wet has time to dry out. And don't over water. Consider watering on an as-needed basis, or use a water timer to ensure plants are getting the right amount of water if you are away for an extended period.

• *Use Mulch*

The benefits of mulch are clearly visible in the garden. For example, I have beds where I started to mulch but didn't finish for some reason. The plants that were

• *Observe Every Day*

A key step in maintaining a healthy garden is vigilance over day-to-day changes. This does not mean you are required to spend time every day in the garden, although I recommend it! It simply means pay attention to what's going on. The earlier you are able to detect adverse changes, the less severe your reaction needs to be. Again, it pays to be proactive, not reactive.

QUICK FACT

?

Keeping water off of the foliage is important.

WHY: Water is a big carrier of fungal disease, so reducing the time the leaf or blade surface stays wet will help prevent fungal growth.

From Joe

I first learned about harpin protein several years ago while touring a private garden that contained hundreds of tomato plants. I've seen plenty of tomato plants, but these were stunning. They were at least 6 feet tall, robust, pest- and disease-free, and full of fruit. And this was in the heat of Atlanta, Georgia. This gardener had my attention! When I found out they were heirloom tomatoes, I was fascinated. How could plants not bred for pest and disease resistance be so healthy, especially when the gardener did not use pesticides in his garden?

Clearly he was doing something different. I had to know more so I asked the owner his secret. He was using a product which I later learned is a naturally occurring protein called harpin. It's benefits were first discovered and made available by Eden Bioscience. He gave me quite a lesson which I barely understood at the time.

I was so impressed with the results I had witnessed that I contacted the company that makes it. Their scientist patiently and clearly explained how this protein boosts a plant's immune system and stimulates growth.

I decided to experiment on the TV set of my show *Fresh from the Garden.* We used harpin on a variety of plants, spraying a test group and treating the others normally. We even wrote our experiment into the show not knowing how it would turn out. This was quite a risky endeavor from a TV production standpoint!

As the season progressed there was a noticeable difference between most of the treated and non-treated plants. The majority of harpin treated plants were healthier and had produced more fruit. Although not a sophisticated experiment, the results really had my attention. I did further research and used it again the following year with similar results.

As I describe above, I was encouraged by the results of using a naturally occurring harpin protein to boost the immune system of my plants.

The earlier I am able to detect adverse changes, the less severe my response to them needs to be.

outbreaks of powdery mildew, black spot, blights, molds and other plant diseases on garden crops and ornamentals. Look for products containing this as the active ingredient for a safe, simple, and effective control.

What Bio-Rational Means

Like my story illustrated, I am constantly looking for a new methods or technology that is eco-friendly to help maintain a healthy garden. One term that has emerged, when it comes to natural pest and disease control, is "biologically rational" or "bio-rational."

Simply stated this control method uses certain biological properties of pests or plants, including natural predators, competitors, parasites, and pathogens. Another approach involves the natural manipulation of a plant's chemistry to boost its immune system.

Although it's doubtful we will ever be able to completely eliminate plant diseases from the garden, it's encouraging to know that there are simple things we can do to minimize their presence. I am also encouraged that there are newer, more environmentally responsible ways to proactively and reactively approach diseases before or after they appear.

• *Anticipate Trouble*

When I resort to spraying anything in the garden, it is to prevent plant disease or promote the health and defense mechanisms in plants. Once plant diseases find their way into your garden, they can be difficult to control. Many fungal and bacterial diseases can be prevented by spraying plants with a simple baking soda (*sodium bicarbonate*) mixture or a copper-sulfate based solution every week or so while the plant is growing. It is important to note this should be done *before* disease becomes apparent. To make your own spray, mix one tablespoon of baking soda and one teaspoon of vegetable oil per gallon of water.

Similar to baking soda, *potassium bicarbonate* has been shown to prevent, effectively reduce, and potentially cure

When I came upon this pond in a private garden near Philadelphia, the serenity reminded me just how much water adds to the pleasure of any garden. In this case, its beauty was in the simplicity. I could have stayed here for hours!

Ponds and Water Features

Pond and Water Feature Basics

Entire books are written about ponds and water features—from how to make them to what to stock once the pond is ready. There are clubs and societies devoted solely to the fish that go into them. This chapter is designed primarily to introduce you to the fascinating world of water gardens and ponds, equip you with some basic information, and possibly stimulate your interest in pursuing one for your own garden.

Space limitations are no longer an excuse for not having some type of water feature, even if only on a deck or patio. We've all seen the small tabletop model and have enjoyed its soothing sounds. A small feature like that is the perfect solution for someone with a busy lifestyle or space limitations.

Why Have a Water Feature?

A pond or water garden is not fully appreciated until you actually have one. Then you find yourself trying to imagine how you got by without it for so long! Although you've appreciated them in other's gardens, the real pleasure comes from having and enjoying your own. I think there is no sound more relaxing and soothing than that of moving water. Add the sound of birds chirping and a soft breeze whispering through the trees, and you have heaven on earth. If you already enjoy your garden or landscape without water, just wait until you add it!

If you are lucky enough to have a natural pond or stream running through your property options abound for ways to enhance these water features. Line them with rocks to prevent erosion or direct water flow or build bridges to traverse them. Incorporating a pond into your landscape plans is easy enough providing you give it thoughtful consideration.

The Bigger the Better

Space permitting, every pond owner I know says bigger is better. The larger the pond, the greater the opportunity for diversity in its appearance, the plants you can add, and the wildlife it attracts. This is good advice assuming you're willing to either do, or hire, the work that needs to be done to keep a large pond clean and maintained. But plan ahead. Once a pond is in place and filled with water, it is highly unlikely that you will go to the trouble of enlarging it. A water garden can only support so much life and that truly is a matter of size.

Types of Ponds

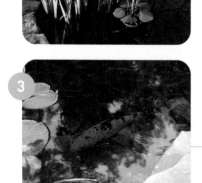

Not every pond is large and some don't have even a single fish by design. In general, there are *three basic types* of ponds.

1. *Water garden:* The least complex, this is simply a collection of aquatic plants contained in water. There are plenty of striking aquatic and water-tolerant plants for you to feature in a dedicated garden.

2. *Combination pond:* These consist of water-loving plants and a few basic fish, such as goldfish. These ponds require only a bit more maintenance and many include a mechanical filtration system of some sort.

Although not everyone has a natural water feature on their property, there are ways to bring those sights and sounds to your landscape.

3. *Koi pond:* This type of pond requires the most attention to detail. It is appropriately named because this pond can hold quite a collection of expensive fish, known as Koi. They usually get very large and need proper attention to ensure a suitable environment. Because Koi eat plant material, you'll have to be extra careful to protect your plants when adding them. Koi ponds have pumps and filtration systems as well.

Planning for a Water Feature

Assuming you have decided to move forward with adding a pond or water feature to your landscape, there will be a number of issues to consider. The following is a list of some of the most important.

In general there are three pond considerations, (1) plants, (2) plants and fish, and (3) koi.

Space permitting, every pond owner I know says bigger is better.

• *Site selection*

If you are considering adding a water feature to your existing landscape, you are likely thinking about a general area in which to put it, as well as its overall appearance. Assuming your water garden or pond will be out in your yard or landscape as opposed to on your deck or patio, you'll need to find an appropriate location. Having it close enough to the house or where you entertain outdoors allows you and your guests to enjoy its sound and beauty.

Important: *Keep runoff out of your pond.* Do not locate it in a low area that poses a risk of runoff water draining into your pond. The concern, besides overflow, is the runoff of silt and potential chemicals: herbicides and pesticides which could be lethal to the fish and entire pond ecosystem.

Check for high water tables and wet weather springs. The hydraulic pressure created under the liner can push the liner up, empty the water garden, and even push large rocks away from the edges.

⚠️ **Call before you dig.**

Before deciding on a site for your water feature, call your local utilities' locating service so that all underground lines and cables can be identified. Make the call well in advance of placing that first shovel in the ground. Utility locating services will come to your

As a safety precaution, have underground utilities marked before you embark on an excavation project.

house at no charge to inspect the area and mark any buried lines. The standard listings for this number is usually "Call Before You Dig." You can find the listing in your telephone book, online, or many times it is included on your utility bill. In addition, irrigation lines should be located and marked. Depending on what obstacles you face, you may be dissuaded from using certain areas of your yard.

Once you've settled on a location, it's time to lay out the water feature. Will you use a pre-formed mold or dig your own pit for a more custom look? Molds are great for quick, uniform results, plus they rarely leak. On the other hand, a manually dug pond will be unlike any other. You can really create a unique look, but it can have its own

Children are naturally attracted to water; plan ahead for their safety.

share of challenges. We'll address that more in the Troubleshooting section.

- *Children and safety issues*

These should be at the front of your mind whenever you are building an area to hold water. As you determine the size and depth of your pond, be sure to take into consideration how children might factor into the equation. Will you need a protective barrier around it? Can all children who have access to your yard swim? How deep do you want the pond? Also, check with your county building inspector. There may be safety issues that must be approved based on specific sites, locations, and depths.

 Children are naturally attracted to water.

Take into consideration all safety risks and precautions when planning your water feature:

- *Convenience, including access to water*

It might go without saying, but there are a lot of reasons for placing the pond or water feature close to the house. One is **access to water** as you fill and add water to it periodically. What about a **source for electricity?** You will be able to enjoy your pond longer in the evening if it is lighted. Consider adding outdoor lighting to your pond or water feature. A low-voltage do-it-yourself kit would be fine, or you might hire an electrician to install a more elaborate system. In either case, a nicely lit pond or water feature is beautiful in the evening, and it adds to safety. Another consideration is **maintenance.** Just like most things, out of sight means out of mind. A neglected water garden eventually becomes nothing more than an eyesore and a mosquito breeding ground.

- *Terrain*

If your water feature will incorporate a waterfall or stream of some sort, you need an elevated section. Many homeowners take advantage of a hilly or less desirable location

Simple low-voltage lighting will allow you to enjoy your pond longer into in the evening.

stone or soil excavated from the pit.

•*Clean-up (tree debris, etc.)*

Although a certain amount of leaf litter, branches and the like inevitably find their way to your pond, you should still take into consideration the surroundings—especially as it pertains to falling leaves and messy trees. In addition to leaves and branches, fruit and seed pods are a natural part of a tree's seasonal changes. If you don't care to make frequent pond cleaning one of your tasks, consider the options before deciding on a final site. In all cases though, no matter where you end up locating your pond, plan on a thorough spring cleaning.

in their landscape and use that hill or slope as a natural fall area for the water. As they say, it's like making lemonade out of lemons.

However, even if you don't have a hilly area for a waterfall or babbling creek, you can still create a hill with stacked

•*Preparation*

Once you find a spot you like, it's time to lay out the pond. If it is a preformed hard liner, then placing it on the ground and painting an outline around it will suffice for figuring out where you need to dig. Use a can of water-based spray paint that is designed for marking lines in the ground. It sprays straight down. You can also use flour or sand, and sprinkle a small amount around

Taking advantage of hilly terrain allows you to have one or more waterfall features.

the liner to make your outline.

If you decide on to use a soft liner, then the shape can be whatever you'd like. An easy way to experiment with the design is to lay out a flexible garden hose or rope into various shapes until you find a size and form that pleases. Once you decide how the pond will look, spray paint the outline with water-based paint or spread powdered lime or flour down over the hose. Remove the hose and dig the outline. I like the rope method best. It's easy to nudge here and there with your foot to fine tune the shape.

Depending on the size of your pond, it will usually be to your advantage to start excavating it from the inside out. This makes for easier work as the size of your pit increases and you haul the dirt away. As you excavate the soil, consider that you may want to use some for a waterfall area.

It is a good idea to create shelf areas for shallow ledges that allow for submersible plants in containers, or plants that just like to have their feet wet. Preformed hard liners often have shelves already incorporated into the mold. Be sure to create those same

shelves into the soil to allow for their support. A layer of sand can be used on the top of the shelves and the bottom of the pit to make leveling the liner easier.

Once the hole is dug and shaped to the desired form and depth, it is extremely important to remove all sharp

Ledges are great spots for plants and make wonderful hiding places for fish.

196

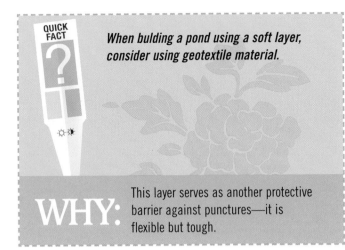

QUICK FACT

?

When bulding a pond using a soft layer, consider using geotextile material.

WHY:
This layer serves as another protective barrier against punctures—it is flexible but tough.

objects from the bottom or sides of the pit. This is especially true for soft liners. The slightest puncture can create a nightmare of problems as you try to locate a leak in your pond after filling it with water, plants and fish. You can easily eliminate this risk with a thorough examination.

In my book, you can't be too careful when it comes to taking precautions. It is much easier to take the proper steps now, while everything is accessible, than to deal with a puncture or leak when your pond is full of thousands of gallons of water.

• *Installation*

The next step in the process is to install the liner. Assuming you've dug the hole properly, pre-formed hard liners will drop nicely into the pit you've excavated. High quality soft liners are also readily available at many home improvement stores, garden centers, and stores specializing in water gardens. A liner that is at least .45 mils thick will give you adequate protection and durability.

 Purchase the highest quality liner for your budget.

The liner is one of the keys to having a leak-proof pond. Paying a little extra now could save you plenty of time and added expense later, not to mention frustration! Also, make sure that the liner is more than ample to cover your pit. It must fit into the pond and overlap the edges to function properly.

Fortunately there is a formula to determine the size of the liner you'll need. First, think of your pond design as a rectangle, even if it is an irregular shape. Determine the smallest rectangle that your pond's shape will fit into.

The *length* of your liner needs to be the overall length of the pond, plus twice the maximum depth, plus 2 feet. The *width* of the liner is the overall width of the pond plus twice the maximum depth, plus two feet. Example: A pond with overall dimensions in terms of a rectangle of 6 feet × 12 feet and a depth of 3 feet will require a liner size of 14 feet × 20 feet.

Length calculation for liner: 12 + (2 × 3) + 2 = 20 feet long

It is better to have extra liner and not need it than to need it and not have it.

Ponds are suitable for formal gardens and lend themselves to uniform shapes and edging.

Width calculation for liner: 6 + (2 × 3) + 2 = 14 feet wide.

Your optimal liner dimension therefore is 20 x 14 feet or larger.

Plenty of overlap and excess material is important to make sure that water does not seep underneath the liner. If you feel that 2 feet is not enough overlap, then allow for more. You can always trim off the excess and bury the remaining liner under soil or stones. You never know what sort of adjustments you may have to make in the future. It is definitely better to have too much than too little liner!

Once you are happy with the placement of the liner and you have plenty of overlap, begin filling the pit with water. The weight of the water as it fills the hole will compress it against the pond walls. However, try to smooth out any overlapping fabric, pleats or creases as the pond fills. When the pond is filled, trim away the excess liner making sure not to cut it too close. As stated earlier, the excess can be concealed.

 Keep runoff out of your pond.

This excess material may come in handy at this point to create an impervious barrier from potential runoff. You should create a lip or raised edge to ensure that any potential runoff is stopped or diverted before reaching the pond.

The material you choose to place around the perimeter of the pond is strictly personal preference. An informal look lends itself to a gently curved outline and looks great with natural stone and boulders randomly stacked along the sides and edges. A more formal, uniform shape would look better with stones, bricks, or pavers that are of a consistent symmetrical shape and texture.

• *Water quality*

Without getting into the science of water quality, it is important to know that the proper pH level in your pond water plays a major role. Fortunately, this range is wide enough to allow for some variance and there are easy ways to monitor these levels with test kits, along with simple remedies to bring them in line. Fish and plants do well when pH levels are between 6.5 and 8.5.

Keeping your pond debris-free, which includes the removal of dead or diseased plants, will help keep the pH balance within range. Leaf debris is one of the biggest detriments to clean and balanced ponds. Although most leaves float for a short time, they all sink eventually, creating problems with removal. As the leaves decompose, they rob the pond of oxygen and contribute to an accumulation of toxic wastes.

Keep your pond as debris-free as possible to help it stay healthy and reduce maintenance.

add fish that are hard to see. However, in the defense of less popular fish, they are every bit as effective at eating mosquito larvae and helping to maintain the ecosystem. If function comes before looks, then your options are many.

Adding fish to your pond is easy to do, but there are some common mistakes to avoid. It can mean the difference between life and death for your fish.

When stocking your pond with fish and plants, resist the temptation to overdo it! Too many of either can upset the levels required to sustain a healthy pond environment. There is a balance and, more often than not, it is found by trial and error. But I'll give you a formula you can start with a little later on.

The right combination of filters and plants is great for keeping the water clean and within the proper pH range. An easy way to ensure that your pond water stays healthy is to renew about 20 percent of it each month. Pump or drain out this much and replace it with dechlorinated water.

Preparing for Fish

The most common types of fish to add to any pond are Koi, comets and goldfish. The mellow, cruising fish you see in ponds are likely Koi. They are also the largest. The smaller fish darting around are usually goldfish or comets. Other fish types will work well in a pond, but some are less colorful and therefore not as popular for viewing.

Let's face it. One of the biggest reasons for adding fish is so we can enjoy watching them. It doesn't do a lot of good to

When is the Best Time to Add Fish?

First, don't add fish too soon after you've filled the pond. It is easy to be excited and want to see your new water feature come to life. But wait! Give the pond water time to acclimate. This may take up to several weeks. The delay will make sure of certain chemical balances such as pH, ammonia, chlorine, fluoride, nitrates, and nitrites. Thankfully there are test kits available at pond supply stores that will let you know if your water is acceptable for adding fish. It is also advisable to test the water every week or two thereafter to ensure that the quality is appropriate for keeping your habitat in top shape.

The ideal chemical balance of your pond can change for many reasons. Some of the most common include fertilizer runoff, excess buildup of fish waste and food, changes in the amount of sun exposure, plant introductions, and quantity of plants and fish relative to the pond size.

How to Add the Fish

The fish you buy should be placed in a plastic bag with water from their tank and captured air to ensure their temporary environment stays oxygenated for as long as possible. Place this bag into the pond and allow it to float for fifteen minutes or so; longer if water temperature differences seem rather extreme.

Once water temperatures are approximately the same, open the bag and add some pond water. Wait another fifteen minutes or so and add some more of your pond water. These steps will acclimate the fish to their new environment. After another fifteen minutes, slowly remove the bag, allowing the fish to swim gently into the pond.

⚠️ If possible, never handle the fish directly.

Handling the fish directly can remove essential protection they have against diseases. When you begin adding fish, do so slowly. Consider starting out with the cheaper, smaller goldfish. Although they'll serve as the "guinea pigs," you'll know soon enough if your water is ready.

Once you determine that everything looks good, begin adding other fish. Be sure they are acclimated to their new surroundings using the steps I just described. *Never dump newly acquired fish into a pond directly from the bag.*

Use moderation! It's exciting to see your pond come to life, and fish are the stars of the show. Unfortunately the ideal amount of fish may be far less than you think. Adding too many to the pond and overcrowding the environment can add more waste than the filtration system can handle. It's best to add only a couple at a time.

Knowing the right amount of fish that can be safely added is not an exact science. It depends on a lot of factors including the size of the

Add fish to your pond in the appropriate manner to ensure a successful transition.

QUICK FACT

Never dump newly acquired fish into a pond directly from the bag.

WHY: Fish must be introduced slowly so water temperatures can match. Quite frequently, water from an indoor environment will be much different than outdoors. Making sure the water temperature and chemistry is the same between their past and future homes can make the difference between a successful transition and failure.

fish, the size of the pond, the number of plants, the size, quality and waste handling capacity of the filter system (if any), and even the amount and quality of food you provide for the fish.

How Many Fish are Too Many?

There are various formulas for knowing the fish limit of a given pond. One common rule of thumb is to add only as many fish as you could line up end to end across the

The right balance of plants and fish reduces the chance for future problems.

approximate diameter. This rule applies to a pond without supplemental oxygen. Adding a waterfall or pump can increase this oxygen in the water.

Another rule applied to established ponds: every three to five gallons of water can support one inch of fish. Small fish grow large in an open pond, plus they have babies. It is likely you will need to reduce the population of fish in your pond before you know it. Koi, due to their larger size, need much more water per fish, about 4 to 12 times more water than an adult goldfish.

 Make sure fish are healthy.

Avoid adding any fish that appear to be sick or diseased. It is advisable to purchase your fish from a reputable dealer in your area. Most of the time these fish will have been quarantined before being introduced for sale. This increases the chance that the fish will be healthy when you add them to your pond. In mass market settings, this extra precautionary step may be skipped, and your chances of purchasing sick fish are increased.

Feed your fish, but not too much. This is a common mistake. Food goes in one end of the fish and quickly comes out the other. Overfeeding increases waste and contributes to a higher level of nitrogen. Algae flourishes in this environment causing pea soup green water and high ammonia levels. I recommend that you only feed your fish what they will eat in two to three minutes. Use floating food and use a net to get out what they don't eat. Otherwise it will sink to the bottom, adding even more waste.

Choosing and Establishing Plants

It doesn't matter if you have a simple water garden or an elaborate pond, there are three basic types of plants that are suitable in a water setting. They are considered *emergent, submerged,* or *floating* species. I enjoy a mix of all types, no matter the size of the pond.

- *Emergent plants* have their roots in the water, but their shoots are above the water surface. These plants should be

QUICK FACT

Strive to cover the total pond surface about 50 percent by using a variety of water plants.

 **WHY:** This cuts down on the amount of sunlight which would promote algae growth, helps keep the water oxygenated and clean, and gives the fish plenty of hiding places from predators.

contained and anchored in pots using a heavy soil. Soil that is extremely light such as a container mix is not appropriate for this type of application. It will not stay in the pot and will likely float to the surface. Examples of emergent plants include water lilies and lotus.

Some Tips for Planting Emergent Plants:

1. Whenever you're placing containers with plants underwater, always top off the soil with rocks or gravel. This will keep the planting contained and prevent fish from disturbing the soil around the roots.

2. Place the containers slowly into the water to allow air to escape and water to fill the voids.

3. To adjust the height of the submerged pots, place bricks underneath to vary the depth to appropriate levels.

The flowers of water garden plants can be as visually stimulating as any perennial border.

EMERGENT PLANTS		
COMMON NAME	BOTANICAL NAME	ZONE*
Arrowhead	*Sagittaria latifolia*	4-11
Bog Lily	*Crinum americanum*	8-11
Brass Buttons	*Cotula coronopifolia*	8-9
Canna	*Canna x hybrida*	7-11
Cattail	*Typha latifolia*	2-11
Chameleon Plant	*Houttuynia cordata*	6-11
Cyperus	*Cyperus alternifolius*	9-11
Dwarf Bamboo	*Dulichium arundinaceum*	6-10
Flowering Rush	*Butomus umbellatus*	3-7
Golden-Club	*Orontium aquaticum*	6-11
Horsetail	*Equisetum hyemale*	3-11
Japanese Iris	*Iris ensata*	4-8
Lizard's-tail	*Saururus cernuus*	4-9
Lotus	*Nelumbo*	4-11
Louisiana Iris	*Iris giganticaerulea*	6-9
Monkey Flower	*Mimulus luteus*	Annual
Pickerel Rush	*Pontederia cordata*	3-11
Spider Lily	*Hymenocallis liriosome*	8-11
Spike Rush	*Eleocharis montevidensis*	6-9
Sweet flag	*Acorus calamus*	4-11
Taro	*Colocasia esculenta*	9-11
Water Lilies	*Nymphaea tetragona*	3-11
Yellow Flag	*Iris pseudacorus*	4-8

• *Submerged* plants live their entire lives under water and are most often used to remove impurities, which helps keep the water clean, and allows the exchange of oxygen for carbon dioxide. Anchor these plants in pots the same way you would secure emergent species.

• *Floating plants* are just as they sound. They have no anchors and do not need to be planted in pots. Besides being pretty to look at, they serve the important purpose of helping to keep the water clean, primarily by shading out some of the water surface and filtering impurities and CO_2 with their exposed roots.

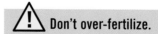 **Don't over-fertilize.**

Although you can add fertilizer spikes to your water plants on occasion, such as once a year, native plants usually don't even need it. Overfertilizing any of your water plants can cause unwanted algae bloom due to the introduction of excessive nitrogen from the fertilizer. A direct consequence of this problem is that as algae growth increases, it

QUICK FACT

Choose a diverse selection of plants that help keep the water clean.

HOW: Water plants have different roles. Some shade the surface or filter the water and others contribute oxygen. Using varieties of each improves water quality.

depletes much needed oxygen from the water.

What Should Influence Your Plant Selections?

When selecting plants for your water feature there are several considerations:

1. *Depth:* Some plants need a depth of 2 to 3 feet to thrive.

2. *Size:* Is your pond or feature large enough to support full sized plants? You may need to look for dwarf varieties.

3. *Available Light:* Will your water garden be in full sun, full shade or somewhere in between? You should pick plants that are appropriate for your conditions.

4. *Overwintering:* Do you have a place or the ability to overwinter tender plants to protect them in the coldest months? Some of the most popular water plants are tropical and will not survive a winter outside of their hardiness zone.

Troubleshooting: Protecting Your Investment

There are four main responsibilities to consider in order to protect your pond properly:

1. *Control algae:* The rapid appearance or buildup of algae is referred to as "algae bloom." It is a common problem in new ponds while they are becoming established and

in ponds that are located in full sun. Adding floating and large-leafed plants such as water lilies helps reduce the light. Water that contains too many nutrients is another contributing factor to excess algae.

It is not necessary to drain the pond to control the problem. Beyond plants, filters help tremendously in controlling algae. Chemicals are also available to help deal with the problem.

2. *Screen against predators:* If you own a pond, sooner or later you will experience a mysterious disappearance of one or more of your prized fish. Birds of pray, small animals, and reptiles all look to your pond as a possible food source.

There are several methods for helping deter predators of your fish. A few of the most popular include creating a

SUBMERGED PLANTS COMMON NAME	BOTANICAL NAME	ZONE*
Canadian Pondweed	*Elodea canadensis*	5-11
Hornwort	*Ceratophyllum demersum*	6-9
Pondweed	*Potamogeton crispus*	7-11
Spike Rush	*Eleocharis acicularis*	5-8
Water Crowfoot	*Ranunculus aquatilis*	5-8
Water Jade	*Crassula helmsii*	6-9
Water Lobelia	*Lobelia dortmanna*	4-8
Water Milfoil	*Myriophyllum aquaticum*	9-11
Water Moss	*Fontinalis antipyretica*	6-9
Water Starwort	*Callitriche hermaphroditica*	5-9

FLOATING PLANTS COMMON NAME	BOTANICAL NAME	ZONE*
Bladder Wort	*Uticularia*	8-11
Common Duckweed	*Lemna minor*	6-11
Fairy Moss	*Azolla filiculoides*	7-11
Feather Foil	*Hottonia inflata*	5-11
Frogbit	*Hydrocharis morsus ranae*	6-11
Water Chestnut	*Trapa natans*	8-11
Water Hyacinth	*Eichhornia crassipes*	10-11
Water Soldier	*Stratiotes aloides*	5-11
Water Violet	*Hottonia palustris*	5-11

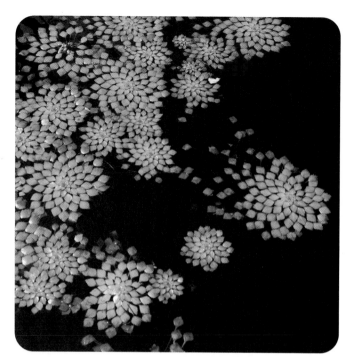

Floating plants provide shade help keep the water clean and protect fish from predators.

physical barrier over your pond to prevent birds of pray from landing. I've even talked to pond owners who have had success by simply stringing a few lines of monofilament across their pond in a crisscross pattern.

Another is to provide ample hiding places for your fish. Large-leafed plants, submersible tubes, and rock outcroppings all provide hiding places which are essential to survival when animals come looking for a meal. By creating areas in your pond that are deep enough, you can prevent birds of prey, even long-legged blue herons, from wading into position for a prime hunting spot.

3. *Prevent a leaking pond or liner:* This can be one of the most aggravating mishaps when dealing with the challenges and pleasures of having a pond or water feature. A leaking pond is the result of a puncture or water slipping underneath or behind the liner.

Conducting a thorough inspection of your site when you excavate is another good way to ensure watertight containment. Adding a geotextile under-layment beneath the

pond liner can help make up for any items you may have missed, On occasion, something may enter your pond from above and puncture the lining. But this is very unusual, and you would certainly be able to find evidence of it.

Sometimes though, loss of water from your pond is simply due to the process of evaporation. In very hot weather, it's not unusual to lose water volume—especially if you have waterfalls or a fountain. This can appear to happen quickly if you aren't used to visiting your pond frequently.

Before you panic, refill the pond, adjusting the pH balance if necessary. This will depend on the amount of water you add. Then keep an eye on the water level. If it is a leak, you'll notice the level will drop rather quickly. More often than not it's just evaporation which will slow as temperatures drop.

4. *Protect your pond and fish over the winter:* As temperatures cool, fish slow down. In fact, they go into a stage of semi-hibernation. At this point, *do not feed them* while

Adding plants such as water lilies is a beautiful and functional way to reduce the chance of algae blooms.

> **QUICK FACT**
>
> ?
> i
>
> **Do not feed your fish when the water temperature drops below 55 degrees F.**
>
> **WHY:** Fish will continue to eat during a stage of semi-hibernation if given food. However, they will not metabolize it. This leads to bloating and possible death.

the water temperature remains below 55 degrees F. They will be unable to metabolize the food, which can possibly lead to death.

As long as the pond is at least 24 inches deep, you should be able to overwinter most fish. Larger sized Koi need about 36 inches. However, you don't want to let a solid sheet of ice form over the pond. An easy way to keep the area open is to make sure water is in constant motion. Even so, it may get cold enough for the pond to freeze

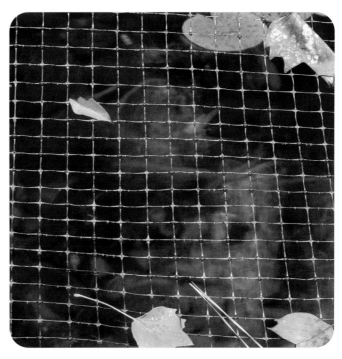

Netting is available to help protect your prized fish from many types of predators.

over. Should this occur, the best way to open an air hole in a frozen surface is to pour boiling water over it. It is necessary to melt that area slowly. Do not attempt to crack the ice with a hammer or other instrument. This causes a vibration or shockwave that can be fatal to the fish.

Water features need not be limited just to ponds or natural streams. The sight and sound of moving water can be accomplished in a variety of other ways. Fountains both large and small provide a way to incorporate these attributes. A birdbath or container filled with water to float candles, colorful petals, and the like can be used as a treat for the eye. However you choose to do it, adding water to your environment—whether inside or out—provides yet another element of interest.

A water feature doesn't have to be large or elaborate to please you and others.

"I can't think of anything that creates a more welcoming feeling at night than a home warmly lit from the outside. Add to that the safety and security night lighting provides and, to me, it's the best of both worlds."

The **Beauty** of Outdoor **Lighting**

It's Practical and Pleasing

As the work day gets longer, sometimes the only time we have to enjoy our gardens and landscapes is after sunset. Combine that with the desire to spend more of our precious free time outdoors, and the concept of outdoor lighting makes sense—especially when you consider the ease and affordability of installing a system yourself. Besides the aesthetic benefits, lighting a dark space is one of the most important deterrents to burglars and vandals. It also illuminates potentially hazardous areas for family and visitors.

Outdoor illumination today is not only appropriate for safety issues, it creates ambiance by accenting places in your garden. Lighting can draw attention to a special tree or prominent feature in the landscape. In all cases it allows our gardens to be enjoyed after dark, not *in* the dark!

Innovations in technology allow for even the most project-challenged homeowners to quickly and easily install a complete system with the look of a professional job. Kits are readily available for purchase at home improvement and lighting stores. They're sold with everything you need to get the job done.

Types of Outdoor Lighting

Do-it-yourself outdoor lighting kits are referred to as "low-voltage" lighting. These systems work by using a transformer to reduce standard 120-volt household currents to a far less harmful 12 volts. Low-voltage kits include everything you need to install and power the system your-

DIY kits are easy to find, easy to install, and with a little planning will add ambiance anywhere you'd like.

self, without the aid of an electrician. The typical kit includes all of the following: light bulbs, fixtures, wiring, transformer, and timer.

Lighting kits come in a wide range of prices to suit any budget. For example, basic, inexpensive plastic kits are good for lighting a walkway or row of foundation plants along the front of the house. Additional components are available, but it may be necessary to upgrade the transformer as you increase the demands on it. It's a good idea to plan ahead for growth and allow for a little cushion.

Before purchasing your kit, make sure you provide enough power to light your system. Consider the total lighting requirements that one transformer will supply. For example if you have ten 15-watt bulbs for a total of 150 watts ($10 \times 15W$), then you'll need a 150-watt, or higher, transformer. More expensive kits include metal fixtures and halogen lights. They may also include more components. Be sure to examine the listed contents to know exactly what you are buying and whether there are enough lights to handle the job you want to do.

Get lasting results from your system

The key to a great looking low-voltage system is to use high quality fixtures. They will be more expensive, but they'll last much longer and you will quickly recover the additional up front cost. One of the most popular high quality choices are fixtures made of copper.

To achieve the best looking and functional system when it matters most—at night—don't take shortcuts when selecting the bulbs that go into them. For a high quality, well lit system, consider using halogen lights. They look natural in the landscape, they're brighter, and they'll last longer.

Designing the system

When designing your outdoor lighting system, consider the following:

• *Ambiance and Interest:* Most of the time, the first intent when considering a lighting system for our outdoor environment is to add beauty to the evening landscape. There are a number of ways to do this with the lighting options available.

• *Pathway Lighting:* The most common application is pathway lighting. Even basic kits are appropriate for this. Lights are placed from about ankle to knee height to light the walking path. It certainly has an aesthetic appeal, but its most important function is to provide safety.

• *Security Lighting:* On the theme of safety, security lighting is placed strategically to eliminate dark areas.

Although this type of lighting can serve to accent special features, its primary purpose is to provide safety and security.

• *Area Lighting:* This type of lighting is generally intended to cover a broad area, as opposed to spot or accent lighting which features a specific object. Again this lighting is primarily used for safety and security.

• *Spot Lighting:* Unlike area lighting, spot lighting is intended to illuminate a specific feature such as a piece of art or a special accent tree. There is no denying that when an object is lit with spot lighting, you simply can't miss it.

A well lit pathway provides a way to add ambiance, along with safety and security.

Mood Lighting

Mood lighting offers a number of different lighting techniques to accent specific features in the landscape or around your home. These features, although helpful to illuminate the general area, are usually not intended for safety and security as their primary purpose. The following are some specific examples for mood lighting:

• *Moon Lighting:* This is a technique where lights are placed high in the trees to wash over a large area giving the appearance of a full moon—all month long.

• *Shadow Lighting:* This type of lighting is used to cast a shadow from a tree, sculpture, or other garden feature

Although a bit more expensive, quality fixtures will reward you with lower overall maintenance and will last longer.

Lighting up an area rather than a specific object is another way to create after hours safety and security.

onto the ground or a wall for added drama.

• *Silhouette Lighting:* In this case, lighting is placed low near the object to highlight the "bones" or shape of the structure. Silhouette lighting is ideal to feature architectural details.

• *Down Lighting:* Down lighting, as the name implies, can be placed against a wall or up in a tree or structure to throw light in a downward direction. When placed above an object, it can have a similar effect to silhouette lighting. I love to see tall trees with down lighting, especially in winter when the branches are void of leaves. Down lighting always creates a dramatic effect to enhance the interesting branch structure.

If simply against a wall, down lighting can accentuate the wall's texture while providing additional security. One of the most pleasing effects of this type of lighting, often referred to as *"wall wash lighting,"* is to soften the wall, accent the texture of the surface, or both.

• *Up Lighting:* Another dramatic effect is created when lights are placed at the bottom of a structure or tree and aimed upward. This type of lighting always commands attention and interest.

Installation

As easy as it is to install low-voltage lighting, planning will make future additions even easier. If you are working in an

As the name implies, moonlighting gives you the special feeling of a full moon all month long.

Shadow lighting is a technique used to highlight a garden feature and to create additional drama.

existing landscape, installation is still easy and only slightly more involved for maintenance and repair.

If you are someone who is organized enough to plan as early as the construction process, congratulations! You'll be quite proud of yourself down the road when it comes to maintaining your system. Here are a few tips to make the process even easier:

I love to see tall trees with down lighting, but especially in winter when their branch structure is more apparent.

• *Plan your lighting needs ahead of time.* Decide what type of lighting you would like to provide, such as for pathways, spot lighting, down lighting, etc.

• *Have electrical outlets installed where you will have the lighting placed.* At a minimum, install an electrical outlet in the front and back of the house to accommodate future transformers. Shielding these outlets from view will make the area a bit more attractive, but more importantly, it will reduce the risk of tampering.

• *Dedicate an electrical panel breaker to all outlets controlling outdoor lighting.* This will simplify your life if that breaker ever trips.

• *Consider installing 2-inch PVC conduit pipe* under walkways and driveways and along any area where you think you might like to have outdoor lighting in the future. Imagine how easy it would be at that time to simply "feed" wire through an existing underground runway rather than digging through hard soil, rocks, and roots.

 Use PVC pipe for protection.

By planning carefully these homeowners were able to highlight a special architectural feature in their garden.

An added benefit to running your low voltage power line through PVC pipe is that it will be protected from potential nicks or cuts by any number of tools including edger blades, shovels, weeders, etc. When using buried PVC pipe, make a notation as to where to find the access openings in the future.

Troubleshooting Lighting Failures

Many times, the most common problems associated with lighting failures are simple to resolve. We often overlook the most obvious solutions first. I, too, am guilty of this. Having made my confession, here is a list of primary—and

Light features near the vicinity of water may be tripped more often than most; it pays to check the GFI first.

sometimes obvious—reasons for lighting failures:

1. At the risk of insulting your intelligence, the most common reason for your lights not working is that *someone has unplugged the transformer*. It happens! Don't rule out the obvious before moving on to other possibilities. It will only take a moment to check.

2. Next, check to see if *the breaker in the transformer has been tripped*. When trying to determine the root cause of a tripped circuit breaker, first try to recall what recent changes could have resulted in this problem. Circuits can be tripped for a number of reasons, but it is usually associated with a short in the wire or an excessive load on the transformer. Locate the breaker which is usually under the transformer, and check to see if it has popped out. Reset it by pushing it in until it clicks or locks. If it pops again you'll need to investigate the problem more thoroughly.

3. Another very common occurrence is that *the GFI (Ground Fault Interrupt) button within the electrical outlet has tripped*. This is designed to happen with the occurrence of excess moisture, commonly associated

QUICK FACT

Have extra electrical outlets installed early-on to accommodate future lighting additions.

WHY:

Installing outlets all at once saves time and the expense of calling in an electrician later. It makes troubleshooting even easier and builds in flexibility for future enhancements.

with pond areas, a hard rain, or when excess loads have been placed on that outlet.

4. *Next check to see if the breaker in your electrical panel has tripped or been turned off by someone.* These breakers can trip for the same reasons listed for the GFI. Reset the breaker. But if it trips again, you should investigate further or call for professional help.

5. Outdoor lighting systems are typically set on a timer. *It is possible that the timer has been altered or has stopped working.*

6. Are your *light bulbs working?* Although it would be highly unusual for all bulbs to burn out at the same time, they may burn out gradually. You don't notice the slow but steady decline in light quality until they are all gone. If the bulbs have worn out due to wear and tear, it is possible to loose all bulbs within a few weeks.

7. *Severed electrical line:* It happens all the time! These lines are usually placed very shallow below grade, or laid on top of the soil and covered with mulch making them easy to nick or sever.

 Don't take chances.

If none of these solutions resolve the problem, you may need to call an electrician. Even though low-voltage

lighting is relatively safe, *the power that is supplied to the transformer can be deadly.*

Care & Maintenance

The easiest and most effective routine maintenance job you can perform is to simply *change the light bulbs about once every year.* Bulbs gradually fade and become dimmer. Because the process is gradual, you likely would not even notice it from day to day or even week to week. To achieve the best looking, high impact lighting, change all the bulbs at the same time. In this way you ensure even, consistent lighting.

No doubt, over time your *fixtures will need to be straightened and cleaned of cobwebs or plant debris.* Anytime is a good time for this, but do so at least once a year as you change your bulbs. At the same time, *check to see if your timer is still operating properly.* If it has a battery back-up system, this also would be a good time change the batteries.

Use care when working around light fixtures as the supply lines may be very shallow.

Once all the work is behind me and the kids are safely tucked in bed for the night, I love to hear the chirping of the crickets and tree frogs and to study the structure of the branches against the evening sky. These are experiences that aren't the same at any other time of day. "

Extending
Your Outdoor
Living Space

Adding Fire Features

Outdoor living in our own gardens would not be complete without creating a welcoming environment that we can enjoy and share with family and friends. Sometimes a lot of work goes into creating a great-looking garden, so why not get the most out of it?

One of my favorite simple pleasures is to retire to a comfortable chair outside at the end of the day, once all the work is behind me and the kids are safely tucked into bed for the night. To hear the chirping of the crickets and tree frogs and to study the structure of the branches against the evening sky are pleasures that simply can't be appreciated as much at any other time of day.

Just as I can be transfixed by the many sights and sounds of the garden at night, we all know what staring at a fire will do for relieving stress and passing time comfortably. Imagine combining the best of both worlds by placing a fire feature outdoors such as a fireplace or fire pit.

If the proper care is taken, an outdoor fire feature can be one of the most enjoyable aspects of your garden experience and one that you can share with family and friends as well.

How to Start

Creating a fire feature in your garden can be a simple matter. Some basic information will have you well on your way to adding a whole new dimension to your outdoor living experience.

Before you begin, carefully consider your placement options.

WHY: Extreme temperatures and hot embers created by fire are detrimental to trees overhead, the ground beneath, and any surrounding vegetation or objects.

• Before you begin, *remember you are adding fire to your environment.* Consequently, you must keep in mind the associated hazards. Consider the impact of hot embers spilling out onto a wood deck, scorching overhanging tree limbs, or radiating heat baking the turf underneath.

• *Always take precautions* that will enable you to deal with any unforeseen situation or emergency. Keeping water or a fire extinguisher at the ready are critical and might help avert a serious problem.

⚠ **Be aware of outdoor burning bans in your area.**

When in effect, they may apply to all outdoor burning, even in contained fire pits.

• *Do you want it to be permanent or portable?* Permanent fireplaces are nice for many reasons. You can create an entire room around one, complete with furniture, cooking facilities, landscaping, and hard-scapes. It will undoubtedly become

a regular gathering place, and you can have all the necessary items to make the experience perfect, right at your fingertips.

Fixed structures are generally safer because they are usually sturdier, built into the area, and not subject to tipping over or being knocked down. However, once a fixed structure is in place, it would take heavy work to remove it. Therefore, before deciding on the final site, be sure that it's ideal: accessible, yet away from any overhangs, and in close proximity to water.

Entire outdoor rooms have been created around permanent free-standing fireplaces.

Outdoor Fire Features

One of the easiest ways to extend the time spent in your garden is to create non-gardening activities that can be enjoyed anytime of the day or night. An outdoor fire feature is a simple and easy place to start. There are a couple of popular choices. One of the least expensive and more popular versions is the "chiminea". A chiminea is an affordable way to experiment with adding this new dimension to your garden.

• *Chimineas:* These can be described as any portable, free-standing fire feature that contains a flue or chimney. Originally intended for cooking, the heat generated was quickly embraced as a way to warm the chill of a cool evening while serving as a visual and social focal point in the garden. Depending on the weight, they are generally easy to set up, move, and remove—especially when compared to the cost or work needed to move a fixed structure.

The most common materials used to make chimineas are: *clay, steel, aluminum, cast iron,* and *copper.*

• *Clay:* The look of a clay chiminea is usually what people think of first when visualizing a freestanding fireplace. They have been around for centuries because they are easy to fabricate. Although clay styles are fairly inexpensive, beautiful, and rustic, they are also subject to breakage and deterioration.

If that isn't bad enough, the bigger concern is that when they fail, they can do so at any time, without warning, even when you are burning an active fire. As with any fireplace environment, it is especially important that the area underneath the fireplace is burn-resistant. A tile or concrete base is a very good choice for protection.

• *Sheet Metal:* Just as with most things in life, you get what you pay for. Sheet metal is a popular choice for low-cost outdoor fireplaces. They look great in the display and right out of the box. But, sheet metal is not a durable choice for an outdoor application, and the material will

A deck should be appropriately protected with a tile or concrete base before using a chiminea.

rust and degrade quickly.

Sheet metal comes in various thicknesses. Some of the cheapest versions have metal that is so thin, it could actually melt—never a good choice for housing a fire! If you visit a mass merchant and buy one of these because of an irresistible price tag, don't expect it to last very long.

• *Copper:* Popular for ages in cooking pots and utensils, copper takes the heat well and looks great early on. However, just like that shiny new penny, copper tarnishes quickly outdoors, so be prepared for some work to keep it looking as good as when you first brought it home. Also know it's likely that not all parts of the fireplace will be made of copper. The non-copper parts are subject to the

Chimineas are an easy way to add a fire feature and are readily available.

wear and tear of that particular material.

• *Cast Iron:* Cast iron is thick and heavy. Just like your grandmother's skillet, this material can take the heat and last for years with only a little maintenance. Chimineas made of cast iron are also built to last and offer that rustic feeling better than anything else. Although virtually indestructible, they can rust over time. Covering them between uses and using steel wool every now and then, along with an occasional repainting using a high temperature appliance paint, can keep the rust at bay for years.

Getting that campfire feeling at home is easy to do using a variety of fire features.

• *Cast Aluminum:* This is the best of all worlds. It has the look of cast iron without the weight, and as an important added benefit, it won't rust. Aluminum is the best investment if you are looking for durability and low maintenance. Although you will spend more money up front than with other options, the cost is well worth it over time.

Since chimineas are portable they are not the sturdiest option. So, you will want to be sure it is situated on a firm, level surface that is burn resistant. If placing it on a deck, be sure to create a generous tile or concrete base for it to sit on. Do not use it in a space with a ceiling, such as a screened porch or portico. Likewise, place it away from the house eves or overhanging tree branches.

• *Permanent Fire Pits:* Who doesn't love the feeling of sitting around an open fire? However, for most of us, we usually only get to enjoy this experience while on a camping trip. A simple project many people can do at home is to add a permanent backyard fire pit. This way you can have the pleasure of that camping experience whenever you want it.

To add an outdoor fire pit to your landscape, there are a

Appropriate ventilation is necessary for that well-fueled, blazing fire we all enjoy.

where it can comfortably accommodate seating around the entire perimeter. That way you can maneuver around the smoke depending on which way the wind is blowing. Make the seating area wide enough to give you the flexibility to move a reasonable distance away if necessary.

• *Will the pit be above or below ground?* Fire pits don't have to be literally a hole dug below grade. Rather, simply picture a contained area, with access to the fire all the way around. A big advantage to creating an above ground pit is that it more easily gets much-needed ventilation. This is important for a well-fueled, blazing fire.

few important considerations:

• *Have you thought of safety first?* Make sure your pit is in an area that is away from the house and not under any overhanging branches or structures. Place the fire pit

• *How deep should you make it?* Other than the foundation, the depth of your pit is a matter of personal preference. The higher the sides, the more important ventilation will be. Creating small open spaces in the first course of materials ensures better draft and more consistent combustion. You will also want to be able to see clearly into the fire. However, the sides of the pit should be tall enough to safely contain whatever you are burning.

• *What about the width?* Again, there are no real hard and fast

A round fire pit provides 360 degrees of fun for entertaining two or twenty.

rules for the width of your pit. But, you should make it large enough to accommodate a reasonably sized fire. You would regret building a fire pit too small to fully enjoy. Building it bigger allows you to have fires of different sizes. Don't limit your options.

There is a wide range of choice in materials when building a fire pit. You can complement the style of your house by using *brick, stone, or stucco coated cinder blocks.* A simple way to build a uniform pit above or below ground is to use interlocking blocks that are available at most home improvement stores.

For me, the benefit of a fire pit over a chiminea is the ability to entertain a larger number of people. The

Although never intended as an outdoor feature a stately old fireplace remnant always leaves an impression on me.

chiminea is only viewed from one direction but certainly makes for a more intimate setting. A fire pit on the other hand can be viewed from all sides, accommodating a wider range of social situations and providing the opportunity to enjoy the fire from every angle.

Since the fire pit is considered a permanent structure, it can be as large as your space and budget allow. Chimineas, because of their portability, must be made only in sizes that are practical. For this reason, the fire pit can create the large roaring fire that throws heat out in every direction.

Fire pits are generally easy to make and a satisfying do-it-yourself project. The materials for construction are readily available. Fire pits are easily adapted for cooking. Add a grill grate made of cast iron or stainless steel to expand the pleasurable experience of using your fire pit for something more than viewing.

• *Outdoor Fireplaces:* A stately outdoor fireplace, like the one you see as the last remaining remnant of an old home-stead, always leaves an impression on me. Each time I see one, I think of how attractive it looks, even though it was never intended to be an *outdoor* feature.

Outdoor fireplaces can be as attractive as they are lasting. Using one as a functional, statuesque garden focal point really makes a statement and provides an additional way to extend the garden season and your outdoor pleasure.

Scale your fireplace to fit appropriately within the landscape design.

sure the firebox will accommodate it without additional cutting of the logs. Most pre-cut firewood is approximately 18 to 24 inches in length. You'll want to make sure the firebox is at least that wide.

 Hire a professional.

This is not a project to be taken on by the weekend warrior without considerable engineering skills. In most cases, using a professional mason is the best way to go.

The durability of **brick, stone, or stucco** allows a permanent freestanding fireplace to last for decades. Formal or casual, the options for design are limited only by your imagination.

As a grand focal point in the garden, entire rooms have been created around a fixed fireplace with plants for walls, and sky as the ceiling. Why not enjoy an outdoor fireplace as you enjoy the one in your den or family room, with comfortable seating and lighting?

Furniture options for outdoor use are abundant these days, as are conveniences such as weatherproof lamps. Patios complete with gourmet kitchens make it even more possible to "live" in your garden.

While scale is important in the grand scheme of landscape design, the benefit of a fixed structure is that you can make it any size you want. You are not limited to what is available from a box. The ability to customize it to your landscape gives you many choices.

When deciding on the size of your fireplace, think of the size of the wood you will be burning. Then you can make

The cost of an outdoor fireplace can certainly be a factor, as can building codes in your area. Check with your local code enforcement authorities as well as your neighborhood architectural control committee for specifications and limitations.

Wood-burning is Not the Only Option

Just about any fire feature, whether portable or fixed, can be adapted to burn wood or operate on natural gas or propane. There are pros and cons to each.

Wood-burning fireplaces are of course, more natural, complete with the heat, sound, and smell only a real fire can provide. There is no denying the allure of a natural wood-burning fireplace. However, you'll need wood, and the lack of it can certainly pose a problem without some advance planning.

Here are some other issues to think about:

• *Size:* You need to consider the size of the fire feature you choose. One that is too small may not accommodate standard firewood lengths. Some can also be less stable, having a smaller base that is not as practical. A larger fireplace offers more options. Remember, the objective is to enjoy

A burning ban in the dry desert area of Taos prohibited the use of even this covered fire pit.

your outdoor environment while keeping things simple.

- **Smoke:** Although there is no substitute for the ambiance of a natural wood burning fire, the rising smoke can be a distraction or irritant. The chiminea or fireplace smokestack has the advantage of directing the smoke up and away from your seating area.

- **Clean-up:** Just as with any natural fireplace, a mess results from the burning wood. You'll need a way to easily retrieve and dispose of the ashes once they've cooled. Gas-fueled fireplaces are convenient and free of any smoke or mess. They have the added benefit of being free of the risks associated with flying sparks or hot burning ash that float through the air.

- **Convenience:** Gas offers the convenience of an instant on and off option—but convenience comes at a price. Gas can get expensive, yet it is certainly a tradeoff worth considering. Do you want your outdoor fireplace to be portable? Portability will depend on how large a system you choose and whether it is gas or wood-burning. With gas-burning units, portability depends on how the gas is supplied—whether it is by a removable tank or directly through a fixed supply line.

Outdoor Fireplace Safety Tips

- Pressure-treated woods emit toxic gases when they are burning, making them an unsafe fuel source. If in doubt as to whether your wood is treated or not, play it safe and don't burn it. Chances are if it has a greenish tint, it's treated wood.

- Wood that is stained or painted is not considered safe to burn. It, too, emits gasses that are unhealthy.

- Do not burn railroad ties or any wood treated with creosote.

- Aerosol cans can explode or become dangerous missiles and should never be put into, or next to, a fire.

QUICK FACT
?

Examine wood carefully before you burn it.

WHY: Pressure treated wood emits toxic gasses when it is burned making it an unsafe fuel source. If in doubt as to whether your wood is treated or not play it safe and don't burn it.

• Always read the instructions on, and inside, any packaging. Important safety information unique to that product will be listed there or in the enclosed instructions.

• Be sure any freestanding fire feature is secure and stable.

• Do not leave fire unattended.

• Supervise children and pets around fire at all times.

• Have water easily accessible until you are sure the fire is out and cold.

• Placing the ashes in a metal container for at least twenty-four hours should ensure they can be safely disposed of properly.

• Fully extinguish the fire before leaving the area.

• Do not burn on windy days. Wind fuels the fire and sparks can be blown a great distance away to ignite other objects.

• Check with local authorities to see if any burning bans

Reading the morning news is made more palatable with good coffee and a warm fire!

or ordinances are currently in effect for your area.

• Avoid using flammable liquids. Remember, lighter fluid is intended for your grill, but not to start an outdoor fire. Use only appropriate materials.

• Do not place your fire feature under an over-hanging structure, below branches, near dry grass, or by leaves.

• Keep excess wood and fuel far enough away to prevent accidentally igniting them.

• Don't burn trash. The resulting embers are light and can easily be blown around.

Use common sense and follow general safety precautions when adding fire to your outdoor environment.

USDA Cold Hardiness Zone Map

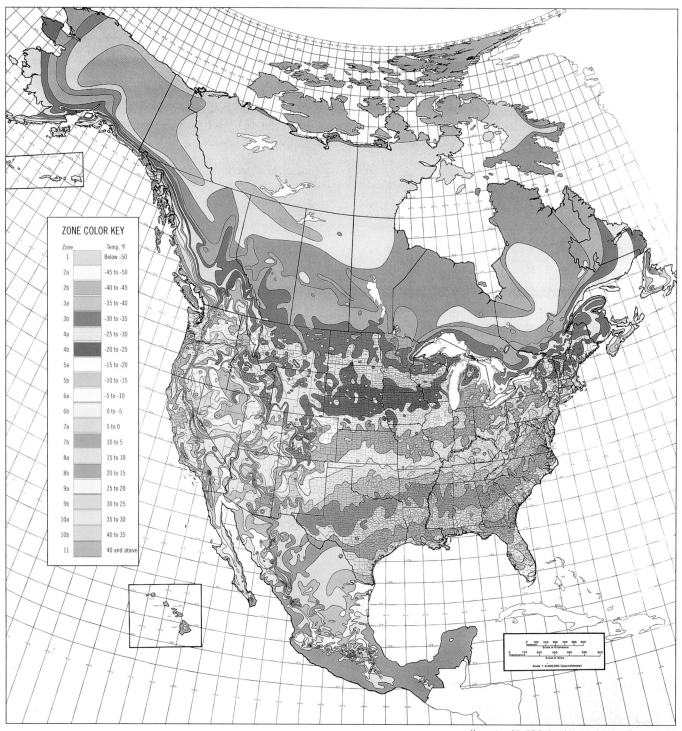

ZONE COLOR KEY

Zone	Temp. °F
1	Below -50
2a	-45 to -50
2b	-40 to -45
3a	-35 to -40
3b	-30 to -35
4a	-25 to -30
4b	-20 to -25
5a	-15 to -20
5b	-10 to -15
6a	-5 to -10
6b	0 to -5
7a	5 to 0
7b	10 to 5
8a	15 to 10
8b	20 to 15
9a	25 to 20
9b	30 to 25
10a	35 to 30
10b	40 to 35
11	40 and above

Map courtesy of the U.S. National Arboretum, Agricultural Research Service

Meet Joe Lamp'l

Joe Lamp'l is not only a gardening expert; he's a passionate educator, dedicated to sharing his knowledge of horticulture by providing resources to gardeners of all levels.

For three years Joe hosted *Fresh from the Garden* on the DIY Network and is currently host of *GardenSMART* on PBS. His fresh, inspirational, and nurturing personality along with his ability to present complicated subjects in an easy to understand manner, make him a sought-after communicator around the country.

As a Master Gardener and Certified Landscape Professional, Joe's work is highly acclaimed. As the founder of The joe gardener® Company, an organization committed to helping people of all skill levels learn, create, and grow beautiful gardens and landscapes, he introduces gardening to beginners and helps seasoned veterans perfect their skills.

His weekly syndicated column, *The Gardener Within*, is distributed to approximately 400 newspapers nationwide. Through television, radio, personal appearances, seminars, books, articles, and the organization's website **joegardener.com**, gardeners are given straightforward instructions and the latest ideas for improving their outdoor lifestyle.

For Joe, gardening personally or professionally has been a passion and a way of life for more than thirty years. Joe enjoys and appreciates the support of his wife Becky and their two young daughters, Rachel and Amy.

Plant Index *(Botanical Name)*

Plant Index *(Common Name)*